The Unquiet Nisei

Palgrave Studies in Oral History

Series Editors: Linda Shopes and Bruce M. Stave

Sticking to the Union: An Oral History of the Life and Times of Julia Ruuttila, by Sandy Polishuk; foreword by Amy Kesselman (2003)

To Wear the Dust of War: From Bialystok to Shanghai to the Promised Land, an Oral History, by Samuel Iwry, edited by L. J. H. Kelley (2004)

Education as My Agenda: Gertrude Williams, Race, and the Baltimore Public Schools, by Jo Ann Robinson (2005)

Remembering: Oral History Performance, edited by Della Pollock (2005)

Postmemories of Terror: A New Generation Copes with the Legacy of the "Dirty War," by Susana Kaiser (2005)

Growing Up in The People's Republic: Conversations between Two Daughters of China's Revolution, by Ye Weili and Ma Xiaodong (2005)

Life and Death in the Delta: African American Narratives of Violence, Resilience, and Social Change, by Kim Lacy Rogers (2006)

Creating Choice: A Community Responds to the Need for Abortion and Birth Control, 1961–1973, by David P. Cline (2006)

Voices from This Long Brown Land: Oral Recollections of Owens Valley Lives and Manzanar Pasts, by Jane Wehrey (2006)

Radicals, Rhetoric, and the War: The University of Nevada in the Wake of Kent State, by Brad Lucas (2006)

Order Has Been Carried Out: History, Memory, and Meaning of a Nazi Massacre in Rome, by Alessandro Portelli (2007)

The Unquiet Nisei: An Oral History of the Life of Sue Kunitomi Embrey, by Diana Meyers Bahr (2007)

The Unquiet Nisei

An Oral History of the Life of Sue Kunitomi Embrey

Diana Meyers Bahr

Department of the Interior
National Park Service
Cultural Resources Library

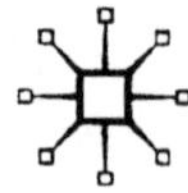

THE UNQUIET NISEI

First published in 2007 by
PALGRAVE MACMILLAN™
175 Fifth Avenue, New York, N.Y. 10010 and
Houndmills, Basingstoke, Hampshire, England RG21 6XS
Companies and representatives throughout the world.

PALGRAVE MACMILLAN is the global academic imprint of the Palgrave Macmillan division of St. Martin's Press, LLC and of Palgrave Macmillan Ltd. Macmillan® is a registered trademark in the United States, United Kingdom and other countries. Palgrave is a registered trademark in the European Union and other countries.

ISBN-13: 978–0–230–60067–6
ISBN-10: 0–230–60067–0

Library of Congress Cataloging-in-Publication Data

Bahr, Diana Meyers, 1930–
The unquiet Nisei: an oral history of the life of Sue Kunitomi Embrey / by Diana Meyers Bahr.
p. cm.—(Palgrave studies in oral history)
Includes bibliographical references and index.
ISBN 0–230–60067–0
1. Embrey, Sue Kunitomi. 2. Japanese Americans—Evacuation and relocation, 1942–1945. 3. World War, 1939–1945—Personal narratives, American. 4. World War, 1939–1945—Japanese Americans. 5. Japanese Americans—Biography. 6. Oral history. I. Title.

D769.8.A6B28 2007
940.53'1779487092—dc22 2007019585

A catalogue record for this book is available from the British Library.

Design by Newgen Imaging Systems (P) Ltd., Chennai, India.

First edition: December 2007

10 9 8 7 6 5 4 3 2 1

Printed in the United States of America.

Dedicated to
the Issei, who endured with dignity,
the Nisei, who insisted on historical truth,
and the Sansei, who asked the right questions.

Contents

Illustrations

Series Editors' Foreword

Oral history narrators typically place themselves at the center of the story they tell. Indeed, the structure of an oral history interview—a one-on-one conversation focusing on the narrator's personal experience—almost requires it. Yet this same structure can lead narrators to overstate their own role in events, to make themselves the hero (or sometimes the antihero) of their tale, the pivot around which other actors revolve. Not so Sue Kunitomi Embrey, the subject of Diana Bahr's *The Unquiet Nisei*, who differs from this norm—as she did from many others over the course of her life.

The American-born daughter of Japanese immigrants in California, Embrey both respected and pressed against the rules of her family and her culture, rules that demanded discipline and decorum and did not sanction critical thinking or outspoken behavior. Like all Japanese-Americans living on the West Coast, she, along with her mother and seven siblings (her father had died earlier), was interned during World War II, spending eighteen months, when she was nineteen and twenty years old, at the Manzanar War Relocation Center in eastern California. Unlike most other internees, however, Embrey, temperamentally curious and restless, left the camp seeking not to return to life as it had been but to participate in the political life of her community. Beginning in the postwar years and for a half-century afterward, she engaged in many forms of progressive activism. Most notably, however, during the late 1960s she became one of the few Japanese-Americans willing to break the silence about the internment. For the next three decades, she became a pivotal figure in educating the public about the internment and in the national movement for redress and reparations for internees. Her most significant achievement came in 2004 with the establishment of Manzanar National Historic Site, which officially recognizes this painful—indeed shameful—episode in U.S. history. In this Sue Embrey was the driving force

Yet she remained a modest person, passionate, but never self-aggrandizing. Interviewing her for more than 50 hours, Bahr found Embrey to be scrupulously accurate and fair in her rendering of the past. She understood—and never overstated—her own role in events and suggested that Bahr interview others to accurately and fairly place Embrey herself within proper historic context. These interviews, together with the evidence of the documentary record, clearly demonstrate how central a role she played in enjoining the American polity to face—and account for—the injustices of the internment.

Curiously, given the numerous oral history interviews that have been conducted with internees, there are few published collections of interviews; there are fewer still single biographical accounts of the internment and its aftermath. For the singularity and significance of Embrey's life and for its contribution to the historiography of the internment, we are pleased to include *The Unquiet Nisei* in Palgrave Macmillan's *Studies in Oral History* series, designed to bring oral history interviews out of the archives and into the hands of students, educators, scholars, and the reading public. It forms a trilogy of sorts with two other books in the series, Sandy Polishuk's *Sticking to the Union: An Oral History of the Life and Times of Julia Ruuttila* and Jo Ann Robinson's *Education As My Agenda: Gertrude Williams, Race, and the Baltimore Public Schools.* Collectively, these books present three women, one Japanese-American, one black, one white, whose passion for justice—for internees, for urban students, for laborers—led them to lives of activism. Through the medium of oral history, their stories move beyond their own communities to educate and inspire a broad community of readers.

Linda Shopes
Pennsylvania Historical and Museum Commission

Bruce M. Stave
University of Connecticut

Acknowledgments

I am deeply indebted to Arthur A. Hansen, who encouraged me to write Sue Kunitomi Embrey's life story and answered innumerable questions with unfailing authority and sympathy. I was able to do greater justice to Sue's life story because of the distinctly intelligent editing of Linda Shopes. Alisa Lynch has been a constant facilitator in her responses to my many questions about Sue and Manzanar. I am grateful to Neil and Carroll Reuben for their generous assistance with the photos, and to Mario Gershom Reyes for his dramatic photos of Sue. Martha Nakagawa was considerate and very helpful in providing significant material on the Nisei Progressives. Paul Spickard answered my questions about a blood quantum policy of the federal government with generosity and expertise. Marjorie Lee of the UCLA Asian American Studies Center Library was especially accommodating to my research requirements. Once again, I am grateful to Linda Stowe who transcribed the taped interviews with efficiency and sincere interest in Sue Embrey's life story and as my first "reader" gave me thoughtful feedback. When I needed a supportive and perceptive ear, I turned to my husband Ted Bahr, whose responses to my requests for his opinion were enhanced by his admiration for Sue. Family, friends, and colleagues of Sue Embrey shared their recollections garnered not only from their memories but also from their hearts: Gary Embrey, Bruce Embrey, Barbara Becker, Monica Embrey, Michael Embrey, Jack Kunitomi, Garland Embrey, Bill Michael, Kerry Cababa, Nancy Iwata, Paul Tsuneishi, Phil Shigakuni, Rose Ochi, Warren Furutani, Takinori Yamamoto, and Alisa Lynch.

INTRODUCTION

Manzanar National Historic Site: Fulfillment of a Mission

The Grand Opening of the Interpretive Center of Manzanar National Historic Site in Independence, California, was the realization of a dream, the fulfillment of a mission, for which Sue Kunitomi Embrey had struggled for more than 30 years against opposition that was often bitter and virulent. Her petite figure nearly obscured by the large sunhat she wore to protect her from the desert sun, Sue was barely visible behind the podium when she stood in response to the introduction by John Reynolds, retired Regional Director of the Pacific West Region of the National Park Service. Reynolds's declaration that he regarded her "with joyful awe" brought the audience of more than 2,500 people to their feet. They rose in unison to give her a standing ovation, an expression of profound gratitude, before she had spoken a word. The older Japanese Americans in the audience, the Nisei,[1] had been uprooted from their homes, removed to desolate camps in remote areas, confined by barbed wire, and armed guards during World War II. They had come on this day, April 24, 2004, to Owens Valley in Inyo County, eastern California, with their Sansei children and Yonsei and Gonsei grandchildren, to commemorate the long-awaited Center that dramatically tells the bitter story of their imprisonment.

As Sue spoke, her emotion-laden, tremulous voice revealed the poignancy of the moment for herself and for every former internee.

> On May 9, 1942, my family and I, along with 300 people, all of Japanese ancestry, living in Little Tokyo of Los Angeles, came to Manzanar under orders of the Western Defense Command of the U. S. Army. We walked to the train station, the old one [in Los Angeles] to board the train. It took us about eight hours to get to the Lone Pine train station. We waited on the platform for the bus to take us on the last leg of our journey into exile.

> My brother, Hideo, who had come [to Manzanar] as a volunteer in March of 1942, met our bus and my mother was especially happy to see him because we were originally supposed to go to the Santa Anita Assembly Center and she was afraid we would never see him again. We went through a large building and registered, got a cursory medical examination, a tetanus shot, and then out the door.
>
> We struggled through the dark and finally got to Block 20. Our apartment was Apartment 1, Building 3. When we walked in, it was a room 20 by 25 feet, with canvas army cots and mattresses filled with hay. My mother sat down on one of the cots and said in Japanese: *"Ma a kon na to kon ni,"* loosely translated, "A place like this." That's all I remember of the first night. Our luggage was still on the train. I don't remember if we had dinner, or whether we were able to wash up, or if we slept in our clothes or our nightclothes.
>
> Twenty-seven years later, I came back to Manzanar with a group of young students and community activists, who declared that this was their first Manzanar Pilgrimage. But for two Japanese American ministers, one Christian and one Buddhist, it was their 25th year. The national media was there. NBC and CBS brought a third generation newscaster named Tricia Toyota.
>
> In the week that followed people called me to tell me that they had seen me on national TV, but the Japanese American community was very disturbed by the publicity. Several people came up to me and said in no uncertain terms: "Don't bring up the past, don't talk about the camps." Well, today, 35 years of our pilgrimages and two weeks to the 62nd anniversary since I first arrived in Manzanar, we have lots of voices in this beautifully restored auditorium. The exhibit, which is stunning, is a first rate interpretive center which is now under the jurisdiction of the National Park Service.
>
> People ask me why it is important to remember and keep Manzanar alive with this Interpretive Center. My answer is that stories like these need to be told, that too many of us have passed away without telling our stories. The Interpretive Center is important because it needs to shout to the world that America is strong and it makes amends for the wrongs it had committed and we will always remember Manzanar because of that.

The thirty-fifth annual Manzanar Pilgrimage, a journey back to the site of World War II incarceration by former internees, had taken place earlier in the day at the northwest corner of the former camp site near the cemetery monument, a white obelisk, inscribed on its front, the east side: *I Rei To* and on its back "Erected by the Manzanar Japanese, August 1943." *I Rei To* is generally translated as "Soul Consoling Tower," but Sue has always called it the Tower of Memory.

Objects placed on or near the monument included coins, an empty jar that had held rice seasonings, a rusted spatula, a Batman doll, athletic shoes, a colorful teakettle, and a small rock on which had been written: "Man fears what he does not understand."

Figure I.1 Sue at Manzanar Pilgrimage, 2002 (photograph by Mario Gershom Reyes)

In addition to the ceremonies at the *I Rei To* monument, this pilgrimage, with the theme "Keep It Going…Pass It On," followed the pattern established over 35 years by the Manzanar Committee, the founding organization of the pilgrimages:[2] welcoming remarks by Sue Embrey, and Takinori Yamamoto, both long-standing, esteemed members of the Committee; comments by Frank Hays, then superintendent of Manzanar National Historic Site, who spoke on the significance of the site and how it differs from National Park Service sites renowned for their natural beauty;[3] performances by Taiko drummers, performing a uniquely Japanese American music; readings from *Zine*, a publication of poetry inspired by the Manzanar Pilgrimages; and a roll call of all ten camps. A deeply rooted custom followed, an interfaith memorial service conducted in both Japanese and English by spiritual leaders of Shinto, Rissho Kosei-Kai, Christian, and Buddhist faiths. All who wished to do so participated in the offering of flowers and incense, and later in *Ondo*, Japanese folk dancing, which concluded the Pilgrimage.

Throughout the day, visitors, many of them former internees, walked on self-guided tours around the barren, dusty, campsite. What is left to remind them of their years of incarceration on the 550 acres that had housed 10,046 Japanese Americans in an "instant" town of tar-paper barracks surrounded by five-strand barbed wire fence? Where are the guard towers? The mess halls, the hospital, and morgue? Where are the structures built with their own hands: the camouflage net factory, the mattress factory, the garment factory, the experimental station extracting rubber from guayule shrubs? What has happened to the 450 acres of cultivated

Figure I.2 The *I Rei To* Tower at Manzanar Cemetery, constructed by internees in 1943 (photograph by E. Bahr)

farmland and the chicken and hog farms? What is left of the rock gardens, the victory vegetable gardens, Pleasure Park with over 100 species of flowers, two small lakes, a waterfall, and a bridge, all created by the internees with no power equipment? Where are the baseball and football fields? The *Manzanar Free Press* office? The outdoor theater? The Orphans Village?

Very little is visible other than the cemetery, the auditorium, which is now the Interpretive Center, and the military police sentry post at the entrance that was built by internee Ryozo Kado. The National Park Service plans to partially re-create the Manzanar internment camp by restoring two of the original 504 barracks, one of the eight guard towers, several rock gardens, and a mess hall.

The chronicle of the Manzanar camp is the latest dramatic chapter in the history of Owens Valley. Scholars have estimated a pre-contact population of 2,000 Paiutes living in permanent villages throughout the valley.[4] Within 10 years after contact with whites, a centuries-old lifestyle of hunting, fishing, and gathering was virtually destroyed, and Owens Valley Paiutes became dependent on wage labor at white-owned mines and ranches.

The town of Manzanar, established in 1905 as an orchard community, maintained a flourishing agricultural enterprise until its water supply was depleted when, beginning in 1913, abundant water in Owens Valley became attractive to the city of Los Angeles. The city built a 233-mile aqueduct to siphon Owens River water. By 1933 Los Angeles had bought 95 percent of Owens Valley agricultural acreage and 85 percent of its town property in order to secure the water rights. The town of

Manzanar was abandoned when lack of water forced farmers and ranchers out of the valley, and the Paiutes had neither their traditional lands nor employment on white-owned ranches to rely on. After decades of conflict between the city of Los Angeles and the U.S. Department of the Interior over "the Indian problem," the Land Exchange Act of 1937 created Paiute reservations at Bishop, Big Pine, and Lone Pine.

In 1940 the Mono Basin Extension Project, drawing water from Mono Lake, added 105 miles to the aqueduct, and in 1970 a second Los Angeles aqueduct was opened, both increasing its import of water from Owens Valley. The conflict persisted until Los Angeles, in a series of concessions between 1994 and 1997, agreed to relinquish some of its Owens Valley water, to limit groundwater pumping, and accepted responsibility for controlling toxic dust blowing from the dry bed of Owens Lake. Water from the Los Angeles Aqueduct now flows into the Little Owens River for the first time since 1913. The revitalization of the 62-mile stretch of the river is expected to create thousands of acres of habitat for fish and wildlife, providing opportunities for birding and fishing, enhancing the economy of Owens Valley.[5]

When Manzanar was selected as a War Relocation Authority camp on March 2, 1942, the 6,020-acre site was described as "an arid, barren area of sand-swept desert . . . [with] a frowzy, dilapidated orchard of old apple trees surrounded by sagebrush, rabbit brush and mesquite."[6] While Sue and her family were being forcibly removed from Little Tokyo to this desolate camp in the spring of 1942, I was 12 years old, living with my working-class parents in south-central Los Angeles. I was keenly aware, as were all Americans, that the United States was at war with Japan following the bombing of Pearl Harbor the preceding December 7. I was not, however, aware that the United States was at war with its Japanese American population. Walking home from school one day in March 1942, I was bewildered to see the furniture and personal effects of Japanese American neighbors strewn along the sidewalk. It was explained to me that these neighbors had to sell, store, or give away nearly everything they owned because people of Japanese ancestry were being taken away, no one was sure where, or for how long. The image of my neighbors hovering disconsolately over their belongings never left me.

In the early 1970s considerable literature began to appear on the compulsory removal and internment of 110,000 persons of Japanese ancestry, two-thirds of whom were American citizens.[7] To avoid acknowledging that Japanese American citizens were being incarcerated, the federal government labeled them non-aliens. They were forced into exile during World War II on the rationalization of "military necessity." Executive Order 9066 issued by President Franklin D. Roosevelt authorized the forced removal and incarceration of Japanese Americans. This action and others by the federal government in violation of basic civil rights had been obscured for a variety of reasons, not the least of which was the profound reluctance of Japanese Americans to talk about "the camps."[8]

Gil Asakawa on his website "*Nikkei View*"[9] has written: "The facts of internment are written out in dozens of books. But what's missing in most of them is the personal perspective that can give the facts of internment the resonance of reality. That's why the telling and recording of oral histories is so important, and why it's critical for those who lived through internment to tell their stories... People are hungry for these stories."[10] The Oral and Public History Program at California State University Fullerton has been the vanguard of organized efforts to record the oral histories of Japanese Americans who are former internees.

There is a chapter on Manzanar in my book *Viola Martinez, California Paiute, Living in Two Worlds*. Viola, an Owens Valley Paiute, had worked at Manzanar War Relocation Authority camp as an employment counselor. Writing this chapter revived the memories of my Japanese American neighbors in 1942. With the encouragement of Arthur A. Hansen, director of the Fullerton program, I contacted Sue Kunitomi Embrey, the Nisei whose name had become inextricably linked with Manzanar because of her resolute efforts to have the former camp achieve state and national recognition. Hansen believes that her most important legacy will be her leadership role in the Manzanar Pilgrimages, drawing hundreds of visitors, many of them former internees, to commemorate the site annually since 1969. "She more than any other person made Manzanar an important site and symbol, and this played a HUGE role in the success of the redress movement[11] and in the recent legislation converting first Manzanar and [eventually] the rest of the camps into protected national park sites."[12]

Although family, friends, and colleagues insist that Sue Embrey's legacy is greater than her activism on behalf of Manzanar, the reality is that the greatest impact of Sue's diverse activism over five decades is the fact that Manzanar National Historic Site has become a national icon for the World War II internment of Japanese Americans. Successfully campaigning for Manzanar enabled Sue to create genuine social change. Her activism on behalf of other issues of social justice, including efforts to improve working conditions for women, advocacy for United Farm Workers, and anti-Viet Nam War campaigning, is also acknowledged in this book. In an interview Hansen added: "She was schooled in a principled kind of progressive ideological movement for a long time."[13] How she expressed this ideology is explored in her life story.

In response to my letter conveying that I would like to collaborate on an oral history of her life and her significant work in liberal activism, Sue said that she would be "honored and humbled."[14] Concurring with Diane C. Fujino, who argues that oral history is a means of "empowering those who have been marginalized by traditional writers of history,"[15] and having written two former life histories based on interviews, I have employed oral history as the optimum methodology for Sue's life history.

Sue and I began working together on November 13, 2002, and during the following 18 months completed over 50 hours of interviews. I recorded approximately 30 additional hours with 17 individuals, all of whom were selected by Sue.[16] Literally hundreds of individuals consider themselves friends of Sue, but since she was unquestionably aware of her role in Japanese American history, the interviews reveal that she selected individuals who would advance the story of her activist legacy.

Family members interviewed were Yoshisuke (Jack) Kunitomi, Sue's older brother; Gary and Bruce Embrey, her sons; Barbara Becker, her daughter-in-law; Monica and Michael Embrey, her grandchildren; Kerry Cababa and Nancy Iwata, her nieces; and Garland Embrey, her former husband. Interviews with colleagues who worked on the Manzanar campaign and on the redress movement included those with Arthur Hansen, Paul Tsuneishi, Rose Ochi, Warren Furutani, Takinori Yamamoto, Philip Shigekuni, Alisa Lynch, and Bill Michael. I prepared for each interview by discussing with Sue the history of her personal and/or professional relationship with the individual, emphasizing activism and experience with or knowledge of the internment camps generally and Manzanar specifically. For each interview I asked questions that were common to all regarding progressive activism and civil rights, and also questions specific to the interviewee's relationship with Sue.

Without exception all 17 interviewees were eager to be involved in documenting Sue's life history. I posed follow-up questions by email to clarify certain topics with all interviewees with the exception of Sue. She and I reviewed each of her interviews during the following session, clarifying and augmenting that segment of Sue's life story. Because all of the interviewees were assured in expressing themselves, editing was minimal and used only to improve the flow of the narration. Although each interviewee was remarkably focused on conveying his/her relationship with Sue and their activism collaboration, the editing process at times combined segments of interviews on the same topic to make details more cohesive. The interviewee is identified in the text, and the name of the interviewer and date of the interviews from which the quotations are taken are cited in Notes at the end of the book. If I thought a quotation may be unclear or confusing to the reader, I added or changed words. These are enclosed by brackets. Rephrased or paraphrased comments appear without quotation marks, but are attributed to the interviewee. To avoid redundancy by a speaker or to eliminate digression, both of which rarely happened, words or lines are omitted and indicated by a line of spaced periods.

Sue's memories were shaped by her research and activism on behalf of Japanese Americans for more than 30 years. This integration of personal memory, action, and scholarship is shown, for example, in Sue's vivid memories of the fear and dread experienced by her family following the attack on Pearl Harbor, while her recall of the situation in the Japanese American community at that critical time has been enhanced by her research in an attempt to educate herself and others. Clearly, because of Sue's reading, writing, and speaking about the Japanese American experience for more than three decades her narrative is remarkably articulate and knowledgeable. Her interviews were congruent with the research I had completed before each interview and remained consistently so when I confirmed her statements with follow-up research. Even when scholarly opinions vary, as with the literature on the Manzanar Riot,[17] she presented the various views objectively. Sue had no agenda other than raising awareness of the truth of the Japanese American experience, and her personal and intellectual modesty precluded exaggeration to make a point. Because of failing eyesight, Sue was not able to read the entire transcripts. When I had a doubt that the transcript did not state what she had meant to say, I read the segment aloud. With her keen perception and confident responses, we resolved ambiguities and other possible misinterpretations. The author's primary responsibility is to assure that the narrator's individual voice is heard, thus the focus and flow of our collaboration were guided by Sue, a compelling authority on the Japanese American experience.

Her account is a dramatic portrayal of what she calls "the lost years, 1942–46," during which Japanese Americans were deprived of their civil rights, and her resolute efforts to make the loss of those years meaningful. As her life story unfolded, it became evident that Sue had been witness to and an intimate participant in crucial phenomena over nine decades of Japanese American history: the anti-Japanese crusade in the western United States during the 1920s and 1930s; the attack on Pearl Harbor on December 7, 1941; the consequent incarceration by the U.S. government of 120,000 people of Japanese descent during World War II; the decades-long campaign for redress for Japanese Americans from the mid-1940s to 1988, when President Ronald Reagan signed the redress act into law; and, as the result of a three-decade campaign, the designation of Manzanar War Relocation Center as a National Historic Site on March 3, 1992.

Significant growth in political awareness and subsequent advocacy for progressive causes were atypical for a Japanese woman of her generation. While it would be unrealistic to attempt to precisely pinpoint when Sue became an activist, it is constructive to explore the origins of her activism as suggested in her oral history: the profound influence of her father on her identity as a Nisei woman; the internment, particularly her association with liberal thinkers on the *Manzanar Free Press;* her independence and relationships with non-Japanese individuals in Madison and Chicago, immediately following her internment; the postwar resettlement in Los Angeles; her marriage to the liberal activist Garland Embrey; and her involvement with Nisei and Sansei activists. In her responses to these factors, including those that were not of her choosing, Sue eventually became one of the few Nisei women leaders in the Japanese American redress/reparations movement. Others include Michi Weglyn, author of *Years of Infamy,* who documented in incriminating detail the monumental violation of civil rights by the federal government; Aiko Herzig, who discovered the "smoking gun," a memo in federal archives that destroyed the rationale of military necessity for the incarceration of Japanese Americans and became instrumental in the fight for redress; Tsuyako "Sox" Kitashima, redress movement leader, and Yuri Kochiyama, who began her activist career in Harlem, and inspired by Malcolm X, campaigned for four decades for civil rights for African Americans, Puerto Ricans, and political prisoners, as well as for Asian Americans.

Sue's determination and resilience are similar to that of her peers in the redress efforts but these qualities were elevated to a unique stature in her Manzanar campaigns. There is a Japanese saying: *Mukashi banashi ni hanagasaku*. "Stories of the past are embellished with flowers."[18] There are, indeed, flowers in the life story of Sue Kunitomi Embrey, but among the flowers are lingering shadows of sorrow, pain, and humiliation.

CHAPTER 1

Growing Up in Little Tokyo

The first wave of Issei, which included Sue's father, came to the United States between 1885 and 1924.[1] Following the pattern of single young men who left Japan to work on Hawaiian sugar plantations, some moving later to mainland United States,[2] Sue's father, Gonhichi Kunitomi, emigrated from Okayama prefecture in Japan to Hawaii on a passport dated September 14, 1898, on a three-year contract to work as a farm laborer on a Hawaiian plantation.[3] The Japanese came to the United States for the same reasons as other immigrants, for economic opportunity. Japanese, however, sought short-term economic gain so they could return home and live with no financial worries.[4]

When he had completed his labor contract, Gonhichi moved to the mainland, arriving in San Francisco with no knowledge of English other than what he had picked up in Hawaii. Sue related what she knew about her father's immigration:[5]

> My father was a very independent person looking for adventure. After his years in Hawaii, he didn't go back [to Japan] like many others did.[6] He never really talked about it, except one time, when he said he never wanted to go back. He said: "When you die, they put you in a plain pine box. In the United States, even in death you can sleep on a pillow, a nice pillow." That was the only thing he ever said.
>
> "He traveled up and down the coast working on farms with a bedroll on his back," Sue recounted. "He met a lot of other people [working] like that. He and a bachelor who lived with us for a while, used to talk about the funny things that happened to them. The first time they ever saw a western-style toilet, they didn't know what it was and decided to wash their hands in it."[7]

The second phase of Issei immigration comprised predominantly of women who came to the United States to marry men they only knew from photographs.

Figure 1.1 Sue's father Gonhichi Kunitomi, ca. 1935 (photograph courtesy of the Embrey family)

These picture brides usually married Issei men ten to twenty years older than they, as did Sue's mother.[8] Two or three years after he came to the mainland, Gonhichi was working in Hollywood as a domestic or gardener—Sue is not sure which—when he asked Komika to come to the United States and marry him. Komika knew Gonhichi's family slightly.

> "They were not really related," Sue stated. "They were sort of from the same family tree because my mother's name was also Kunitomi. On my last trip to Japan over

> Labor Day weekend [2002] I found out that there are a lot of branches of the Kunitomi family. We went to the family cemetery. There were Kunitomis all over the place. My father's name, Gonhichi, means seven. My mother's name, Komika, means pretty bird."

"I don't know if my father asked my mother directly or through someone, but I do know that she had somebody else in mind she wanted to marry," Sue stated, "but her mother insisted that she go to America. Although my father wasn't making much money in America, they thought there was more opportunity here."[9] Despite her insistence that Komika emigrate to America, her mother said: "Once you leave, I'll never see you again." Sue reported: "She never did."

Traveling alone to the United States, Komika landed in San Francisco, but was sent back to Japan because of an eye infection. She successfully emigrated on her second attempt, arriving on January 22, 1910, and married Gonhichi Kunitomi on January 24, 1910, when she was 24 and he was 34.[10] Had Sue's mother talked about her expectations of America? "She said [in Japan] they were always reading about discrimination against [Asian immigrants], but she was ambitious and really wanted to make a go of [living in America]."[11]

Gonhichi and Komika settled in the Little Tokyo community of Los Angeles. Although it developed later than the Japanese American communities in Seattle and San Francisco, Little Tokyo in Los Angeles, since 1910, has been home to more Japanese Americans than any other city in mainland United States.[12] The core of the Japanese community's business and cultural life for nearly 100 years was located in the blocks converging at the intersection of First and San Pedro Streets.[13]

Sue described the neighborhood in which she grew up in a 2004 article, "Little Tokyo—My Neighborhood, My Community, My World."[14]

> Little Tokyo stretched from Temple Street on the north and flowed south into the wholesale market that was the centerpiece of the fruits, vegetables and flowers grown by Japanese farmers throughout Southern California. The Honpa Hongwanji Temple...served as a cultural center.... the grocery store with fresh fish and piles of fresh Japanese vegetables such as *nappa* (cabbage) and *daikon* (white radish) would send their fragrant smell out along the street. There was a clock repair shop, a sushi restaurant, a shoe store and a department store. The prominent businesses on the south side were the Fuji Kan, a Japanese owned theatre, a barbershop, and the studio of Toyo Miyatake, who was already a recognized photographer.[15]
>
> On the east side, the boundary was the foot of the First Street Bridge. This was one of the bustling residential neighborhoods which supported the businesses, which could not have survived without the patronage of this population.

While undoubtedly welcoming outsiders, the small retail stores and medical and professional services in the heart of Little Tokyo relied primarily on Issei customers.[16]

Figure 1.2 Sue's mother Komika Kunitomi, date unknown (photograph courtesy of the Embrey family)

Mainstream department stores would not cater to nonwhite customers. As Sue recounted: "There were a lot of stores that refused service to minorities in the [19]30s. I didn't try to enter those stores. It was common knowledge that they wouldn't serve you." Despite this awareness, Sue described the Little Tokyo of her youth as insulating her family somewhat from racism: "[It was] a closed society of poor, working people, small businesses, churches and temples, several Japanese language schools and public schools. It was also a tight-knit community.... For those of us growing up in Little Tokyo, there was a sense of strength and protection from a hostile world."

Little Tokyo was not homogenously Japanese, but rather a mix of Caucasian, African American, Mexican American, and other ethnic groups.[17] Sue alluded to this multiethnic population when she wrote: "The area to the west was bounded by Los Angeles Street, which was the beginning of Manila Town, where Filipino bachelors lived in run-down hotels and sat on wooden chairs on the sidewalk watching the traffic go by."

Some historians have portrayed Little Tokyo as one of the poorest places in town, with substandard housing units, most of which lacked flush toilets.[18] Others, however, describe Nisei in Los Angeles as living in fairly comfortable homes of *hakujin* (Caucasian) style, with trees, lawns, and ample back yards.[19] Descriptions by Sue of her childhood home indicate that the latter description is more appropriate for the Kunitomi family home.

Sue began her life in Los Angeles' Little Tokyo on January 6, 1923. "I was born on Central Avenue, which is behind what is now the Japanese American National Museum. There were a lot of small, bungalow houses, where the police department parking lot is now." Like most Japanese American children, Sue and her siblings were delivered by *osama* (midwives).[20] "All of us were born at home. I'm number six out of eight children. My father named me Sueko. The [Japanese] character for siet [six] also means last. He was hoping I'd be the last child. I guess," she laughed.

> I had five brothers. My oldest brother was Frank [born in 1910]. My father called him Koya, but he went by the name of Koichi, Ichi meaning number one. I had a sister, Choko [born in 1913]. [Next in birth order] I have a brother Jack [born in 1915]. Jack's Japanese name is very fancy, Yoshisuke. We used to call him "Yosh" growing up. "Somewhere along the road he changed it to Jack.[21]

Jack explained his name change.

> "Yoshi means good or well done. Suke is a common addition to Japanese names. I was an avid reader in grade school, especially in summertime... I would be reading out on the porch in the morning sunlight, and an old vet, who lived down the street in a boarding house would take his daily walk to where all the vets would assemble at Pershing Square." The veteran offered Jack reading material. "He had

magazines, [including] *Argosy Magazine*, and paper bound, rough edged adventure stories. He would drop them off to me when he was finished with them. One day he asked me my name. [When] I said: 'Yoshisuke,' he said: 'This is America. You were born here. You are an American.' 'I'll call you Jack.' I adopted it. Of course it wasn't legal so I couldn't change my name in school, and my Caucasian teachers stumbled over Yoshisuke."

Sue continued with the chronicle of her siblings:

After Jack was my brother Kinya [born in 1918]. It means golden arrow. All my brothers had fancy names. We call him Kim or Kimbo, a nickname that he grew up with. Then after Kimbo was my brother Hideo [born in 1921]. We called him Hide (pronounced Heeday). I came after him. Then my younger sister, Midori [born in 1925]. Midori is another way of saying pretty bird. Then my youngest brother, Tetsuo [born in 1930]. We called him Tets.[22]

Sue described the cultural and social life of Little Tokyo as she and her siblings were growing up. "The west side of San Pedro Street, which is now Parker Center [headquarters of Los Angeles Police Department] housed a cultural center with judo and kendo dojo, a sumo [wrestling] ring and an archery field."[23] Cultural programs, including Japanese plays and Kabuki dances were produced in Yamato Hall, a huge place with a stage on the first floor, located across the street from the Kunitomi home. Sue remembers her parents attending for an entire day. "They would bring their lunch. My father loved it."[24]

Sue was aware of a less innocent activity in Yamato Hall, illegal gambling. "It was very popular in those days, mostly with the Issei. They had some arrangement with the police department so they wouldn't be arrested." The Tokyo Club of Yamato Hall was a significant phenomenon in Little Tokyo, having grown from a loose network of gambling clubs into a syndicate, headquartered in Los Angeles, with links in most major cities in the western part of the United States. Although gambling and prostitution activities were linked with kidnapping, extortion, and even murder, the club had the tacit approval of the community. Tokyo Club provided for the needy, feeding 60 to 80 people a day during the Great Depression, and supporting cultural activities and scholarship funds. In the early 1930s the Club made over 1 million dollars per year and had the local civic and police officials in its pocket.[25]

Jack Kunitomi remembers one night when the arrangement with the police evidently was not in effect.

We lived right across the street from the entrance to Tokyo Club. One night, in the late '20's—prohibition was still in effect—federal agents had blocked off Jackson Street between San Pedro and Central Avenue. They were on the second story, dumping cases of liquor over the balcony, right in front of our house. It kept up all night.[26]

Figure 1.3 The Kunitomi siblings, Little Tokyo, Los Angeles, ca. 1927. Seated: Midori; middle, left to right: Hideo, Kinya, Sueko; rear, left to right: (Jack) Yoshisuke, (Frank) Koya, Choko (photograph courtesy of the Embrey family)

The Kunitomis, together with the Miyatakes and other neighbors and friends in Little Tokyo, served as surrogate family for each other.[27] Few Issei immigrants had kin in the United States, horizontal or vertical.[28] This was especially true of the Kunitomis, because both Sue's father and mother came to the United States alone.[29] Because of the absence of relatives, Japanese Americans relied on *kenjinkai,* an association of immigrants from the same prefecture in Japan, for economic and moral support. In addition to presenting networking opportunities in business, the *kenjinkai* served as a welfare agency. When a member died the *kenjinkai* arranged the funeral service at which enough *koden* (mourners' donations) were offered to pay for the funeral and assist the bereaved.[30] "Japanese families didn't appreciate welfare," Sue stated. "They avoided it, so a lot of help came through *ken* organizations. This still goes on. I donate *koden* to help a family."[31]

The Japanese American community was also effective in exercising control over its members. Nisei were admonished to remember that their actions would reflect not only on their family, but also on the community and Japanese people in general.[32] Sue expanded on this: "When young kids were getting into trouble [the community] put a lot of pressure on the families. If it didn't work, they had the family ship the kids back to Japan." Who had the authority to take such drastic action?

> Mostly peer pressure from the school, the church, and the big wigs, who would put pressure on the family. It was a very strong force to make sure that everybody behaved and did not bring attention to the community. There is a saying: "If the nail sticks out, it is going to get hammered down." The Japanese community was law abiding. There was very little crime, because of that pressure to conform.[33]

Authorities generally left Japanese youth to the discipline of their parents, reinforced by the power of gossip, an influence dreaded by children.[34]

Sue personalized the control: "My mother used to watch when we were playing outside. The kids used to say: 'Your mother doesn't have to say anything. We can tell by her face that we were doing something wrong and we'd better stop.'"[35] What kind of behavior would result in a youngster being sent to Japan? "Mostly boys," Sue said, "continually starting fights or stealing." One nine-year-old boy, suspected of stealing a car, was sent to Japan because his parents apparently were unable to control him.[36] Given these strong internal controls authorities usually left the discipline of Japanese youth to their parents. Youth delinquency was never the problem in Little Tokyo that it was in other ghetto communities.[37]

Sue continued: "When I was growing up, there was no Social Security, no Medicare. My mother used to go around visiting people [in need]. There was an understanding, neighbors helping neighbors."[38] Sue remembered that growing up during the Great Depression her father managed fairly well. "Mostly because he had a transfer business, moving people, delivering flowers and distributing things to businesses. My mother said he was not a good businessman because a lot of the time he would barter rather than take cash, but that is what people had to do in those days."[39]

Her brother Frank, 13 years older than Sue, evidently had harsh memories of the early 1930s. "He remembered that he didn't have enough to eat. He was the only one I've heard say that."[40] One account does indicate that food was carefully distributed within the community. Sue has written:

> I can remember long ago when I stood in the doorway of the Japanese style bathroom in a boarding house and watched as the men brought in the huge albacore and threw them on the cement floor with a drain in the center.... Quickly and deftly, the fish would be cut up and piled in a corner, this one for old man Fujino... the next big piece for that family down the street. They're always hungry, those kids. And I'd whisper: "Papa, are we going to get any?" Papa would shush me and say: "Don't be impolite. There won't be any left over from this one. But there's another fish over there and we're going to get a piece from that."[41]

Evidently the lean years were made more tolerable by the most memorable events sponsored by the *kenjinkai*, elaborate annual picnics, a rare occasion when gravity, restraint, even sobriety were set aside.[42]

> For the Okayama picnic my father would build a stage for dancing usually in Elysian Park, near Little Tokyo. They would have races for both kids and grown-ups. There was a watermelon game where they blindfolded the women, who had to try to smash the watermelon with a stick. I remember my mother doing that. They would also have a sack race. They would have prizes for everybody, including bags of rice. People would donate money and food. [It was] the one time when we could have lots of soda pop and ice cream. It was really a pretty elaborate and fun day for families.

In response to a question about Issei men becoming tipsy, Sue said: "Oh yes! Most of them were, partly because the donations included saki and beer." She claimed, though, that her father rarely drank alcohol and she never saw him drunk.[43]

While the Japanese American family brought to America many traditional values, the new circumstances nonetheless required adjustments, which over time became significant.[44] Two aspects of tradition, however, remained firmly in place in the years prior to World War II: male dominance and privilege, and shared responsibilities and effort on behalf of the family. Sue's narration dramatizes these and other values of prewar Japanese American life.

CHAPTER 2

Old Values in a New Home

Male dominance and privilege were unmistakable in the Kunitomi family. Gonhichi Kunitomi was often portrayed in the interviews as stern and inflexible. Sue remembered hearing about a fistfight her father had with his business partners, after which they separated and he set up his business in his home. "I could believe that story because my father was a very impatient guy who had a short temper."[1]

Scholars have found that, while both Issei parents were undemonstrative, Nisei generally felt closer to their mothers and feared the wrath of their fathers. Sue recalls that her mother was a disciplinarian, but mostly by scolding.

> She never spanked us. My father did. He would get really angry, if we didn't follow his instructions immediately. With the girls he was very strict. My sister Choko was 10 years older than I. She wanted to go out on dates, but he wouldn't let her. She would put on her lipstick after she left the house. I think he thought she was going out with a group of girls.[2] Sometimes my father had physical scuffles with my brothers when he thought they were not obeying him. My brothers never complained. They just said: "Oh, he has a bad temper."

Jack has recollections of harsh parental discipline. "My father was very stern about things and my mother, too. She said: 'Don't bring disgrace to the family name.' The Japanese had incense sticks called punks. Parents would put one on our back then light it. It burned into the skin. That was our punishment for misbehaving. That, my father did."[3] This practice, known as moxibustion, from Japanese *mokusa* or *mogusa,* is still used as an alternative treatment for medical conditions for which acupuncture is not appropriate.[4] However, as Jack Kunitomi testifies, it was once used in Japanese American families as a punishment.[5]

Consistent with both the belief in male dominance and the conviction that one must assume responsibilities on behalf of the family, Sue's brothers became surrogate fathers. Sue remembered a time when she and friends were innocently talking in front of the house. "My brother Frank said: 'You get in the house right now.' We obeyed him because he was our older brother."[6] Jack also has memories of Frank being protective. "Being the oldest he felt responsibility for us younger ones. I remember we used to go play at the L. A. River. Crossing the last street to the riverbank there were railroad tracks with trains going back and forth all the time. I remember Frank pulling me off the tracks because trains were coming."[7]

In his own role as older brother to Hideo, Jack says:

> I tried to set a good example. He was athletic like I was. You had to play football; that was a macho sport. Hideo also played basketball. Later he organized the basketball league for the Japanese American youth. Because he was the founder of the basketball league they have an award named for him that is given to the best scholar athlete of the [Little Tokyo] Community Youth Council.[8]

About Kinya, Jack said:

> He was more involved with mechanical things. He used to hang around the bicycle shop. He had cronies there that repaired bicycles. And he got into motorcycles. Tets was the youngest and I had a lot of interest in him. I remember giving him a bath when he was an infant. I was in my teens [15 years older]. I was like a second father.[9]

Jack remembers Choko in ways that seem to contradict the model of male privilege. "Being the oldest girl in the family she was catered to and given music lessons. I remember her practicing on the *koto* and violin." Jack was interested in music and became a talented ballroom dancer, but music lessons were considered unmanly.[10]

Many Nisei women spent more time with their sisters than with friends.[11] Sue had a lifelong close bond with her younger sister Midori, grieving profoundly when she died August 9, 2001. She remembered affectionately: "She used to follow me around. We took care of each other as siblings. The older ones took care of the little ones. We took care of Tets a lot." Sue was seven and Midori was five when Tets was born. "He used to follow us around a lot until he started school and was able to have his own friends." [12]

In the prewar Japanese American family there was an acceptance of distinctly different gender roles.[13] After school Sue liked playing baseball, but her father insisted that the girls stay home and help. The young men used to go to the pool hall and to the movie theater on First Street. But the girls were pretty much tied to the house.[14] As Jack recounted: "We hung around the pool halls." He laughed at the memories. "Of course that was a bad thing because the pool halls were associated with gamblers and Mafia. That was a no-no for us, but where else could we hang around?" He also has vivid memories of the Samurai movies. "Before the talkies came in, they had a voice imitator, a *benshi.* He would even imitate ladies' voices and the sounds of war. Before the talkies came in, he would imitate all the speaking parts and all the noises."[15]

Male privilege in the Kunitomi family was also evident in the difference between the celebrations of the traditional Japanese holidays, Girls' Day, March 3, and Boys' Day, May 5. "Some families used to have elaborate dolls that they put in their window for Girls' Day," Sue related. "We never had dolls, and I don't recall doing anything ceremonial for Girls' Day. For Boys' Day my father used to 'Fly the Carp,' one carp [pennant] for each son. He had a flagpole in our yard, and he would have five carp, black and red and very big."[16]

Nisei expected to marry Japanese Americans and both Nisei sons and daughters had arranged or semi-arranged marriages.[17] The choice of husbands for his daughters was unquestionably Gonhichi Kunitomi's prerogative, but only Choko was married before he died. "My sister was 19 or 20 when my father arranged the marriage," Sue said. "The prospective husband [Kiyoshi Teshiba] had come from Japan when he was a young man. He was not much older than Choko, although he was Issei."[18] Like many Nisei women who avoided assertiveness and found it difficult to express strong personal feelings,[19] "Choko didn't say very much," Sue remembers. "I guess she just accepted the arranged marriage. I don't think she had any boyfriends. My father was very strict about her going out."[20]

Sue's narrative reveals, however, that although Gonhichi Kunitomi was autocratic and hot-tempered, he was a complex individual with some surprisingly benevolent characteristics. Sue remembered her mother as always being accepting of people, whereas her father was less so. She did remember one incident with amusement: "A homeless man came to the door and said he was hungry and needed money to buy food. My father made him a sandwich."[21]

The Kunitomis, although typical of their Japanese American peers in family structure and dynamics, were nonconforming in a transformation of gender roles on Thanksgiving. "It was a big holiday for my mother. I remember my brothers helping by bringing home biscuits and fruit. My mother made the turkey, but my father cooked, too. He always helped her cook Thanksgiving dinner." Sue laughed quietly at another memory. "On one birthday he baked his own birthday cake. I was really surprised. I don't know where he learned to cook."[22]

Sue remembered with affection her father's occasional generosity with his family. "We were still in the Depression, and we did not have much money, but my father was one of the few that had a business so he could afford a treat for us occasionally." The Chinese Far East Café on East First Street in Little Tokyo is now one of 13 national landmarks on or near that street.

> "It seems strange," Sue said, laughing, "but Japanese people love Chinese food. People used to go there after weddings and after funerals. Every once in a while my father would order food to be brought to our house, five blocks from the café.

> They would bring food in porcelain dishes with covers on them, on big trays that they carried all the way with two hands up in the air. After supper we would wash all the dishes, pile them back on the trays and my father would take them back the next day. I remember that so vividly, waiters coming up the hill with five trays of food. Nowadays they bring plastic packages."[23]

Sue remembered that although her father did not speak much English, he attempted to read the comics to his children on Sunday.[24] The attempts to amuse the younger children shown by their father at these times were adopted by Sue's brothers.[25] Hideo carved Halloween pumpkins for his younger siblings, and the older brothers made sure their sisters and younger brother had Christmas presents.

Sue acknowledged the powerful influence of her father. "He said: 'Have character, be honest, don't treat people badly and take care of your parents.'" These principles reflect the Issei belief in *giri,* the sense of duty and obligation that encouraged continuous interaction and the strengthening of bonds among people. Filial piety, taking care of one's parents, is a manifestation of the ideal of *giri ninjo,* meaning, in part, obligations and responsibilities that are conducted with one's heart.[26]

Sue was instructed, as were her siblings and other Nisei, that to be a good Japanese person, one's actions must reflect the self-respect of the Japanese community. To do so one must adhere to the principles of *gaman,* perseverance; *enryo,* self-restraint; and *sunao,* obedience. *Haji,* shame, was an especially potent concept used to inhibit behavior. Misbehaving brought *haji* not only to the individual and his or her parents, but also to the community and, in fact, to the Japanese race. These values, stressing the impact of an individual's actions on the community, had as a consequence an emphasis on group orientation. Nisei were admonished about violating group norms, and the negative consequences of such a violation were nearly impossible to avoid. Sue was exceptional among Nisei women in her lifelong endeavor to develop independence and assertiveness, in defiance of these compelling traditional values.[27]

Japanese Americans were able to sustain time-honored values, partially because religion in the new country reinforced generational and racial ties. Temples and churches were firmly rooted within Japanese America. For some Issei, including Komika Kunitomi, Buddhist organizations and the ethics of Buddhism played a significant role in their lives. Other Issei were strongly attracted to Christianity, believing that becoming a Christian was a factor in assimilation, but, ironically, these churches segregated them into all-Japanese congregations, thus perhaps delaying assimilation.[28] While Komika Kunitomi was devoutly Buddhist and sang in the choir of Koyosan Temple in Little Tokyo, she did not insist that her children attend.

Sue related the family's religious history. "The first church my parents went to was the Koyosan [Temple]. It was a big house behind the [present day Japanese American National] museum. Just before the war, they bought land on First Street to build a temple. They asked each family to donate money to build it. It is still there." Recalling her mother's tolerance, Sue said: "Although she would have liked for us to attend the Buddhist Temple regularly, she only asked us to participate in the *Ondo* (Japanese Folk Dance) Festival. 'Honor the dead with your dancing. It's a celebration of joy and not sadness.' Only Midori and I went with her." Sue acknowledged that she and her sister, although they started going to the Buddhist Temple to please their mother, never were actively involved.

Sue expressed great respect for her mother having a strong faith, yet accepting that Choko was the only one of her children who practiced Buddhism. Frank later became an active member of the Hollywood Independent, a Christian church. Both Jack and Midori married into Christian families and attended church regularly. Midori, however, astounded her family when they discovered after her death that she had arranged a Buddhist funeral for herself.

Traditional values of family life in Japan, which were combined with American customs, included the celebration of holidays. Sue remembered Christmas parties in the Hongwanjii Buddhist Temple. "We had a Santa Claus. A lot of the program was in Japanese, although we used to sing songs like Jingle Bells. I guess it was a strange combination, but I didn't think it was strange at all."[29] The Kunitomi family celebrated Christmas in a secular way. "We exchanged gifts, among the kids, anyway. They always made sure we got something, usually clothes. We always had a Christmas tree."

How much did Sue know about the Christian meaning of Christmas as a small child?

> I had read the story about Jesus when were in Sunday school classes in storefront churches. When I was growing up in Little Tokyo, there used to be storefront religious groups. They would come around with little sayings from the Bible, asking us to come to church. We never had real affiliations with any of them because they would be gone in a year or so. My mother didn't mind. She said it would be good for us to go to church and not be out in the streets. My mother also liked to celebrate holidays. It didn't matter whether they were American or Japanese.

Following their observances of Thanksgiving and Christmas, the Kunitomis prepared for *Oshoogatsu,* Japanese New Year, the major holiday for most Japanese Americans.[30] Identical to American New Year celebrations, it is observed each year on December 31 and January 1. Sue remembered:

> My mother would cook for days. We had an elaborate table with a cooked lobster as a centerpiece with vegetables and tofu around it. The lobster represented a long life. The vegetables indicated good wishes for the New Year, the black bean *mame,* for good health and bamboo shoots for always bending but never breaking. On

> New Year's Eve my mother would cook buckwheat noodles that were supposed to be eaten before midnight to give you good passage into the New Year. Our neighbors would come and we would all eat the buckwheat noodles for supper. Before the war we used to pound our own *mochi* (rice cakes).
>
> My mother would wash the sweet rice and put it in square wooden steamers. We steamed the rice over a huge galvanized container heated on the stove. My father and brothers would pound the steamed rice until it was like taffy. My father made the pounding tools. Now they have machines that do that. The neighbors would bring their rice and have us pound it for them. My father would pound *mochi* for the whole neighborhood.

The Kunitomi family learned to function in a bicultural environment, like most Japanese American families, relying on the Nisei to doing most of the mediating between the two cultures. Sue and her brothers engaged in American sports, including baseball, basketball, volleyball, and football, while their mother taught them Japanese games she remembered from her childhood. Komika also taught her children Japanese songs, while Sue's older brothers were keen on American songs. Scholars have determined that the critical dimension in acculturation, learning American values and demeanor, is education.[31] Sue's parents were typical Issei parents in expecting their children to excel in school. The dedication to achievement was resolutely linked with a profound belief in the importance of education, a belief reinforced by both family and community.[32]

CHAPTER 3

A Father's Shadow

Of all the influences in Sue's life, one of the most potent is the shadow her father cast on her education. "My father always looked at our report cards to make sure we had all good grades," Sue remembered. "We would wait until the last day to show him our cards. One time I had a B in something. I had all A's in everything else. He was very angry. 'How come you have this B?' 'You've got to have an A!' "[1] This attitude toward achievement in school was not limited to Japanese American parents. Nevertheless, more than 60 years later, Sue's memories of her father's harsh words and inflexible decisions distressed her.

Sue's schooling began in Amelia Street Elementary School, which her older brothers also attended. The Kunitomi family had moved from Central Avenue, because of redevelopment, to a neighborhood in Little Tokyo that also included the Japanese language school. Like most Nisei women, whose parents emphasized achievement in education, Sue had rewarding experiences in school, although she did not totally avoid interracial tension or prejudice.[2] Mabel Colerick, who was later to prove her trustworthiness to the Kunitomis, became principal while Sue was attending Amelia Street School. Sue recalled the principal and the Caucasian teachers as being exceptional. "They made a real effort to bring people in from other groups. We had Native Americans and Mexican groups who talked to us about how they lived. The teachers would also take us on fieldtrips, like the La Brea Tar Pits."[3]

Most of the students in the grade school were Japanese American, 98 percent by Sue's estimate. "There were Chinese families that lived a block away toward Chinatown and their children were in that school. There were only two Caucasian kids. One was a blonde, blue-eyed, gal, Dorothy, who became my best friend."[4] The Japanese American students were clearly aware of the boundaries of interracial socializing. A small minority of Nisei had Caucasian friends, but their association was confined to the school playground.[5] About Dorothy Sue said: "I don't know where she lived, but we were good friends at school through the eighth grade. Then we went to Lincoln High School and I lost track of her."[6]

Sue evidently began to develop her eclectic interests and independence at an early age. "The thing I liked [in school] was the multi-cultural activities. I was always curious about how other people lived. I got interested in world affairs and listened to the radio a lot. My brothers all listened to the baseball games. I was listening to the news. I knew about Walter Winchell and the other commentators."[7]

While Nisei learned American history and traditions in school, more importantly they learned English. Most Japanese American children first confronted the English language in grade school.[8] "When I started in kindergarten at age five, I thought English was my first language," Sue said. "At home we did speak Japanese, but my brothers spoke English to us."[9]

While public schools prepared Nisei for their roles as interpreters of America to their parents and the Japanese American community, at the same time, Japanese language schools, the *gakuen,* endeavored to strengthen in Nisei a knowledge of their parents' language and culture. The Issei hoped the Nisei would learn to appreciate their heritage by becoming conversant in Japanese.[10] Although most Nisei did not become fluent in Japanese, the *gakuen* did strengthen ethnic ties, but the Japanese Language School was conversely also a conduit to cultural pluralism. The president of the Southern California Japanese Language School Association asserted: "[W]e must not forget that we are educating American citizens. We must study more diligently in order to select character traits which will be suitable to the American nationality."[11] The first *gakuen* opened in Los Angeles in 1911. By 1933, about the time Sue began attending, 4,000 students were enrolled in Japanese Language Schools in Los Angeles County.[12]

Although most Japanese Americans report that they were not attentive in the language school,[13] Sue, atypically, was from first grade through high school a diligent student in the Rafu Daiichi *Gakuen* in Little Tokyo. "I liked it. I would do my homework regularly. With Midori and me, my mother insisted that we go. My brothers weren't interested, so they didn't go. Boys got more spoiled than the girls."

Although her brothers were "great readers," they read mostly books in English.[14] Jack corroborates Sue's memories of her brothers' lack of interest in the *gakuen.* "My parents were paying for Japanese School tuition but instead of going to school we were playing football, basketball, baseball, whatever the season was. The teacher or the principal would notify our parents. And wow!" Did his parents' wrath force him to attend Japanese Language School? "No. We finally dropped out because we were in high school and rather independent."[15]

Although Jack was indifferent to Rafu Daiichi *Gakuen,* he was a devoted and enthusiastic member of the Olivers, which met on the second floor of the same building as the Japanese Language School. One of the remarkable stories of Little Tokyo is that of the Olivers, an athletic club for Japanese American boys, founded in 1917 and sustained for a quarter century by Miss Nellie Grace Oliver, a kindergarten teacher at Amelia Street School and Hewitt Street School, who became Director of Kindergarten for the Los Angeles City School District in 1906. The Olivers, Little Tokyo's first youth organization, became a second home for hundreds of Nisei, including Jack Kunitomi. Because Japanese ancestry excluded Nisei from swimming pools, skating rinks, and organized sports that white teenagers enjoyed, the Nisei could achieve popularity and respect only in their own groups. Thus the Olivers quickly became a uniquely Nisei phenomenon and Japanese American boys turned to the club to construct a positive self-image.[16]

Although the Olivers had started a girls' club in 1925, tutoring girls in good manners and other feminine virtues of that time, Sue was instead involved in the *gakuen,* diligently learning Japanese. Many Nisei, even those who had done well in Japanese Language School, now say that they do not know Japanese. As Sue said: "I lost a lot of it." She explained: "Ability with the Japanese language was lost because of the war. To be American you couldn't speak any language but English. The Japanese language schools were all closed after Pearl Harbor.[17] The principal was picked up by the FBI that night."[18]

Following Amelia Street Elementary School, Sue and her older brothers attended Lincoln High School, for which their elementary school teachers had tried to prepare them.

> Our teachers were concerned that we were going to an integrated school after we had been in almost all Japanese classes. We had an after-school program where we learned to do social dance, the waltz and the foxtrot and *La Bamba.* They did a lot of counseling so we would be able to get into the mainstream because most of us had never been out of the Japanese community.

Lincoln High School was multiethnic, Russian, Chinese, and Mexican, but mostly Italian. However, Sue remembered: "Everybody stuck to their own group. The school never did anything to try to integrate. I guess in those days they didn't think about that." Sue was in the minority among Japanese Americans in making friends with Caucasians, but her friendship with a non-Japanese was confined to school hours.

Despite her friendships with Caucasians, Sue has valued her Japanese heritage. The Lincoln High School Yearbook of 1938, *The Lincolnian,* includes pictures of Sue and Midori in the campus club, The Mikados. The yearbook states, ironically in retrospect: "The Mikados undertook the project of introducing the student body to the culture of Japan, which everyone appreciates."

The 1937 yearbook has two references to Sue's being Japanese. One, "Best wishes to the daughter of the east, Japan," is signed "Smiley." I asked Sue how she had felt about this description in 1937. "My father always said: 'Don't forget that you are Japanese, but you are an American citizen.' Later I think a lot of people were embarrassed to be Japanese because of the war, but not in our family." Another entry in 1937 states: "Lots of luck to my little Japanese pet." It is signed: "Your pal, Lita." Sue said: "I don't know who that is. That's a little patronizing."

All of the other messages in the yearbooks have comments about Sue's intelligence. One 1939 entry states: "Knowing you has taught me new things. I only hope I can someday be as smart and intelligent as you are." It is signed by Leo Garcia. "He was our student president," Sue said. "He was really a great friend." In an entry in 1940 teacher Paul Church Greene wrote: "Every once in a while I find a real student among the crowd, and such a one are you. Keep it up."

The most potent restraint Sue's father imposed on her was when she entered high school. Although the Issei placed great emphasis on education, Nisei women generally did not expect to go to college.[19] Sue differed significantly from her peers in this respect.

> My mother let my father control our schooling, and he told me to take a business course, bookkeeping and typing. I got brave enough to tell him that I wanted to go to college, but he emphatically said: "No!" That's the first time I heard him talk about prejudice. "You're Japanese. You're a woman, and women don't have any value in the United States." So I took bookkeeping. I took typing.

Although she did well in business courses, Sue was frustrated, repeatedly expressing her hope of attending college. Her father responded: "You are going to get married and have kids. You don't need a college education." During the last year in high school Sue worked in the office of the school counselor, where she looked into her student file and found this notation: "Recommended for college." Sue was bewildered because no one had ever told her that she qualified for college. She remembered thinking: " 'I may not be able to go, but I'm going to try.' "

In contrast, Jack remembers his father encouraging him to go to college. "He knew immigrants, especially then, didn't have much chance of getting up in society, but he said: 'Try your best.' " Although Jack earned a bachelor's degree and a teaching credential after World War II, Frank, Hideo and Kinya did not attend college. Jack remembers Frank being more interested in making innovative radio crystal sets, Hideo being sports minded, and Kinya being mechanically inclined.[20]

Sue's father was conforming to contemporary values when he told her that she would get married and have kids, that college was not an option for her. There were three major reasons for most Nisei women viewing marriage and motherhood as their future.[21] First, most families could not afford college for the daughters, especially if there were sons, who usually had priority. Second, Japanese Americans, both men and women, were limited in career choices. Even civil service was not open to them; a job with the city or county of Los Angeles was extremely rare. While teaching was attractive to Nisei women, no Nisei was employed as a public school teacher in the city of Los Angeles during the 1940s. Nor was there a single Japanese American fireman, policeman, or mailman. Sue's father was correct about the lack of employment opportunities. Third, most Nisei young women viewed marriage and motherhood as predestined. Sue was an exception, but she was never able to answer my question: "Where do you think the idea of going to college came from?" She responded: "I really don't know. Even my teachers didn't talk about college. None of my friends went to college."[22]

In December 1937, when Sue was almost 15 years old, her ambition had to be set aside. Gonhichi Kunitomi was returning from Glendale after delivering flowers. Driving on San Fernando Road alongside railroad tracks, he evidently missed a turn. His pickup truck, out of control, rolled over onto the railroad tracks. According to family accounts, he was 61 years old, in good health. He died from his injuries that night.[23] Sue remembered the trauma:

> I was home with my mother when the phone rang, around 5 o'clock. It was the police department. My father was at the Georgia Street Receiving Hospital, at that time an emergency hospital. The hospital wanted him transferred to another hospital. My mother called a Japanese taxi firm. I called around looking for my brothers. We went to the hospital, just me and my mother. The nurse gave me all of his belongings and they put us in an ambulance with the siren screaming to the Japanese Hospital in Boyle Heights in East L. A. The doctor told us that my father was unconscious with a skull fracture and he did not know whether he would pull through. By that time my brothers had gotten the news. The whole family was there.

Jack, who was 22 when his father died, recalled:

> I was working at Grand Central Market. That's where our work entry used to be for most of the young people, retail marketing, selling fruits and vegetables. We were in the process of closing for the night. A young fellow that lived across the street from us came running in and said: "Your father got into an accident and he's in the hospital." I excused myself and walked down to First Street to the bicycle shop where Kinya was. When we got to the hospital, my father was in a coma. We waited, the whole family. I was close to my father because I worked with him more than the others when we moved things for the big *kenjinkai* picnics.

All of the siblings were living at home when their father died. Sue described the impact of her father's death on the younger ones. "Tets was crying because he could not give his Papa the Christmas gift he had made at school. He also told us: 'Those big bullies are going to beat me up now that I don't have a father.' He was only seven."[24] Sue remembered Midori, who was 12, not saying anything. "But she cried a lot. She stuck close to me. At the funeral she was always right next to me crying."[25]

The funeral for Gonhichi Kunitomi was held at the Koyasan Buddhist Temple. "It was packed with people," Sue remembered. "Lots of flowers and wreaths, I think a whole truckload. The Fukui Mortuary brought the casket in. First to offer incense was my mother and then my siblings, from oldest to youngest. Then everybody else in the congregation offered incense." Sue found the service comforting: "... to have all my father's friends there; I had not realized that he was that popular."[26] Komika Kunitomi received aid from the Okayama *kenjinkai.* "My father died in the middle of the Depression, 1937 [but] my mother received enough *koden* to cover most of the funeral expenses."[27] How did her mother manage to pay the hospital and doctor bills? Sue did not know. "There was no medical insurance. She didn't worry us about how she was going to do it. She didn't complain. She just did it."[28]

When I asked Jack how his mother responded to this crisis, he responded: "Japanese women were stoic. *Shikata ga nai.* It cannot be helped. I was working in the market so I would bring home fruit and a few groceries. Then we were able to buy the store next door to our house."[29] Midori later wrote a brief family history, never published, in which she stated that when their father died, 19-year-old Kimbo took over the transfer business. Sue explained: "He was the only one that didn't have a full-time job. He had been helping my dad all along. He continued with it by himself, although there wasn't a lot of work."[30]

Komika Kunitomi revealed an assertive independence following her husband's death. "She went around to collect all the debts that were owed to my father. My older brothers were working. They had part-time jobs even while they were in high school. I guess that's how she managed."[31] Komika purchased a grocery store from neighbors who returned to Japan. She financed the purchase by borrowing from Frank's and Jack's life insurance policies. Since Issei could not own property, Komika did not actually own the store. "The grocery store and our house were owned by the same Caucasian," Sue explained. "We paid rent for the store and we paid rent for the house. The neighbors [who had returned to Japan] sold my mother the good will and the business."[32]

Many Nisei report never having a sustained discussion with either parent.[33] In this respect Komika and her sons were atypical. Possibly because Komika, being a single parent, felt the weight of responsibility, she talked at length with her sons. "My brothers used to sit around the dinner table and talk about what they had been doing. She liked that, knowing what they were doing, that they weren't in trouble. My mother always tried to have all of us eat together. That was important."[34] When Sue turned to her older brothers for help or advice, they continued in their role of surrogate fathers. "I asked them for money to buy my high school athletic sweater with the letter 'L'. I was in the Girls Athletic Association and got my Lincoln letter in baseball and basketball. The sweaters were very expensive. Then we had to buy the yearbook, also very expensive for us, but my brothers helped."[35]

Shortly before she graduated from Lincoln High School in January of 1941, Sue had an appendicitis attack requiring surgery. "I got out of bed just long enough to go through one rehearsal at the high school. I could barely stand, but I did go through the graduation ceremony. I couldn't go to any of the parties."[36]

Although Sue had been helping her mother by working part-time in the store, she began working full-time after graduation.

> It was seven days a week. They would come banging at the door at 6 o'clock in the morning, wanting us to open, even on Sunday. My brothers, when they came back from work, would help, but mostly it was just my mother and me. We didn't have time for much else. We bought it, in March [19] 41, not quite a year before Pearl Harbor.

Sue speculated: "We were pretty young when my father died, so I don't know what kind of influence he would have had on us. He probably would have wanted me to get married."[37] She vividly remembered that when her mother bought the store, Sue told her that she wanted to go to college. She was given hope when her mother replied: "Maybe we will make some money from this grocery store. In a couple years Midori will be graduating. She can help me and you can go to school." Sixty-three years later, Sue said poignantly: "I was really counting on that."[38] But ensuing events intervened that disrupted the entire family and tested Komika Kunitomi's resolute independence.

CHAPTER 4

The Impact of the Attack on Pearl Harbor

Although Japanese comprised only one percent of the population of California, by the early 1900s they controlled nearly one-half of the state's commercial produce market. Agricultural skills brought with them from Japan enabled the Issei to grow crops on land deemed infertile by other farmers. The Japanese farmer, working unusually hard in a cooperative and innovative manner, was able to sell high-quality produce at low prices. Success in both wholesale and retail produce markets led to further collective endeavors in floriculture, commercial fishing, and gardening. Japanese Americans had developed a thriving niche economy most notably in southern California.[1] Fuming that Japanese immigrants and their descendants were unfair economic competition, organized labor in California launched an anti-Japanese campaign based on racial stereotypes and fear of the "Yellow Peril." that ultimately became a national movement.

White supremacists achieved significant victories through legislation, including alien land laws enacted by several western states in the early 1900s that prohibited aliens ineligible for citizenship from owning, leasing, or sharecropping agricultural land. Asians were ineligible for citizenship by naturalization, which was limited until 1952 to "free white persons" and persons of African descent. Thus the land laws impeded agricultural competition from Japanese Americans.[2]

The anti-Japanese legislation created a diplomatic problem for President Theodore Roosevelt, who had negotiated an understanding with Japan that came to be known as the Gentlemen's Agreement of 1907–08. Under this agreement Japan discontinued issuing exit visas for laborers to the continental United States, although Japanese labor was still allowed on Hawaiian sugar plantations. The two nations, however, could not agree on the definition of a laborer and the status of picture brides, whom the United States claimed were not covered in the agreement.

In response to growing pressure from anti-Japanese forces, Congress passed The Immigration Act of 1924, the most restrictive immigration policy in American history, which ended all further immigration from Japan.[3] Despite the impact of this restrictive legislation, the fears of white supremacists were inflated by an upsurge in Japanese Americans emigrating to California through Hawaii and bringing picture brides from Japan.

The harsh legacy of the anti-Asian crusade in the western United States created the environment for the mass hysteria that led to the forced removal of Japanese Americans during World War II following the bombing of Pearl Harbor.[4] Nowhere was this hysteria more evident than in Little Tokyo, Los Angeles.[5]

At 7:55 a.m. Honolulu time on December 7, 1941, Japanese bombers had attacked Pearl Harbor, the major U.S. naval base in Hawaii, sinking or disabling 19 ships, destroying 150 planes, and causing 2,403 fatalities.[6] Like many Americans, Sue learned of the attack when the news was broadcast on the radio.

> I was in our store listening to a radio show, Al Jarvis' Big Band music. They interrupted the program around noon, announcing that Japanese planes had attacked Pearl Harbor in Hawaii. I didn't know where Pearl Harbor was. I ran next door and told my mother the news. "Ah," she said, "they are always saying those things to try to sell newspapers. I don't think that's true. How could they? They would be too far from Japan."

Sue herself had trouble believing the news until her brothers came home saying that police had surrounded the streets of Little Tokyo. Jack's recollection of Pearl Harbor Day is as vivid as that of his sister.[7]

> We knew from newspapers and the radio that the embargo was going to hurt Japan and we were wondering what they would do about it. We also knew about the Japanese envoys in Washington.[8] We were going to a football game that Sunday morning at Gilmore Field. An announcement came over a loud speaker outside the stadium where we were waiting to get tickets that we had been attacked by Japanese bombers.

Jack remembers that when he and his friends drove back to First and San Pedro streets, Little Tokyo was "buzzing with Caucasian policemen, FBI, and plainclothesmen. They were going into the different shops, arresting the proprietors. Terrible confusion for all the employees. That went on through evening because there were many, many shops." Stores operated by Japanese Americans were closed; Issei bank accounts were frozen, depriving Little Tokyo and other communities of both its leadership and its financial resources. The Japanese American community in Los Angeles was in chaos.[9] Jack Kunitomi remembers the acute uncertainty and anxiety in Little Tokyo. "At the wholesale market where I was working, the company was owned by a Japanese alien. Our store was closed. We were jobless. Even in many Nisei-owned shops. Money was tied up because it was in Japanese banks."

> "I was scared," Sue remembered. "We didn't know what was going to happen to us. My mother didn't think it was true, but by nightfall she had to believe it. By then we heard that our Japanese language school teachers and neighbors who were active in civic affairs had been arrested. My mother was worried that they were going to arrest her, because she was a member of the Women's Federation at the temple."

The Japanese community was diligent in keeping membership lists and minutes of meetings, making information easily accessible to the authorities, but despite Komika's fear, far fewer women than men were arrested.

On December 8, President Roosevelt addressed a joint session of Congress with his legendary "a date which will live in infamy" proclamation, asking Congress for a Declaration of War against Japan. "We all listened to that," Sue recalled. "Most of us supported the President. He had done some good things domestically like the WPA (Work Projects Administration). My mother didn't understand much English, so we talked to her about being at war with Japan."

As early as 18 months before Pearl Harbor, Japanese Americans living on the Pacific Coast had been placed under intense scrutiny. In October of 1941 FBI agents had visited Little Tokyo, questioned leaders of Japanese American organizations and seized documents and records.[10] On December 7 and 8 President Franklin D. Roosevelt authorized the FBI to arrest aliens in the continental United States who were deemed "dangerous to public peace or safety." Since Issei were not allowed to become American citizens, Japanese American community leaders were considered enemy aliens. By December 8 the FBI had picked up 736 Japanese Americans, and by the end of the week, the number had doubled.

Sue clearly remembered who was detained by the FBI. "Our Buddhist ministers were picked up, also judo teachers, cultural leaders, sports managers, teachers, the Chamber of Commerce president. All of the people who were active in the community and those who had gone back and forth on business to Japan were all picked up."

Among those arrested by the FBI was Togo Tanaka, Nisei editor of the English edition of the Japanese newspaper *Rafu Shimpo,* whose life later intersected with Sue's. He was never charged with violation of the law, nor was the reason for his arrest explained during the 11 days of his incarceration.[11] Jack has a personal memory of another Japanese American journalist arrested by the FBI, his future father-in-law, Shiro Fujioka, the Japanese editor for the *Rafu Shimpo,* who was also working for the Japanese Chamber of Commerce as the Executive Treasurer/Secretary.

> They took him to Tujunga Canyon [14 miles north of downtown Los Angeles] where they had vacant CCC [Civilian Conservation Corp] buildings. We were all worried. Evidently they had been following Fujioka for a year or so. We found out later that they even had a history of when he took the bus in Hollywood, when he got off on Sixth and Olive [in downtown Los Angeles.] We were not able to talk to anyone in the FBI then. They were too busy rounding up more suspects.[12]

In picking up virtually every Issei who had been active in the life of the community, the government was aided by members of the Japanese American Citizens League (JACL), a national organization founded in 1930, as a response to xenophobia expressed by white Americans. The JACL was the largest Japanese American organization when the war started, although the membership was relatively small. Since only American citizens could join at that time, JACL was entirely Nisei, whose average age in the community was 18.

> "The JACL wanted to show that they were patriotic and loyal citizens," Sue explained. "They would turn in anybody who seemed to be suspicious. They have a reputation even now of having sold people down the river. We knew all through the war about the JACL helping the government. They didn't keep it a secret. Even though the national organization was claiming to be representing us, many people said they were not."[13]

Within hours of the attack on Pearl Harbor, influential Nisei of Los Angeles had formed an Anti-Axis Committee, with Tokutaro Slocum, an active member of the JACL, as chairman, to uncover "subversive activity."[14] The "constructive cooperation" policy of the JACL had numerous critics, some of whom accused the organization of having a "petty entrepreneurial position . . . with middleclass aspirations." However, the majority of Japanese Americans preferred accommodation to confrontation, and the JACL gained a legitimacy that allowed them to claim leadership of the Japanese American community in the immediate postwar years.[15]

Although there was considerable distress in Little Tokyo, Caucasians for a brief period following the attack on Pearl Harbor were relatively amiable toward Japanese American residents. Los Angeles Mayor Fletcher Bowron maintained a friendly, if distant, attitude. The County Board of Supervisors expressed concern that innocent Nisei schoolchildren might be attacked.[16] Sue remembered that her younger siblings were in an all-Japanese class. "I don't know how much they worried; they never said anything."

For Sue the most distressing aspect of the weeks following the attack on Pearl Harbor was the uncertainty. "Were we going to be able to go about our lives like we had before? Would my mother be able to keep the store and make a living? However, there wasn't much hostility until the agricultural groups, and The [Native] Sons and Daughters of the Golden West became very vocal, and the media hyped it up." The Native Sons of the Golden West was formed in 1875; the Native Daughters was created in 1885. The organization has earned the reputation of being one of the most strident and blatantly racist groups in the anti-Japanese movement. California chapters of the group tirelessly campaigned in January of 1942 for the removal of all ethnic Japanese people from the West Coast.[17] One of its members was California Attorney General Earl Warren, who later became a champion for civil rights as Chief Justice of the U.S. Supreme Court.[18]

By the end of January 1942, there was a dramatic shift in public sentiment toward Japanese Americans. More and more were demanding their internment of Japanese Americans, due in large measure to the campaign of the Native Sons and Daughters of the Golden West and to the rhetoric of elected officials. Also on January 25 the Roberts Commission, appointed by the president and chaired by Supreme Court Justice Owen J. Roberts, released its report. Among its conclusions was that Japanese Hawaiian spies were partially responsible for the bombing of Pearl Harbor. Even though it lacked corroborating evidence, the report implied what military officers believed to be true at the time: the attack could have been prevented. The report advocated that counterespionage efforts on the West Coast be augmented immediately.[19]

Sue commented on the report: "The story that I still hear today is that farmers in the pineapple and sugar plantations dug ditches with arrows pointing toward Pearl Harbor."[20] Historian Roger Daniels underscores the absurdity of this myth by pointing out that Pearl Harbor, "a large natural harbor containing dozens of war vessels" would have been "highly visible from the air."[21] Despite its ambiguous language, the Roberts Report had a dramatic effect on newspapers and politicians of the West Coast and was taken as proof of Japanese American disloyalty. The governor of California, Culbert L. Olson, who ironically was chairman of the Northern California Committee on Fair Play for Citizens and Aliens of Japanese Ancestry, announced in a radio address on February 4: "It is known that there are Japanese residents of California who have sought to aid the Japanese enemy by way of communicating information...." Los Angeles Mayor Fletcher Bowron echoed Olson's warnings: "Right here in our own city are those who may spring to action at an appointed time in accordance with a prearranged plan wherein each of our little Japanese friends will know his part in the event of any possible attempted invasion or air raid.... We cannot run the risk of another Pearl Harbor episode in Southern California."[22]

Such rhetoric inflamed the rampant panic in Los Angeles in the early months of 1942. Roger Daniels quotes headlines from the pages of the *Los Angeles Times* to convey what he calls the near hysteria.[23] "Enemy Planes Sighted over California Coast." "Japs Plan Coast Attack in April." "Jap Boat Flashes Message Ashore."

Daniels reports: "Day after day throughout December, January, February, and March, the *Times* and the rest of the California press spewed forth racial venom against Japanese."

Many West Coast newspapers in identifying Japanese Americans used not only "Japs," but also "Nips," "mad dogs," and "yellow vermin." Newspapers and magazines nationwide ran false stories about spy rings, alleging that the FBI had confiscated navy signal flags, illegal radios, and ammunition from Japanese American homes.[24]

On February 11, 1942, President Roosevelt transferred jurisdiction of Terminal Island in Los Angeles Harbor to the navy. Terminal Island had been settled at the turn of the century by immigrant Japanese fishermen, and a Japanese American community with fishing as its economic heart grew rapidly in what became known as East San Pedro. Largely a self-contained group retaining many of Japan's traditional customs, Terminal Islanders were highly suspect as potential saboteurs. The community was also in a strategic location, close to both the harbor of Los Angeles and the U.S. Naval Station at Long Beach.

The urgency of protecting the harbor had been reported in the *Los Angeles Examiner* on December 8. The headline read: "Flash of news that Japan has attacked Pearl Harbor and Manila hit Los Angeles Harbor like a thunderbolt. It tripped the trigger of 'zero hour' preparations and within an hour the entire harbor area was under a virtual state of martial law."[25]

Navy Secretary Frank Knox directed that signs be posted on February 25 ordering all Japanese Americans off Terminal Island within 48 hours, by midnight February 27. Since the War Department had already picked up the Issei men of the fishing village, Issei women and the Nisei scrambled desperately to pack their belongings, find new places to live and locate jobs, any kind of jobs, to support their displaced families. Bill Hosokawa, Nisei journalist and author, reports:

> Near panic swept the community.... Word spread quickly and human vultures in the guise of used-furniture dealers descended on the island, driving up and down the streets in trucks offering $5 for washing machines, $10 for refrigerators... pittances for household goods.... The Japanese, angry, but helpless, sold their possessions because they did not know what to do with their goods and because they sensed the need in the uncertain days ahead for all the cash they could squirrel away.[26]

Sue described the Kunitomi family's involvement in the "cruel overnight ouster":[27]

> People who worked in the wholesale markets, like my brother, took big trucks to help load everything they could and get them off Terminal Island. We put some of them in the Japanese School building. They had closed the school, but the upstairs was open. The community got together to help them. All of my brothers helped, and we took food to the families.

When my brothers helped move the Terminal Islanders, [we were given] their fishing poles. When we were ready to leave, my mother gave them to some of our Caucasian customers. Hideo got mad and said: "You shouldn't have given those poles away. We may have to go fishing for our food wherever we are!" I thought: "God, you mean we have to catch our own food?" That was terrifying.[28]

At the request of the War Department, the Justice Department had created lists of "contraband" items. Without warrants the FBI conducted searches of Japanese American homes on the west coast, confiscating guns, cameras, radios, and other possessions deemed potentially dangerous. Japanese American families, living in anxiety day to day, waiting for the appearance of FBI agents, and apprehensive about dispelling the slightest suspicion, destroyed the possessions that signified their Japanese heritage, including family pictures, letters, books, even clothes and crafts.[29]

Sue remembered:

"Kinya had guns that he used to go shooting in the desert. He turned all those in. My father had brought a sword from Japan disguised in the shape of a cane. Being honest, we decided to turn it in. Hideo made sure he got a receipt for it." She laughed at the futility. "Of course, he went back after the war and they had already auctioned it. A lot of good that receipt did. We had bought my mother a short wave radio so she could listen to Japanese broadcasts. We turned in all our radios, so we didn't have anything to listen to. We were even more isolated. After the Terminal Island removal, we really began to feel that we also were going to be moved; we weren't sure where," Sue said. "I was resigned to the fact."[30]

Sue's anticipation of her own family's removal was confirmed by Franklin Roosevelt's decision to issue Executive Order 9066 on February 19, 1942.

Now, therefore, by the virtue of the authority vested in me as President of the United States and Commander of the Army and Navy, I hereby authorize and direct the Secretary of War and Military Commanders whom he may from time to time designate, whenever he or any designated commander deems such actions necessary or desirable, to prescribe military areas in such places and of such extent as he or the appropriate Military Commander may determine, from which any or all persons may be excluded, and with respect to which, the right of any person to enter, remain in, or leave shall be subject to whatever restrictions the Secretary of War or the appropriate Military Commander may impose in his discretion.[31]

Roosevelt believed that removing Japanese Americans from the West Coast would be admired by Congress and the general population.[32] The executive order did not specifically mention Japanese Americans, the West Coast, evacuation, or internment. Nevertheless, there was no doubt that the purpose of the order was to give the army the power to remove the Japanese Americans from the Pacific Coast.[33]

February was a grim month for the United States. Singapore, Manila, Hongkong, and much of the Dutch East Indies were under Japanese control and it was evident that Burma soon would be captured. On February 23, four days after the Executive Order was issued, a Japanese submarine surfaced and shelled an oil refinery off the coast of Santa Barbara. At 3:15 a.m. on February 26 unidentified planes purportedly flew over Los Angeles in the "Battle of Los Angeles." The 37th Coast Artillery Brigade fired 1,430 shells, searchlights swept the skies, and air-raid warning sirens wailed.[34] The population of Los Angeles was greatly unnerved by these two incidents. "It had more impact on the Japanese American community than the community-at-large," Sue stated. "Most of us were pretty scared. My mother was scared to death. We were wondering what would happen to us. We were Japanese, the lost American citizens."

Many Issei and Nisei still believed that forced removal was an impossibility, "a hideous nightmare that would vanish with the dawn."[35] Their hopes were temporarily buoyed by a congressional committee, chaired by Representative John H. Tolan of California, which had undertaken an investigation of the necessity for removing enemy aliens from strategic military zones. Japanese Americans were encouraged by the Tolan Committee's apparent willingness to hear testimony on their behalf.[36]

During testimony before the Tolan Committee on February 21, California Attorney General Earl Warren insisted that Japanese Americans had "infiltrated themselves into every strategic spot in our coastal and valley counties."[37] In his testimony Warren made a statement, which later became infamous, that the complete absence of sabotage by Japanese Americans was evidence that such sabotage was forthcoming.[38] This leap in logic was articulated by a number of other high-ranking officials, including Lieutenant General John L. DeWitt, head of the Western Defense Command.[39]

Mike Masaoka, the charismatic executive secretary of the JACL, appeared before the Committee, testifying that if the government declared that removing Japanese Americans from strategic military zones was necessary, the Nisei would have no alternative other than accepting it. However, he also argued: "As American citizens believing in the integrity of our citizenship, we feel that any evacuation enforced on grounds violating that integrity should be opposed."[40] Since the decision had been made to remove Japanese Americans from the West Coast before the hearings were held, the Tolan Committee hearings have been described as "a sham."[41]

Japanese Americans who had hoped to be aided by Congress had their expectation shattered when Public Law 503 gave legislative sanction to Executive Order 9066. The law, declaring it a federal offense to violate restrictions by a military commander in a military area (under Executive Order 9066) and providing for enforcement in the federal courts, passed both houses of Congress on March 19 by unanimous voice vote. The "appropriate military commander" referred to in Executive Order 9066, John L. DeWitt, head of the Western Defense Command, declared: "A Jap's a Jap... It makes no difference whether he is an American citizen; theoretically he is still a Japanese."[42]

One of the most persistent rumors that filled the press was that all Issei would be interned in concentration camps, while Nisei might not be interned because they were American citizens. Executive Order 9066 made no direct reference to Japanese Americans. However, on March 2 DeWitt began the process of their removal, and incarceration, as the executive order had authorized, by issuing Public Proclamation No. 1, creating Western Defense Command zones 1 and 2. The area ultimately encompassed the entire state of California, the western sections of Washington and Oregon, and the southern half of Arizona.[43]

On March 11 DeWitt announced the formation of the Wartime Civil Control Administration [WCCA] with Karl R. Bendetsen, chief of the Aliens Division of the Provost General's office, as director to handle the evacuation program. The WCCA, operated by the War Department, was responsible for the mass removal of Japanese Americans from the Western Defense zones and the administration of the 16 assembly centers, where Japanese Americans were temporarily kept prior to being sent to permanent internment camps. Horse stalls of race tracks were among the facilities used for assembly centers. On March 18 Roosevelt issued Executive Order 9102 creating the War Relocation Authority, a civilian agency responsible for supervising the incarceration of Japanese Americans who had been transferred from assembly centers to internment camps. The president selected Milton Eisenhower, director of Information in the Department of Agriculture, to be director of the WRA. Japanese American citizens, as well as Issei, would be excluded from strategic military areas.

All persons of Japanese ancestry were notified by signs posted throughout the community by the WCCA that they were to prepare to be evacuated on a specific day assigned to them. They were further ordered to send a representative from each family to the Wartime Civil Control Administration on April 21 or 22 for registration and instructions. "My mother reasoned that my oldest brother Frank was the head of the household," Sue said, "so he signed everybody up." The Kunitomi family originally was assigned to Santa Anita racetrack assembly center to await removal to an internment camp. Jack was not yet married to Masa Fujioka. He recounted:

> My mother and I talked to Masa's mother [Chiyo Fujioka]. Her husband [Shiro Fujioka] had been picked up [by the FBI] and she had a big family to take care of. Masa and I got married downtown at one of the justice of peace offices, then we walked to the Olympian Hotel, where they were signing up for the evacuation.[44]

On March 24, DeWitt issued Proclamation No. 3 instituting an 8 p.m. to 6 a.m. curfew for German, Italian, and Japanese aliens and Japanese American citizens. The proclamation also required them to obtain military clearance to travel more than five miles from their homes. Sue remembered: "My mother and I closed the store early and stayed home. Frank lived in East L.A., a little more than five miles, so we rarely saw him."

Although the curfew was imposed also on German Americans and Italian Americans who lived in the restricted area, they were not subjected to compulsory mass removal. According to the 1940 federal census, 112,353 persons of Japanese ancestry lived in the United States, nearly all of them on the Pacific Coast. Of this number 71,484 were citizens by birth and 40,869 were aliens denied citizenship by law. In contrast, there were 51,923 Italian aliens and 19,422 German aliens, who were aliens by choice since no law prevented them from becoming citizens.[45] For Europeans suspicion of disloyalty was individual; for Asians it was collective. By excluding both Nisei and Issei, the federal government reinforced the widespread public identification of Japanese Americans with the Japanese enemy.[46] Alien Italian Americans and German Americans, however, did not escape totally intact. Individual Italian and German aliens who were on government lists were interned."[47]

"The notice [from the Western Defense Command] said 'Persons of Japanese Ancestry should prepare for evacuation,'" Sue remembered. "It didn't mention anything about Italians or Germans. I didn't think that was fair, but I thought we should cooperate. What other choice did we have?" Perhaps no experience of the removal and internment was more painful to Sue than her family's suffering as they prepared to leave their home in Little Tokyo for a camp in an unknown desert.[48]

The Kunitomi family received their official notice on May 3. On March 21 the first group of Nisei "volunteers" from Los Angeles, including Hideo Kunitomi, had departed for Manzanar, then an assembly center operated by the army, to prepare the camp for the ones to follow under the compulsory removal program. Sue remembered Hideo's letters telling his family to prepare for severe cold weather. The volunteers "had to heat water on a wood fire in a big galvanized can." Hideo also complained that there was no work for them except to clean up after the union workers. "They had been promised union wages," Sue remembered, "which, of course, infuriated the union. The volunteers never got union wages. And no matter how harsh the living conditions were, once they were there they couldn't come back."[49]

The compulsory removal began with a departure date one week after registration. The Kunitomis were instructed to report to the old Union Train Station in downtown Los Angeles at 8 a.m., May 9, 1942.

> We had a list of things we could bring and things we couldn't bring. No pets. No furniture. No mattresses. We were instructed to bring dishes and utensils for each person. Toiletries. Only what we could carry in two hands. We all were in limbo

> and we felt a sense of relief that something was finally happening, although we weren't sure exactly what.[50]

In addition to relief, however, a predominant response of Japanese Americans was cooperation with the government based on the *enryo* syndrome. *Enryo,* meaning reserve, restraint, diffidence, perhaps explains in part the response of Japanese Americans to forced removal. They understood that they were up against the power of the federal government during wartime and that resistance would be pointless. Moreover, every Nisei had grown up hearing his Issei parents recite the phrases *shikata ga nai* and *gaman suru*—"It can't be helped" and "Just endure it." It was a virtue of Japanese culture to accept what could not be changed.[51] The logistically complex removal was facilitated by the Japanese propensity to obey authority. The evacuees were so cooperative in responding to the orders for exclusion that they won a commendation from Secretary of War Henry Stimson.[52] Michi Weglyn said poignantly: "In an inexplicable spirit of atonement and with great sadness, we went with our parents to concentration camps."[53]

Sue interpreted the collaboration of Japanese Americans bluntly: "A lot of people believed that if they didn't [cooperate], they would just shoot us. We were giving up all our property, our jobs and our freedom to tell the United States that we were loyal citizens, willing to make the sacrifices. But some of us were bitter."[54]

Among the most painful hardships was the loss of property.[55] As with the Terminal Islanders, Japanese Americans in Little Tokyo were given so little time to dispose of their property, they faced the loss of everything they had acquired through years of hard work. They were compelled to sell businesses, household goods, and personal assets for demeaning prices or lose everything. Komika Kunitomi sold her store in April. She refused to abandon it. A handwritten account in the files of Sue Embrey shows that Komika paid $1475 for the business in March of 1941 and sold it for $500 in April of 1942. "We had just bought a 1939 Chevrolet, a used car," Sue said. "We had also bought a Servel refrigerator, and a gas range from the Gas Company." The Kunitomi experience was more positive than that of others because of the help of a sympathetic Caucasian.

> Our elementary school principal Mabel Colerick offered to find buyers for the car, the refrigerator and range. We did get something for them. Other people were selling expensive appliances for five dollars. It was terrible. There were people driving through the neighborhoods looking for things to buy cheap or even get free, because they knew that we had to leave.

Komika, showing an admirable fortitude, even managed to sell her plants. "Most of us didn't want to negotiate, but my mother wasn't going to give anything away," Sue recalled. "A friend had the sewing machine of his mother who had passed away. Nobody would give him a decent price for it, so he took it out to the backyard and broke it up."

Sue sighed heavily when she talked about the distress of deciding what to take and what to leave.

> The most difficult things for me to leave were books and encyclopedias that my father had bought. My brothers and I had annuals from Lincoln High School. We left them with the Spanish American War veteran [who had given books to Jack]. He mailed them to us later. That was really nice of him. The high school annuals were the only things I got back.

Tets, who was 12, was miserable and confused. "He had a box of toys he had to give away to the second-hand dealer, and he cried. My mother hated to leave a cabinet filled with Japanese dishes. She used to say: 'When you get married, I want to be able to give you some dishes to start your home.' " Jack added to his sister's account: "What was hard for me to leave behind were my 78 disk records, all the Big Band sounds. Our neighbors, a Mexican couple, bought the store and we left quite a few things with them, including my records which I never saw again."[56]

Sue remembered acute confusion, as families prepared to leave Little Tokyo:

> We just followed the notices that were posted. We were supposed to leave for Santa Anita, but a couple of days before we heard that people who had relatives who were volunteers at Manzanar could go there and not go to Santa Anita. My mother insisted: "We've got to go to Manzanar because we will never see Hide again if we don't. We all have to stay together. If we get separated, we might not see each other again."[57]

Frank was able to change the registration for all of his family to go to Manzanar. Jack's bride Masa went to Manzanar with the Kunitomis while her family was sent to Santa Anita. Although Choko, ill with tuberculosis, was in the Olive View Sanatorium, she insisted on going to Manzanar with her family and her husband Kiyoshi Teshiba. She was in Manzanar only a few months, however, before her health worsened because of the dust and the poor food and she was sent back to Olive View.

Frank's wife Hide, whom he had married in 1940, was expecting a baby. She asked her doctor: "What can I do to get this baby born now." Following the doctor's advice Hide and her sister Shizu "walked in the morning, walked in the afternoon, walked at night," and the baby, Gene, arrived in time to go with the family to Manzanar.[58]

Hide's family also went to Manzanar, including her mother, Mrs. Hiramo; Shizu, married to Lindy Uyehara, and their two-year old daughter, Linda; Lindy's niece and nephew who were orphans; Hide's and Shizu's brother Ben Hiramo, and a younger sister Kazuko, nicknamed Koo. Others who accompanied the Kunitomis to Manzanar included a bachelor with no relatives who lived with the Kunitomis, and the Miyatakes, neighbors in Little Tokyo, 16 people, an extended family, assigned to the same barrack.[59]

"On the day before our departure we went to say good-bye to our friends who were going to Santa Anita. My mother's best friend who lived across the street was crying. My mother was crying: 'When are we going to meet again?' They did get together after the war. But at that time, it was very…" Sue could not find words for the anguish.[60]

In photographs taken of the departure many of the young men and women are smiling, almost as though as though they were about to embark on a lark.[61] Sue was not smiling.

> A couple of Japanese Hawaiian boys were here going to school; they couldn't get home and were being sent to Santa Anita. I had gone out with one of them on a couple dates. He had asked Ralph, the man who bought our grocery store, to buy a box of candy for me. Ralph came up to me when we were leaving the station and said: "I'm sorry, none of the stores are open and I couldn't find anything. I just wanted you to know that he had asked me." I burst into tears. Ralph didn't know what to do. An MP standing by him turned his head away and I thought: "There is somebody at least who sympathizes."

Hideo had written that Manzanar, in addition to being cold, was dusty and desolate. John L. DeWitt announced the selection of the location for the Manzanar camp on March 7, 1942. The first of the ten World War II internment camps lies in Owens Valley in east-central California, between two opposing mountain ranges with 14,000-foot peaks, the Sierra Nevada to the west and the White-Inyo to the east. The dramatic beauty of Mt. Whitney and Mt. Williamson acutely emphasized the bleakness of the camp, located on 6,000 arid, windblown acres. A dried-up and barren patch of sand-swept desert, it had no vegetation other than the vestiges of an old apple orchard surrounded by sagebrush, rabbit brush, and mesquite. The climate was bitterly extreme both summer and winter.

Jack remembers being told that Manzanar was a desert with snakes. "We managed to buy boots and knapsacks. We thought we were adequately prepared."[62] But how prepared were they for the internment camp that Komika Kunitomi described in dismay as *ma a kon na to ko ni,* a place like this?

CHAPTER 5

Manzanar: Weeping under the Apple Trees

Despite detailed planning by the Army, internees experienced considerable discomfort during their trips into exiles. In some cases they had little or no food, armed MPs guarded the buses and trains, and windows were covered, adding to the anxiety and isolation of the internees.[1] Sue described the train trip to Manzanar.[2]

> We started from the old Union Station. They brought out old trains, World War I trains, I think. They had gaslights turned on because it was dark inside the train. It was my first train ride and I thought: "God, what a ride." The trip took all day, ten hours. We could see out for a while, but later they told us to pull the shades down. I don't know whether they didn't want people outside to see us, or they didn't want us to see out. It was very quiet. None of us were talking. Some people were crying, but normally Japanese people don't want to show their emotions so we were just sitting there with our own thoughts. Even Tets didn't say anything. He just sat there.

Near dusk the train arrived in the town of Lone Pine, in the Owens Valley of eastern California. "We had no idea where we were. We'd never heard of Lone Pine."

Sue thinks she blanked out much of that day and night. She did remember that when the buses that had picked them up at the train station finally arrived at camp, they were lucky because Hideo was there. After more than 60 years, Sue still expressed deep appreciation of Hideo's efforts. "The night air was frigid, and he was leading us around in the dark with a flashlight. He took us to one long barrack, where we got our shots."

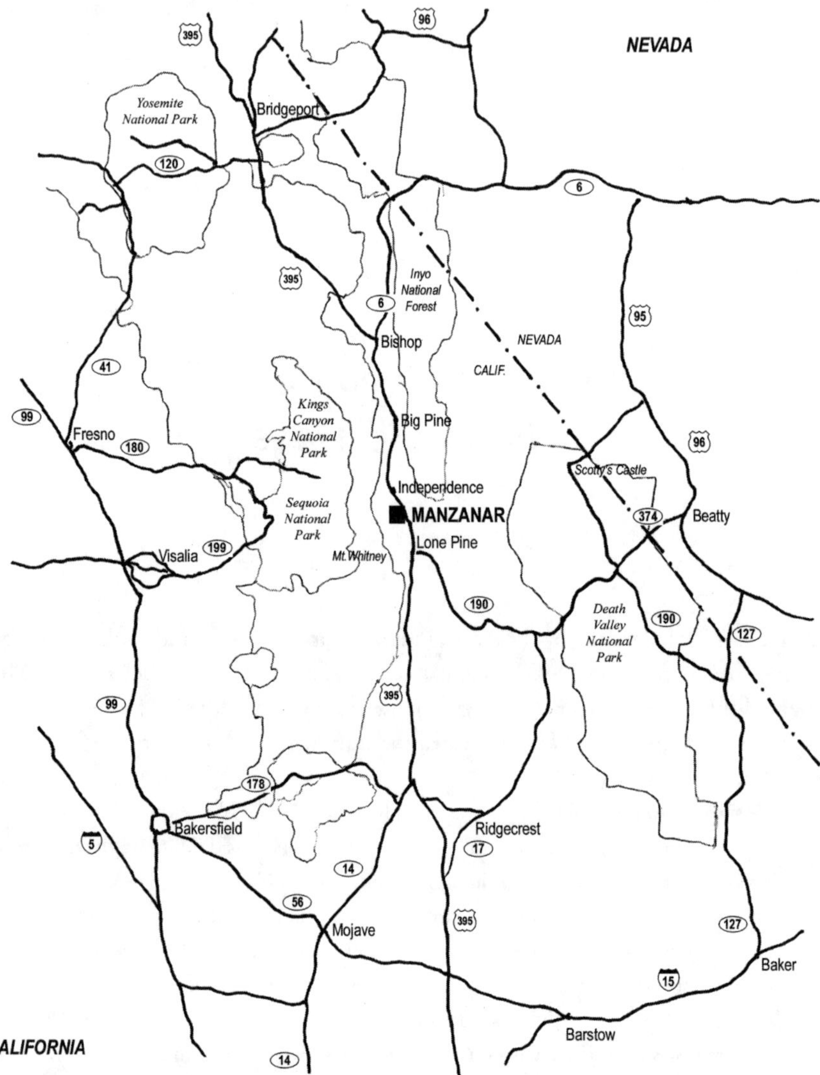

Figure 5.1 Map of California, including the Owens Valley and Manzanar (courtesy of the National Park Service)

Many internees have painful memories of arriving at assembly centers and being confronted with a cordon of armed guards, barbed wire fences, watchtowers, and searchlights. Sue's memories were less painful in one respect, but far more so in another.[3] "I don't remember watchtowers in the beginning, and there was no barbed wire because they were still building." Eventually Manzanar was enclosed with barbed wire and had 8 watchtowers manned 24 hours by 2 armed Military Policemen (MPs) working in shifts. When the Kunitomis arrived, the camp had boundaries made conspicuous by armed sentries. Sue remembered: "One fellow, Hikoji Takeuchi, who was in our block, was shot by an MP a week after we got there." An MP had given Takeuchi permission to get scrap lumber. Evidently he came too close to the boundary and the MP, thinking he was running away, shot him. "I think the MPs were nervous. The government was telling them we have to put these people away because they are all dangerous."[4]

A distinct memory for internees arriving at Manzanar was that of being handed long bags of mattress ticking that had to be filled with hay, a disheartening task Hideo had already done for his family. They were given their family number, 2614D, and assigned to Block 20, Building 3. The buildings of the camp were grouped in a uniform block arrangement, each of the 36 blocks consisting of 15, 20-foot by 100-foot, barracks. Each barrack was divided into five rooms, euphemistically called "apartments." The number of internees per apartment varied unsystematically; sometimes eight to ten persons of various ages and different families occupied one room. Partitions between the apartments left a gap between the walls and the roof. The cold, drafty apartments, which had no insulation, were heated by a Coleman oil burner.[5]

Initially, Sue, her mother, Kimbo, Midori, and Tets were in one apartment. When they entered their room, Hideo turned on the only light, a bulb in the ceiling with a string to pull. Sue remembered seeing eight canvas cots, each with two blankets, and huge bags filled with hay for mattresses. Sue's mother sat down on one of the mattresses, slumped over and said *ma a kon no to ko ni!* (A place like this!) With remarkable understatement, Sue described her own reaction: "I was a little disappointed. I don't remember much about that night except that we could hear people crying in the next unit."

Sue recalled the morning following their arrival.

> We found Frank and his family and Choko and her husband, but it took us a long time to find Jack and Masa. They were in an apartment with a strange family. They were newlyweds! So we took their cots and moved them into our area. Hideo was in Block 2 with the bachelors, but he moved later to our room. He was able to get things for us because of being a volunteer. He knew his way around.

When the Kunitomis arrived on May 9, Manzanar was administered as an assembly center under the Wartime Civil Control Agency. On June 1, it came under the supervision of the War Relocation Authority, which was responsible for administering all 10 internment centers.[6] Milton Eisenhower became distraught by the desolated camps, the deplorable living quarters, and the general treatment of the Japanese Americans. He wrote later that the internment was "illustrative of how an entire society can somehow plunge off course."[7] On June 17, 1942, he resigned and was replaced by Dillon Seymour Myer, who served as director of the WRA from June 1942 until its termination in June 1946.

For more than three decades Myer's reputation was that of a bureaucrat who performed a difficult job adequately and honorably. The JACL honored him in 1946 with a citation commending him as a "champion of human rights and common decency." Myer came under attack in the 1980s, however, as the "deceitful and paternalistic 'jailer' of the internees," as the former internees began to speak publicly about their incarceration.

Roy Nash, former superintendent of an Indian agency in California, was hired as project director, essentially the camp administrator, on May 20, 1942, but was succeeded ultimately by Ralph P. Merritt, who had had a lengthy career in business, agriculture, and politics and had established his residence in Big Pine. Merritt served as project director from November 24, 1942 to November 21, 1945, when Manzanar was closed.

After the Kunitomi family's arrival, the population of the camp rose rapidly, reaching a peak of 10,046 by September of 1942. Approximately 88 percent of the total population, 8,828, was from Los Angeles County, and approximately 72 percent, 7,207, were from the city of Los Angeles. Other evacuees came from counties throughout California, and 227 internees were from Bainbridge Island in Puget Sound, Washington.[8]

The WRA encountered major problems in recruiting staff for several reasons: an acute manpower shortage on the West Coast, higher rates of pay in war-related industries, isolation of the camp site, adverse climate, the belief that the employment would be temporary, and the fact that some people did not want to work with Japanese Americans. Housing of staff was one problem that was effectively resolved when the WRA erected 19 buildings with apartments furnished with refrigerators, electric ranges, and space heaters.[9] The staff at Manzanar during 1942 averaged about 200, many employees transferring from other government agencies. However, because of the inherent problems and administrative inexperience in operating an internment camp, the staff was reorganized several times, causing additional stress for internees.

Within 10 days after the first internees arrived at Manzanar, the WCCA administrators appointed block leaders who were considered by most internees to be stooges for the administration. The WRA instituted direct election of block leaders; as a result their leadership, although still being criticized, was accepted by most internees.[10] Sue remembered:

> "Each block elected its own manager. They called them Blockheads," she said, laughing. "The block managers were supposed to bring the grievances of the internees to the administration. I'm not sure how effective they were. When the block leaders met with the administration, English was required. That's where the change of leadership from Issei to Nisei became apparent, because, although a lot of them spoke English, few Issei were fluent enough to be in leadership positions. Most of the camp leaders were older Nisei."

The attitude of the internees toward the "Blockheads" depended on who the block leader was. Shizu's husband Lindy Uyehara,[11] an older bilingual Nisei, was elected. "He was able to do a lot for the block, because he wasn't hesitant about telling the administration what the internees' complaints were."[12]

Complaints about sanitation and health problems were major concerns.[13] Sue's own health problems corroborate the report.[14] Years later she was diagnosed with sarcoidosis, a disease characterized by lesions that appear in the liver, lungs, skin, and lymph nodes, caused by exposure to a dusty environment. She also had bronchiectasis, chronic dilation of the bronchial tubes, and a heart condition that may have been caused by the sarcoidosis.[15]

Health issues were exacerbated by stress. Despite Hideo's efforts to make his family as comfortable as possible, Sue's mother was overwhelmed by the living conditions.

> "We didn't have a fancy house in Little Tokyo," Sue said, "but at least we had our own bedroom and we had a bathroom. Years later my mother told us for the first time what she did every morning while we were looking for work: 'After that first morning, [which was ironically Mother's Day] I walked up to the apple orchards every day and sat under a tree and cried. I cried every day for about two weeks.'"[16]

Twelve-year-old Tets also manifested signs of stress. Sue remembered him as being "unhappy all the time. He was going to school at Manzanar, but he would say: 'What's the use of studying American history?' He was a bright young boy. He saw the hypocrisy in it."[17]

Living conditions intensified the stress of dislocation. The lack of landscaping or natural foliage resulted in an acute dust problem; large cracks in the floors and walls of the barracks appeared, due to the dried out lumber because of heat and low humidity, and installation of linoleum on the floors was delayed because Caucasian union labor would not work on the project with Japanese Americans. "The dust and wind would come through the cracks of the bare floors," Sue remembered. "The windows and doors had no screens. When the wind was blowing you often couldn't open or close the door because there was so much pressure."

Probably the most disturbing aspect of camp life in the beginning was the lavatories without partitions. Sue remembered:

> You had to go past the toilets to get into the shower room. There was a cement floor with a drain in the middle and I think five or six showerheads for about 250 people. No separations. We realized immediately that we were going to have to do something about that. People found all kinds of ways to help each other. They brought coats and other things and took turns covering the stalls so they had some privacy. Eventually they put in partitions, but it took a long while. It was embarrassing.[18]

The water supply was not sufficient and tests had revealed a high degree of pollution. Dishwashing equipment was inadequate and unsanitary. Sue remembered that the eating utensils were dirty and that people suffered from dysentery from the first days. There was no water supply in the apartments. "They did have a spout outside each barrack, but that was mostly in case of fire."

The laundry room had big tubs in which women washed clothing by hand with scrub boards. The wet laundry was taken back to the barracks and hung on clotheslines installed by the internees. "We were doing laundry all the time in that dusty environment, especially for the babies. The parents would put little kids in the laundry tubs to give them baths. When we were all working, my mother did the laundry for our family, but we helped her, trying to do it on the weekend or at night."

There were 20 mess halls in operation, each one accommodating approximately 500 persons. Sixteen additional mess halls were under construction. An administrative order issued on August 24, 1942 was "to provide good wholesome, nutritious, palatable food at a daily cost of not more than 45 cents per day per resident."[19]

Sue's mess hall memories:[20]

> They rang the bell. They had the mess hall open for an hour. We would stand in line. We had aluminum Army utensils with a handle that folded over. The mugs also had handles that folded. If you didn't hold the coffee cup just right, it would tip over and spill. They had something on the table that we couldn't figure out at first, a white slab on a dish. It looked like lard. It turned out to be oleo [margarine] before they put the yellow coloring in it. They would pile the food one on top of another. We would have hot rice and Jello dropped on top of the rice. Then we had hot rice melting the Jello.

Each block had an internee cook, who was paid wages. The quality of the food preparation varied, depending on the cook. Some blocks had cooks who had owned restaurants or coffee shops before the war and were able to provide somewhat superior food. Sue remembered when former internees met after the war for a Manzanar reunion in a restaurant in Little Tokyo, the men ate so fast they would be finished long before the women. The men explained: "We learned that in Manzanar. We had to eat fast to get to the next mess hall before it closed. We were growing kids."

The arrangement of the mess halls, with long picnic tables and no assigned seats, weakened family ties. Historian Page Smith asserts: "To lose the family meal, especially in such a tradition-bound culture as that of the Japanese, was to lose the essence of family unity . . . [T]he breakdown of the family meal may have been the most demoralizing aspect of [internment] center life."[21] The young people would eat wherever they wanted, leaving the older people to eat by themselves. "My mother tried to keep us together," Sue said. "We all worked and ate breakfast and lunch separately. But at dinnertime she wanted all of us together. Tets had his own group of kids he wanted to run around with, but the rest of us stayed with her."[22]

Several sources describe the discrepancy between the living conditions of the staff and those of the internees. Sue had this to say:

> They had their own little apartment with cooking facilities, although they could also eat in the main [administrative] mess hall. I had a friend who worked in the main mess hall and he said that the best thing about the job was the food. People in Lone Pine used to say: "Oh, look at all the meat and good food that's going into the camp." Well, it may have been going to the administration. It wasn't coming to us.

In an interview conducted by David J. Bertagnoli in 1973, Mary Gillespie, who had lived in Owens Valley since 1909, articulated this unfounded belief: "We had to ration things—we were given so much coffee, so much sugar—and [the internees] got everything... and you know the Japs are used to fish and rice and their own food. The Japanese had ham and bacon, and it was said by some people who worked at the camp that the garbage cans were just full because they weren't used to that kind of food. They got the best of everything. They were treated very, very good."[23] However, Lou Frizell, a music teacher from Los Angeles who volunteered at Manzanar, told Sue about being invited to have dinner with his Manzanar students and being so shocked by the food that he could not eat it.[24]

Perhaps the saddest sector in the camp was the Children's Village, completed in June, 1942 to house Japanese American orphans and abandoned children. More than 100 children eventually lived in the Children's Village. Sue expressed lingering sorrow 60 years later. She may have seen no more compelling example of the evil of bureaucratic racism. Sue remembered: "They just took them out of orphanages in L.A. and San Francisco.[25] They even took them out of foster homes. Anybody who was 1/32nd Japanese had to go to camp." Sue was repeating a common belief that there was a blood quantum criterion for internment, although there is no evidence of such a policy.[26] Japanese American children being taken from orphanages and sent to Manzanar, however, is well documented. Sue asked with residual anger: "Can you imagine the absurdity of taking these kids out of an orphanage? What harm could they do? Bureaucracy just run amuck."[27]

On June 1, 1942, the hospital facilities consisted of a 10-bed improvised infirmary in one of the barracks, an isolation ward, an outpatient clinic, and a children's ward. Sue experienced this early "hospital" firsthand.[28] "I caught measles and had to be isolated. They put me in a barrack with all the little kids with measles. I was trying to sleep, but it was very noisy. The little kids were running around the room in their bare feet. Nurses gave us our meals, but I don't remember a doctor coming in."[29]

Despite the overcrowded living conditions, Sue was the only one in her family to get measles. "Maybe I caught it from the kids when we started the school." Since the WCCA had no money allocated for schooling, all educational programs had to be initiated by volunteers, most of them internees.[30] "The Sisters from the Maryknoll Mission [in Los Angeles] came to the camp and sent out a call for volunteer teachers." Sue and her sister-in-law, Masa, volunteered. "We gathered all the kids. There was nothing. No paper. No pencils. No chalkboard. No chairs or tables. No books. Somehow we managed. It was due to the Maryknoll Sisters that we had a school at all in the early weeks. The Sisters weren't there very long, not more than a couple months."

When it assumed administration of Manzanar, the WRA responded to continuing pressure from parents for a summer school program. Since the children had missed two months of the school term during evacuation, the parents were concerned about loss of academic credit. Internees volunteered to serve as teachers and design an academic program. Genevieve W. Carter, a staff member of the University of California, was hired by the WRA and became superintendent of schools at Manzanar on June 15. The summer program initiated by volunteer internees was thrust upon Carter, who faced the challenges of setting up an education program without supplies, experienced teachers, or even classrooms. She described the hurdles involved in establishing schools in the camp: "Since schools had not been planned for at the time the incoming evacuees had been assigned to their housing, it became a necessary step to move people into barracks already crowded... in order to make room for schools. These problems were desperate ones."

The recruitment of teachers was severely hindered by poor salaries. The $1620 12-month salary offered by the WRA could not compete with the much higher salaries of the public schools for a teaching term of nine to ten months. Most of the credentialed teachers at Manzanar came from states that paid lower salaries than California did. In order to start school in the fall of 1942, it was necessary to assign full responsibility for some classrooms to internees.[31]

On September 14, the elementary schools opened with 1,001 students and on October 15 high schools classes began with 1,376 students. There were no chairs, tables, books, or playground equipment. Some of the younger children carried little benches their parents had made from scrap lumber. There were no heaters in the rooms and no linoleum to cover the cracks and holes in the floors. Cold weather and sandstorms sometimes made attending classes impossible. Schools at Manzanar did not become fully functional until spring of 1943.[32]

Once the schools were established the Nisei continued to exhibit the Japanese American principles of *gaman,* perseverance; *enryo,* self-restraint; and *sunao,* obedience. In the high school yearbook *Our World* a commentary entitled "Democracy at Work" concludes: [Community government] under the capable guidance of Mr. Merritt, has been instrumental in creating a feeling of peace and goodwill, not only among the evacuees, but also with the surrounding communities."[33]

Ralph P. Merritt, project director, wrote an essay for the yearbook, which included statements similar to those of the yearbook staff. He expressed his hopes that former students would remember Manzanar positively.

> [Manzanar] was a city serving a wartime purpose where people lived in peace and goodwill. ... Where there was a school system that taught young citizens the ideals of American citizenship ... I hope you may say that Manzanar was an experience worth living, where the important realities of life were made clear and where there was time and opportunity to prepare for participation in the work of peace based on tolerance, understanding and goodwill.

Sue's responses to Merritt's essay were candid.[34] "I don't think this particular city served a purpose. Peace and goodwill? No. There was a lot of tension, conflicts between regional groups, between people with different political views, between the Nisei and Issei, and between internees and camp administrators. It was not a peaceful place."

Merritt's claim that Manzanar had a school system that taught young citizens the ideals of American citizenship not only appears hypocritical now, it must have been transparent at the time. Sue said: "Sure they tried to teach these ideals but I don't think the kids believed it."[35]

"I hope you may say that Manzanar was an experience worth living" brought Sue's response: "No, I definitely don't think so. I think it negatively affected everybody's life after camp, trying to make up for all those years that they lost."

"Where the important realities of life were made clear," brought Sue's rejoinder: "The important reality of racism was made clear; we were separated from the mainstream of life.... We couldn't get out of that imprisonment of our own free will, and we had lost all our personal property, so we were not secure in our person. Those are the Bill of Rights freedoms that were violated."

Like cities all over America, Manzanar had its own defense industry. The WRA had established industrial sections in the camps, the first of which began to operate in June of 1942, the camouflage net project.[36] Sue left the Maryknoll temporary school during the summer of 1942 to weave camouflage nets.

> They had built a huge, tall building with pulleys. We went voluntarily because they told us we were going to get paid. It was unskilled labor, so it must have been about $12 a month. They had ten [feet] by twelve [feet] patterns of camouflage net that they hung from the ceiling with pulleys that would raise or lower them. In front of that would be another net, an empty one. We would follow the pattern and the colors of the one behind and make exact copies. The pulleys would have the nets low in the beginning so we could do the top portion. As we finished, they would pull the nets up so we could follow the pattern.
>
> We would weave in and out with strips of burlap in a zig-zag pattern in different colors, green fading into yellow or darker green fading into green and brown.

> They would be used to cover Jeeps and tanks. The dust and the lint from the burlap would fly around. We had masks, but I don't know how much help they were.

The camouflage net factory operated until early December 1942, employing 500 internees at its maximum and producing up to 10,000 nets per month. Because Geneva Convention prevented aliens from being recruited for war work, Issei could not work in the net factory and were distressed by this policy. The exclusion of the Issei and labor agitation over the wage scale led to the operation's closure.[37]

There is considerable evidence that people in the camps shared a strong desire to contribute to the war effort. Sue agreed: "Yes, we all did. Some people volunteered for the Military Intelligence, those who could speak Japanese and later a few went to work for the Office of War Information. But those were special people. Every time I go back to Manzanar, I say: 'What a waste of human resources.'"[38]

Sue talked about the various types of employment in which her family members were engaged at Manzanar. "Frank was a truck driver making deliveries. Hideo was working in administration. Choko's husband Kiyoshi was a policeman. Kinya also worked as a policeman in internal security. Midori was in high school, and Tets, of course, was also in school. A lot of us went to work in the camouflage nets, but Jack and Masa were not there very long, before they went on furlough to harvest sugar beets. When the call came to harvest the sugar beets, a lot of people went because they thought this was not only a way to get out of camp, but also to help in the war effort."[39] With the help of 3,500 Japanese American workers the Utah-Idaho Sugar Company increased sugar beet production from 72,000 acres in 1941 to 89,000 acres in 1942.[40]

Limited opportunities for helping the war effort were only one of the many frustrations that made people tense, often resulting in physical problems. When she talked about her own frustrations, Sue recalled her earlier eclectic interests and her inclination toward independence.

> The worst was the fact that I couldn't get out and be with people other than Japanese. I wanted to be in the mainstream of America. We had some Chinese friends who used to send us magazines, *Life* magazine and others, so we knew something about life outside camp. It was painful to look at those pictures and see what the rest of the world was doing.[41]

Inadequate clothing was a major morale problem for many internees.[42] How could they possibly have taken enough clothing in two suitcases? "We just wore what we had and washed them over and over." To meet the need for clothing during 1942, privately donated new and used clothing and outdated army clothing were distributed.[43]

> They gave us huge Navy pea- coats, much too big for most of us. Some enterprising women took them apart and altered them to size. But they were so heavy we

> got stooped down by all that weight. Eventually we got Sears, Roebuck and Montgomery Wards catalogs, but you had to have money to buy those clothes. They gave us each only $3.75 a month for a clothing allowance.

One way to enhance morale was to correspond with people outside the camps. Sue corresponded with a former high school teacher and with the Mexican American friends who had lived nearby (in Little Tokyo). One of these friends enlisted in the navy and frequently wrote to the Kunitomis, "until one day he was told by his supervisor that he couldn't write to us while we were in camp."[44]

People could send packages to internees, but they were inspected by MPs for contraband. "Film and cameras and anything that was used for carving were confiscated. Some people liked to carve wood, but they couldn't do that in the beginning." Having visitors involved a difficult process of getting a permit. "The people that bought our store finally got the permit and [extra] gas rations for their car, but their car broke down. We kept waiting all day at the gate and they didn't come. They didn't try again."

Sue's narrative differed significantly from statements by some former internees, who maintain that they had a good time in camp.

> "When I first heard them, I was shocked. After a while you make friends and try to make the best of it, but to say camp was fun all the time means that they must have suppressed traumatic memories." Asked about her mother's frustrations and worries, Sue replied: "Her worst anxiety was about the draft and my brothers. And they all went [into military service], all three of them."

Sue is especially appreciative of the difficulties her mother and other Issei internees experienced. Komika told her family years later that after crying alone under the apple trees for two weeks, she decided that "was a silly thing to do" and began to take part in camp life, including singing in a choir. Sue's mother was typical in not telling her family for years about weeping under the apple trees. Sue remembered one Issei woman saying irritably: "How could we talk about it? We didn't know what hit us."

CHAPTER 6

Manzanar: A Community of Contradictions

Although Manzanar was enclosed in barbed wire and guarded by armed MPs, it resembled a typical American community for the Nisei, and for the Issei it became a community with traditional Japanese attributes. Internees of both generations were intent on recreating a semblance of normalcy. For the Nisei this meant proving they were Americans. Sue explained: "Kids wouldn't speak Japanese. Many felt that they should not be involved in anything Japanese. We were American. Public schools really did a good job in Americanizing us. Manzanar became a very American city because that's what we knew."[1]

Nowhere is this phenomenon more evident than in *Our World,* the Manzanar High School Yearbook of 1943–44. In the forward is this explicit statement: "Since that first day when Manzanar High School was called into session, the students and faculty have been trying to approximate in all activities the life we knew 'back home.' With the publication of this yearbook, we feel that we have really come closer to our goal."[2] The photos of the graduating seniors are similar to those in other high school yearbooks, even though 168 faces are Japanese.

One, however, is not, the photo of Ralph Lazo. Sue told Lazo's remarkable story.

> He's Mexican American. He was going to school with Nisei at Belmont [High School] and associated with them all the time. Without telling anybody, he registered [for evacuation] with the Japanese Americans. His mother had passed away, and he told his dad he was going to camp with his friends. The day the train left L.A. he got on and was going from one car to the next pretending to say good-bye.

> He was still on the train when they got to Lone Pine. They couldn't believe it when he said: "I decided to come with you." His father was very upset, of course, when he found out that it was not a summer camp. They kept him at Manzanar. He spoke a little Japanese, but, still, I don't know why they allowed him to stay. Even the Issei accepted that he belonged there. They thought he was an orphan and put candy under his pillow. He stayed until he was drafted into the Army in [19]'44.[3]

Ralph Lazo was a contradiction that emphasized a community built on contradictions. In some aspects *Our World* is an example of a classic American high school annual with photos of girls in cheerleader attire, students in band practice, and in theatrical productions, sports, dances, even a Spanish Club. When the publication extends its descriptions to the larger Manzanar community, the ironies are pronounced. A section entitled "democracy in action" reveals the control the WRA exerts on the "community government." An article on industry and agriculture, stressing that the internees must produce much of their own food and clothing, refers to the community alteration shop, which alters GI clothing to fit internees. Then there is the uncaptioned photo on the last page of the guard tower looming over a bleak landscape.

The establishment of The Manzanar Cooperative Enterprises promoted the Americanization of the camp. "The government wanted the camps to be self-sufficient," Sue said, "so they set up the Cooperative." Cooperative members, charged five dollars each, participated in the earnings of the enterprise. A canteen/general store offering merchandise not provided by the WRA carried items that were in constant demand. The canteen sold newspapers, periodicals, smoking supplies, candy, soft drinks, ice cream, and sunglasses. The general store sold toys, fabric, clothing, and shoes.[4] But the ability to purchase merchandise associated with pre-interment life was limited. "Only the ones who worked had money to spend in the canteen or the store, and they had very little," Sue said. "We didn't get paid very much, either eight or 12 dollars a month." Sue pointed out another irony: "The administration argued that we were getting our room and board free.[5] There was terrible financial insecurity. We made do with what we had."

Sue told one very appealing story about trying to approximate life as it was "back home." Given the limitations of Manzanar, it reveals something of the audacity of Hideo Kunitomi.

> My brother bought a pair of Florsheim shoes that he ordered from somewhere. I don't know how he had the money for that. He was furious because they ruined them at the co-op shoe repair shop by putting on the wrong kind of heel. I don't know why he wanted a pair of fancy shoes like that to wear around camp. Maybe they made him feel better about himself. Maybe he thought he would make a hit with the girls.[6]

Sue formed lasting friendships in camp, where the Nisei aspired to be typical American teenagers, despite living behind barbed wire.

> In our block I had a very good friend, Cherry [Yamashita Nakama]. I knew her in Little Tokyo and went to school with her. She was a bright gal. We would talk about the boys, which ones we liked, which ones we thought were special. We loved to dance and we loved the Big Band music so we would talk about that. She and I would walk around the whole camp and talk, because that was the only privacy we had. In fact, we talked a lot about the lack of privacy.

Sue's inclination for making friends with Caucasians, which began in elementary school, continued improbably at Manzanar.

> Cherry and I got to know two of the Military Policemen who inspected the packages that came into the post office. A lot of Nisei didn't want to talk to the white people. There was a young woman who, when she heard me say hello to an MP, confronted me: "You are talking to those white people? As long as I am here, I'm not going to talk to any of them." I thought she was wrong. I told her: "You're not going to be able to avoid talking to people other than Japanese."

Sue's natural open-mindedness was apparent in her friendship with the MPs.

> One of them, Neil Scheeler, said: "You've got to get out of this place." He wrote to me when I was in Wisconsin and Chicago. When I came back to L. A. we saw each other a couple times. Later he was in Olive View [Sanitarium] when he got TB and I went out to see him. He was very happy to see me.

When I asked Sue whether she ever thought she would have a romantic involvement with him, she responded: "No. Never."

Although her friend Cherry married a Kibei (a Japanese American born in the United States, but educated in Japan) while in camp, Sue said:

> I really didn't have boyfriends. There was one fellow, a Kibei, who had been in Little Tokyo before the war. He had come to our house and my mother encouraged him. Before we both went to Manzanar, I had told him that I didn't want to see him anymore. I really did not want to get committed to anybody. I wanted to go to college. I felt that with his Kibei background, he would not want me to be that independent. But he kept trying to get Tets to talk me into going to eat at the mess hall where he was working. I didn't want to hear it. When I left camp, he brought me a carved wooden rose. He wanted to work on the relationship, but I wasn't interested.[7]

Historian Harlan D. Unrau states: "The shock of sudden separation from the 'American way of life'...had made [internees] restless and desperate," craving activities that had been ordinary outside the camp.[8] One of the acute frustrations for the internees, especially in the early days of confinement, was enforced idleness. Sue talked about the ways in which internees coped.[9] In addition to trying to improve their surroundings, the Issei engaged in activities such as haiku, arts and crafts, and gardening, while the Nisei preferred athletics. Frank and Jack, too old to play with the younger internees, were on a baseball team called the Has-Beens; Masa was also on a baseball team; Hideo and Sue played basketball; and Sue was also on the volleyball team. All sports were played outdoors, because the auditorium was not yet built. The gymnasium/auditorium was constructed between January and September 1944, rather late in the internment period, yet evidently it was extensively used. Having been restored, it is now the Interpretive Center for Manzanar National Historic Site.

Despite the American city character of the camp created by Nisei, many of the lifestyle improvements, including a Tea House, had a Japanese influence. Sue remembered the internees in her block collecting money to buy cement for a Japanese hot tub each for the men and women. "My mother and her neighbors would sit [in the tubs] and gossip. They enjoyed that. It was very relaxing, especially on the cold days. The family structure may have been deteriorating because of the lack of privacy and lack of control by the parents, but at the same time there was social interchange involving older people."[10]

Both Issei and Nisei found pleasure in music. Sue's mother belonged to an a cappella choir group. Mary Nomura, a Nisei known as the Songbird of Manzanar, still sings at Manzanar reunion events. Louis Frizell, who later had a career as a character actor, came to Manzanar, vowing "to teach these kids to sing." As head of the music department he was a generous and significant person in what Nomura calls the "cultural enrichment" of the camp.[11] A significant means of coping with frustration and depression for the Nisei were frequent dances, with sometimes as many as three being held on the same evening. A young swing band, The Jive Bombers, often played for these dances.[12]

> "My brothers' age group, the older married ones, wanted to make sure we stayed out of trouble," Sue remembered. "They wanted to keep their eyes on us because young kids were going under the apple trees and necking and fooling around. After dinner we would move all the tables to the wall and mop the floors in the mess hall, then we would have dances. I don't know where people got the player and records, but we had all the latest music. We had all of Bing Crosby. Our theme songs were 'Don't Fence Me In' and 'Don't Sit under the Apple Tree.'"

Sue and her friends also tried to recreate social activities.

> We went on a picnic. We had to crawl under the barbed fence. There were MPs in the guardhouses, but they didn't stop us. One of the MPs came out of the

> guardhouse and asked us: "Are you really Japanese?" He couldn't believe that we were speaking English, singing American songs and doing social dancing. These MPs mostly came from the east or the South and they'd probably never seen a Japanese before.[13]

While the Nisei were trying to stay attuned to the rhythms of mainstream popular culture, the Issei were recreating traditional Japanese attributes. Ironically, the Issei were able to achieve environmental beauty on a far wider scale than would have been possible in Little Tokyo. The bleak and barren surroundings of the camp eventually were transformed by extensive landscaping, including stone walkways, flowerbeds, rock gardens and ponds.[14] "Internees built little gardens in front of the mess halls where people could sit, waiting for the mess hall to open," Sue said. The most prominent garden encompassed the entire 100 feet around the Block 22 mess hall and included a waterfall and an enormous pond with a bridge. "This was initiated by Harry Ueno, a kitchen worker, who felt sorry for people standing in the desert sun waiting for the mess hall to open. He enlisted the mess crew to build a garden and a pond where they could sit and watch the koi." Sue explained how he circumvented the fact that cement was rationed. "He would get one order for three sacks of cement. He told the internees helping him build the pond to bring the receipt back to him. He kept ordering cement with the same receipt. So we called it The Three-Sacks Garden, although it was far more than three sacks."[15]

Internee Kuichiro Nishi worked with wild roses that grew in one area of the camp, budding 15,000 wild shoots, which were later planted between Blocks 23 and 33 in what became Rose Park. In addition to the roses about 100 species of flowers were planted from seeds the administration helped internees obtain. Other beautifications of the camp included the elaborate Pleasure Park, which later was renamed The Merritt Park, in honor of Ralph Merritt, the director.[16]

Many Issei played *goh* and *shogi*, Japanese table games.[17] Was there any gambling activity?

> "The Issei did a lot of it," Sue responded, "but it wasn't very open. People didn't have a lot of money, so betting would have to be pretty small. They also used to make wine from leftover rice. They mixed it with raisins and let it ferment. We could smell where they were making wine. This was illegal, of course."

Sue's narrative illustrates the uncertainty of the administration and guards about regulations in the camp. Although the internees were imprisoned, not free to leave, the administration and the MPs often did not quite know what to do with them. Internee men often crawled under the barbed wire fences to go fishing. One of the internees, later active with the Manzanar Committee, reported an incident in which he was crawling under the barbed wire, coming back from fishing. An MP approached him. The internee was expecting a harsh reprimand at the least. But the MP handed him a fishing line and said: "You probably need this."[18]

Sue's most significant experience while at Manzanar was that of working on the internee paper ironically named the *Manzanar Free Press.* This work became a critical factor in the development of her political awareness. It is unlikely that Sue would have been able to have had journalism experience in Little Tokyo, first because of her father's insistence that she would get married, and second, because of her mother's need for her to work in the store. Over the objection of John DeWitt, Commander of the Western Defense Command Zone, Robert L. Brown, Reports Officer and Assistant Project Director at Manzanar, decided to launch a camp newspaper. "When they finally got the camp going, we all knew that there had to be some means of communication," Brown recalled. "So that's when I got the newspaper, the *Manzanar Free Press,* started. We did it first just on mimeographed sheets.... They hired this tremendous crew of kids. They just ran the damned newspaper. I didn't."[19] The first issue was April 11, 1942. By July it was being printed by the Chalfant Press in Lone Pine. The administration policy alternated between permission and prohibition of a Japanese language version of the paper. Finally, on October 1, 1942, it was announced that a four-page supplement in Japanese would be published regularly.[20]

Sue talked at length about this significant experience in her life at Manzanar.[21] "They had openings at the *Free Press,* because people were leaving to go on harvest furloughs, so I applied for a job as a reporter and was hired. That was the end of May or early June [1942]. My first story was about Block Six finishing their pond and Japanese garden."

Chiye Mori, an older Nisei, served as editor of the paper. Mori had a vital impact on Sue's views. "I marveled because she was smoking and swearing. One time I heard her say to a guy: 'How come you didn't bring me a bottle of whiskey?' A Nisei woman who smoked and swore and drank whiskey! Most Nisei around her age, 22 or 23, were very conservative." Prior to internment Mori had been a member of the liberal Democratic Club, and the staff of the *Free Press* were considered progressive, which created considerable animosity among the more conservative internees. "Chiye would criticize Roosevelt, not in the paper, of course, but in the office," Sue remembered. "I thought that was terrible. I admired Roosevelt, so I was shocked. The other staff members were pretty much [in agreement with] her."

Sue remembered some of the liberals who worked on the paper: "Joe Blamey, who was Japanese and Italian. He was very progressive, a very outspoken person. Jimmy Oda was a Communist.[22] He was a friend of Karl Yoneda who was also a Communist. A bilingual Kibei, Jimmy volunteered for Military Intelligence. He went to the Burma area with Karl. Some of these things were so contradictory." Sue found Tad Uyeno, a newsman before the war, who later became editor of the *Free Press,* to be not as liberal as the others. She considered Togo Tanaka, who had been the English-language editor of a newspaper based in Los Angeles, the *Rafu Shimpo,* an independent. "He was kind of a loner. He wasn't with the JACL group, but he also wasn't with the progressive group." Sue remembers being interviewed with him many years later for a program on British Broadcasting Corporation. She was astounded when he said: "I never think about Manzanar."

Listening to the discussions in the *Manzanar Free Press* office, Sue found herself in a completely different world. "They used to have these long discussions and I would sit there and listen to them, talking about what was happening in Europe and the Pacific. I don't know where they got all that information, except the *L. A. Times* which we did get every day." Further evidence that the *Free Press* office was a meeting place for liberals, where ideas mattered, is expressed in the autobiography of the communist labor activist Karl Yoneda. Learning that a Military Intelligence Service (MIS) recruiting team would be in Manzanar the following week, Yoneda visited the *Free Press* office to announce that anyone who wanted to enlist in the MIS could apply. When asked what would happen to Manzanar if *Free Press* staff members left, Yoneda replied: "This was the opportune time to fight against the fascist Axis which was the main enemy of democratic people everywhere. Enlisting was the best way to guarantee and protect our future." Fourteen Nisei and Kibei, who had been confined by barbed wire and armed MPs at Manzanar because they were considered security risks, were allowed to enlist in the MIS.[23]

Although her early socialization may have prevented Sue from agreeing with them at the time, her association with the staff of the *Free Press* had a major influence on her political development.

> I began to think that you could voice your own opinion and even criticize those in government. They were very free [in their discussions]. They didn't change my mind, though, about Roosevelt. He signed the Order and we had to go. It was a matter of *shikata ga nai*. You might as well try to make the best of it.

In retrospect Sue values what she learned while working on the *Free Press*. "I could better express myself when I tried later to educate people as to what had happened to Japanese Americans."

Chiye Mori was relocated from Manzanar for her own protection following the Manzanar riot on December 6, 1942, and Sue succeeded her as editor. Sue found her work on the *Free Press* a potent antidote to the depressing camp life. "Writing was something I wanted to do and I liked. I had a column called 'Purely Personal.' I would write about things happening outside the camp that I had heard about, generally from listening to the administrators talking, or I had read about, mostly in the *L. A. Times*."

Despite her enjoyment of the work, Sue admitted:

> The human element did not appear in the printed pages. There were no personal views of the writer. We did not write about what was happening to us, the poor food, the poor medical care, the lack of privacy, having to take showers together.

> We knew if we wrote about a certain thing, it wouldn't get in the paper. The complaints of the internees were not voiced in the *Free Press.*

The paper did not originally intend such a stance. An early editorial stated: "We want to repeat again that the *Manzanar Free Press* belongs to the people of Manzanar. That instead of being merely the voice of the administration, it strives to express the opinions of the evacuees and solution of immediate and foreseen problems."[24] Sue explained :

> That editorial was written by the first group of staff people. Especially in the beginning the staff members tried very hard to represent the opinions of the internees and not the voice of the administration, but they weren't successful. I wrote about a strike in one of the defense plants in L. A. My boss, [editor] Roy Takeno, said: "We don't write about things like that." A labor strike against the government during a time of war was not an acceptable topic. Even though there wasn't overt censorship, indirectly we knew. Some of the editorials mentioned that we were in "this unusual circumstance," but they did not say: "In violation of our civil rights."

What was the attitude of the internees at the time toward the *Free Press?* "They would complain about the stories we wrote. [They said]: 'You're not giving a balanced picture.' " None of the camp newspapers raised critical issues about internment. Rather, they emphasized loyalty to the American way of life.[25] Sue remembers one *Free Press* editorial in particular, "Happy New Year to You, America" that was very pro-America and was widely criticized by the young activists, who found it patronizing. It had been written by Roy Takena, and sent to the press nationwide as a New Year greeting from Manzanar. Sue claimed: "Our editorials were widely reprinted nationally."

There were real reasons for the cautious editorial policy that developed on the *Free Press.* The newspaper was very visible, and justice in the camps was erratic and arbitrary. Sue recalled people being deported to Japan for perceived disloyalty to the United States. "This partly explains why we were very careful in what we said in the paper." Although the *Free Press* was constrained from criticizing camp conditions or questioning the fact of the internment, another project was much less restricted in reporting the depressing living conditions. Robert Brown, public information officer for Manzanar, believing that a comprehensive documentary record of Manzanar should be written, selected Joe Masaoka to prepare the reports. Masaoka, the Japanese American Citizens League leader who had gained considerable recognition for his cooperation with military and government authorities, chose Togo Tanaka as his assistant.

Brown hoped that the reports would provide more of a summary of life in the camp than was being documented by the *Free Press*, accurately describing the evolving life of internees. Complete reports or excerpts were sent to the WRA regional office in San Francisco to keep the agency apprised of events at the camp.[26]

> "I don't think internees were aware of the purpose of the reports," Sue said, "and they thought Masaoka and Tanaka were *inu,* spies, working for the Administration. Years later seeing one of the reports, I was shocked that members of the JACL had been complaining about Manzanar so early because they had been so cooperative with the government. The report was very critical, protesting that the food was terrible, the barracks were so flimsy they would probably blow away in a strong wind, and the housing for the administrators was much better constructed.[27] I had assumed, like most of the internees that they were informing on people for being anti-American."[28]

Although Masaoka and Tanaka reported the unhealthy and demoralizing conditions of the camp as early as May 1942, these same conditions were partly responsible for the Manzanar Riot in December of that year. Sue's assertion that Manzanar was not a peaceful place, as Ralph Merritt had described the camp, that there were tensions and conflicts in Manzanar, are confirmed by the riot and its aftermath, in which staff members of the *Manzanar Free Press* were significantly involved.

CHAPTER 7

Violence and Desolation

Despite growing knowledge of the mass incarceration of Japanese Americans during World War II, the general public is not usually aware that internees in all 10 centers persistently resisted the conditions in camp. Defiance often took the form of recurring passive resistance. Obvious resistance rarely occurred, but from the very beginning of the incarceration, there were conflicts, not only between internees and administrators, but also among the internees themselves. There were also legal challenges of the authority of the federal government. Four Nisei, Mitsuye Endo, who challenged the government, not on the basis of the internment, but on the grounds of being denied the right to work; Fred Korematsu, who was jailed for refusing to report to an assembly center; Gordon Hirabayashi and Min Yasui, both convicted of violating the curfew, were working through convoluted court proceedings. Endo's case was decided in her favor by the Supreme Court in 1944, mandating the reopening of the West Coast to Japanese Americans. The Supreme Court decisions against Korematsu and Hirabayashi were reopened and reversed in 1983. Min Yasui died before a decision was reached in his case.[1]

In contrast to these individual acts of defiance expressed through court proceedings, overt resistance to the internment took place at Manzanar.[2] The riot, also variously described as "incident," "revolt," or "uprising," occurred on December 6, 1942.[3] The Western Defense Command had issued a proclamation on May 19, 1942, that declared all "relocation" centers were subject to external military control. So-called protective services around the exterior boundaries of each center were provided by a company of military police. Maintenance of security and order within the camps was delegated to the internees under the supervision of the War Relocation Authority internal security offices.[4] Sue's brother Kinya was a member of the Internal Security Force. Although most of the internees did not want to have anything to do with the Caucasian police, they accepted the internal police, including Kinya, who worked the night shift as part of the routine of the camp.

Manzanar internee Ryozo Kado, under the supervision of the administration, constructed two rock and concrete sentry posts, one within the camp and one at the entrance, both still existing.

Two armed MPs were assigned to each of eight watch towers in day and night in shifts.

> "There was also what they called a 'night checker,'" Sue remembered. "At 8 o'clock we were supposed to be inside unless there was a movie or something. They would make sure all of us were counted. I guess they were trying to figure out if anybody was going to escape. I don't know where we would have gone. Up into the mountains? Or Lone Pine or Independence, where they were harassing the Native Americans because they looked Asian?"

Manzanar had a jail inside the police department barrack, "a jail inside a jail," as Sue put it. Both the MPs and the Internal Police could make arrests. Asked about claims that the non-internee police harassed the female internees, Sue laughed: "Probably true, because some of the women were looking for excitement, and maybe they flirted with the officers. It was boring there."

Togo Tanaka, one of the documentary historians appointed by Robert Brown, has written: "On December 6, 1942, Manzanar was not unlike a powder keg and

Figure 7.1 Manzanar War Relocation Authority Camp Military Police Sentry Post at Entrance (photograph by E. Bahr; this military police sentry post, constructed of rock and cement by internee Ryozo Kado in 1942, still stands at the entrance to the camp)

[conflicting groups had] exceedingly short fuses."[5] A major source of tension was the resentment internees felt at being prisoners against whom no crime had been charged and for whom there was no recourse.[6] Sue's account recognized, however, that not all of the resentment was directed against the WRA. From the beginning of the incarceration, critical tensions existed among factions in Manzanar, some of which had persisted from pre-internment years. The war did not create the generational, class and ideological conflicts that existed within the Japanese American community.[7]

The following three discordant factions have been identified: (1) The Japanese American Citizens League, composed entirely of Nisei, adhered to a policy of "constructive cooperation" with the WRA, thus claiming leadership in the camp. (2) The anti-JACL left-wing group had a reputation in the Japanese American community as being *Aka* (Red) or Communist. Being labeled *Aka* meant ostracism, but some internees considered members of this group liberal or progressive rather than Communist. Those in this group saw themselves, despite their resentment of the internment, as profoundly antifascist and supportive of an allied victory.[8] (3) Internees who were primarily Japanese speaking, notably the Kibei, who were born in America but educated in Japan. Members of this group were both anti-JACL and anti-camp-administration and were reputed to be pro-Japanese.[9]

In its constructive cooperation policy, which began as an attempt to prevent internment, the JACL was recruited by government officials to act as informers on their own community. When war with Japan became a distinct possibility, the federal government wanted to insure that they could identify potentially disloyal Japanese Americans. The JACL reasoned that refusal of the government's request could be interpreted as disloyalty. Cooperation was the only way the Nisei could ensure the safety of their community.[10] At Manzanar, Issei and Nisei competed for leadership, with the latter gaining control when the WRA required American citizenship for internal governance positions. The Kibei, although American citizens, were excluded from the political process because they lacked fluency in English, a requirement the WRA exploited to empower the JACL leaders, who were granted white-collar, supervisory jobs in the camp.[11]

Months of hostility against the JACL by a group of Kibei and Issei, including work slowdowns, strikes against war-related industries, and beatings of suspected *inu*, culminated on the evening of December 5. Fred Tayama, a prominent JACL leader, was severely beaten by six masked men. Because of his close association with the WRA administrators at Manzanar, Tayama was suspected by many internees of being an *inu*, an informer. Tayama identified one of his attackers as Harry Y. Ueno, an outspoken Kibei who was an openly avowed enemy of Tayama. In September of 1942, Ueno had organized the Kitchen Workers' Union at Manzanar to represent the 1,500 Kibei-dominated mess hall workers. This union was in direct competition with the Manzanar Work Corps, sponsored by the JACL and chaired by Tayama.[12]

As a mess hall cook, Ueno had earned considerable internee admiration by reporting to the FBI that Ned Campbell, assistant project director, and Chief

Steward Joseph Winchester were allegedly stealing meat and sugar from the camp supplies to sell on the black-market. Ueno also maintained avuncular relations with the camp's children, baking special treats for them. His arrest and transfer to the county jail in Independence on the evening of December 5 provoked intense hostility among the internees.[13]

At noon on December 6 an estimated 2,000 internees arrived at a meeting called to discuss possible responses to the arrest of Ueno. A Committee of Five was selected to negotiate with Project Director Ralph Merritt for Ueno's release from county jail.[14] Spokesman for the committee was Joseph Y. Kurihara, Hawaiian-born, 20 years older than most Nisei, and a veteran of World War I. He had volunteered for military duty following Pearl Harbor, but was rejected because of his Japanese ancestry and was incredulous that not even service during World War I was sufficient to prove the loyalty of Japanese Americans. In his unpublished autobiography he later recalled feeling "sick" about the JACL cooperation with the WRA. Embittered, he had vowed to fight the JACL in the camps and had become a leading dissident at Manzanar, exhorting both Issei and Nisei that the internment was the result of pure racial hatred.[15]

Meeting with the Committee of Five at approximately 1:30 on December 6, Merritt, who had been project director for only 12 days, agreed to bring Ueno back to the Manzanar jail on several conditions, including the assurance that no demonstrations would be held by the internees. When Ueno was returned from the jail in Independence, a crowd, of several hundred, formed, demanding that Ueno be unconditionally released. A further demand by the crowd was the irrational stipulation that individuals who were on a blacklist be killed. The list named those who, like Fred Tayama, were suspected of informing the FBI about alleged pro-Japanese internees and included several *Manzanar Free Press* staff members.

When Harry Ueno was returned to the camp, the crowd gathered near where he was being held in a steel jail cell inside the police barrack. The MPs were putting on masks to throw tear gas to disperse the crowd. Sue vividly remembered the night of the riot.[16] "Kinya came running home. He said he threw his hat in one of trashcans and took his badge off. 'I'm not going to be a policeman,' he yelled." "I'll get killed!' " Kinya Kunitomi's fears were well founded. The demonstration, now out of control, had reached a deadly focal point, as leaders proposed a plan to liberate Ueno from jail and kill internee policemen, whom they blamed for Ueno's arrest. The plan also included killing Tayama in the hospital where he was recovering. Members of the mob armed themselves with knives, hammers, screwdrivers, hatchets, stones, and anything else they could get their hands on.[17]

Accounts vary in detail, but Tayama was effectively hidden by hospital personnel. The rapid transformation of the original demonstration into a violent mob convinced Merritt to call in the military police. The MPs at first used tear gas to attempt to disperse the crowd, but when a driverless automobile, used by the camp's fire chief, was pushed toward the police station, the military police fired into the crowd. Internee James Ito was killed. Eleven others were wounded. Jim Kanagawa died from his wounds.[18]

Sue, who was in her room in Block 20 as these events occurred, recalled how she and her family responded to the riot.

> Some people say it was a revolt, but I've always thought of it as a riot. During the day I had heard there was meeting in Block 22 because there had been an arrest of a man, but I didn't know who he was. That night about eight o'clock we were inside the apartment when we heard a mass of people walking by. We heard their boots crunching on the pavement. When we looked out, my mother said: "Be careful! We don't know who they are. You better hide yourself." After we heard them pass, we didn't hear anything for a while. Then Kinya came running home. He said: "They just shot some people."
>
> In our apartment were my mother, Hideo, Kinya, Midori, and Tets. It was terrifying. My mother was shaking. She said that they were going to come and shoot all of us because the jeeps were making the rounds up and down the Blocks. We tried to help her, to hold her and calm her but she was too frightened. We were all scared. We never thought there would be any shooting, although we knew the MPs had loaded guns. I think we were all in a state of shock. My mother kept saying: "Just stay inside. Don't go out." She especially wanted me to stay out of sight because she knew that *Free Press* people were in danger.
>
> We just huddled around in the apartment. Then they started to ring all the mess hall gongs. The gongs went on most of the night. I don't think we slept at all. The next morning we heard that a young man had been killed, a boy whom my brothers knew. They also knew his older brother, who was in the U. S. Army. My brothers were very, very upset. They kept saying: "What's going to happen?"

Fred Tayama had been given permission by the WRA to go to Salt Lake City for a national conference of the Japanese American Citizens League.[19] About the attack on Tayama, Sue said: "He was a representative of the JACL and considered to be an *inu*. People felt that he was getting extra advantages, being allowed to go out of camp when nobody else was able to go out for meetings." A notice appeared in the *Free Press* that those who had gone to Salt Lake City were "representatives of Manzanar."[20]

Anxious internees threatened to beat the "delegates" if they claimed they represented Manzanar residents or took any action that they deemed objectionable that was binding upon the internees.[21] Tanaka has written that JACL activity was not the only cause of the riot. He lays blame on the "inadequate, ill-prepared or ill-advised administrators and on the government decision of mass evacuation based upon race and on the basic incompatibility of the conflicting groups." When Fred Tayama was beaten and Harry Ueno arrested,"the powder keg blew."[22]

About the arrest of Harry Ueno Sue said: "I think he was used as a scapegoat because he was head of the Mess Hall Worker's Union. Block 22, where Fred Tayama worked as cook, was the only Block that would not join the union."

Although she knew several *Free Press staff* were on the Black List, Sue also believed that people in the camp considered that reporters for the *Free Press* had a connection with the administrators, and, therefore, were all informers. "People were very suspicious anyway." Sue herself was not on the Black List. "I'm not sure why. My mother worried all the time I worked at the *Free Press*. I kept telling her I was not a big shot so the 'bad guys' would not come for me. She worried, though, because I worked with people who were threatened." Sue, who later became a tenacious liberal, thinks that, ironically, she was not on the Black List because she was not considered a member of the progressive or the left-wing group.[23]

Because of serious threats against the blacklisted internees, 65 individuals, including staff members of the *Manzanar Free Press*, were taken into protective custody. On December 10, they were transported to Cow Creek Camp, an abandoned Civilian Conservation Corps camp adjacent to the headquarters of Death Valley National Monument. Paradoxically, these 65 liberal thinkers who were philosophically antiadministration, were being protected from the other internees who thought they were all pro-administration informers. With the considerable assistance of the American Friends Service Committee, they were able to find jobs and relocate to destinations east of the strategic military zones. By mid-February, Cow Creek Camp was vacated.[24]

Twenty-six internees presumed to be instigators of the riot, including Harry Ueno and Joseph Kurihara, were arrested and transferred to jails in Lone Pine and Independence. Ten were released and returned to Manzanar, while the remaining 16, including Ueno and Kurihara, were sent ultimately to the Tule Lake Segregation Center,[25] which housed internees deemed "incorrigible" by the WRA. Ueno never received a trial or a hearing on any charge that led to his removal from Manzanar.[26]

Harry Ueno's version of the riot, when interviewed by Sue, Arthur Hansen, and Betty Mitson in 1986, differs in critical aspects from other documentary accounts.[27] He believed the riot was partially Ralph Merritt's fault for letting the demonstration get out of control. He steadfastly maintained that internees did not arm themselves with rocks, tools, and other makeshift weapons. He charged the Military Police with shooting internees, with the possible exception of James Ito, in the back as they were running away from the tear gas. He also claimed that before being transferred from Lone Pine to Moab, Utah, he and the other detainees were given a document signed by Dillon Myer, Director of the WRA, promising them a speedy hearing after their transfer. Ueno declared that his detention without a hearing was based on racism. "If we were Caucasian, they never [could] do that."[28] He voiced an enduring regret: "Not many persons know what happened in camp. All they know is there was a riot.... They never [found] the truth."[29]

During the interview Art Hansen asked Ueno to identify the people who beat Tayama? Ueno refused, saying: "I'm not going to be an informer." Hansen asked him outright: "Did you do it?" Ueno answered: "I'm not going to tell you. A lot of the [internees] are still alive; we were all in this place together and we shouldn't be acting against each other." Sue thought he knew, but he would not reveal identities.

Ueno was released from incarceration in 1946. He characterized his early post-war years as "being a tumbleweed." He moved his family around California working as a sharecropper or field hand. Finally, he was able to buy a 10-acre farm near Sunnyvale, California, and began growing fruit.[30] The National Park Service received the following message from Ueno's family in December, 2004: "[We] thought the Park service might like to know that one of the historical figures of Manzanar, Harry Ueno, passed away Tuesday, December 14, at El Camino Hospital in Mountain View, California. Harry was 97. The family is planning a simple, private ceremony as per Harry's request."[31] A memorial service for Ueno was held at the Block 22 garden during the 2005 Pilgrimage.[32]

I asked Sue whether her interview with Ueno had changed her mind in any way about the events of the riot.

> Yes. Most of the people at Manzanar felt that Harry and his group were causing trouble for the rest of us, bringing too much attention to Manzanar. Newspapers were writing about it; a Congressional subcommittee was investigating. In fact, I heard people say: "It's a good thing that some of them went to Tule Lake because now we don't have as much trouble at Manzanar."

However, Sue concluded: "After interviewing Harry and reading about the riot, I've come to the conclusion that all the factions had a legitimate position at that time in that place."

In their final report on the Manzanar Riot Ralph Merritt and Robert Brown claimed it resulted from a struggle for leadership between Issei and Nisei.[33] Sue thought it was a struggle not so much between the generations, as between the different factions of Nisei: the JACL, the progressive group, and the Kibei. Sue also emphasized two factors: the assumption by the JACL that they had a right to speak for the evacuees without consulting them and the exclusion of the Issei from official positions in the camp because of the imposed English-language requirement. "The Nisei were not of age yet. Most of us were around 17 or 18. The Issei, especially the men, thought that they were abdicating their position as head of family in giving in to young people who had no experience in organizing or in leadership roles. That must have hurt [the Issei] quite a bit."

Sue stated that the reliance of the camp administration upon JACL leaders to help manage the camp was undeniably a significant cause of the riot. "Even today, some people say: 'They sold us down the river.'" Sue also referred to quarrels among various factions in the Japanese American community prior to evacuation. "They brought some of these quarrels with them into camp." She does not entirely agree with the WRA assessment that anger at the presence of informers within the camp was an underlying cause of the riot. "I think the assumption of the internees was that anybody who worked with the government was an informer. There were some informers, but not as many as people thought."

The WRA cited talk about the thefts of sugar and meat to be sold on the black market as another cause of the riot. "That rumor went around quite a bit, especially after Harry started investigating. People didn't have anything else to talk about." The rapid turnover in camp directors was also a source of agitation.

> We had three different camp directors, Ned Campbell, Roy Nash and Ralph Merritt. Each one had a different idea about how the camp was to run. They all had restrictions but I think Merritt was the most lenient. You would think if he were more lenient, that would have eased some of the tension, but I think [the dissension] was too far gone by the time he got there. Also, Manzanar, was located in a strategic military zone, so there were a lot of restrictions.

Sue also related underlying dissatisfactions that may have contributed to the outbreak of violence: the delay in making wage payments to the internees caused immense frustration. "People needed to buy things; not everything was provided by the WRA. It got to be a big problem." There also were delays in clothing allowances. "People needed those allowances because walking all the time wore our shoes out. Winter was coming, and we needed warm clothes." Wage differentials were yet another source of frustration. "They had a scale: unskilled labor was $12 dollars a month, semi-skilled, $16 and professional people like doctors and nurses, $19. I got $16 as a reporter and $19 a month as the editor."
Variation in food among the kitchens was a constant irritant.

> I think everybody got the same vegetables and fruits, but we didn't have much meat or chicken. [The quality of food] depended on how the cook managed it. In the beginning it was hard because they were cooking over wood stoves and they couldn't control the heat. I remember eating burnt rice all the time. We had what we called Slop Suey, a mixture of overcooked vegetables.

Sue agreed with the allegation made in the WRA report that an underlying cause of the riot was the widespread dissatisfaction among internees with the apparent pro-government policy of the *Manzanar Free Press*, but she argued: "They didn't let us write anything else. We did a lot of the reporting for the WRA because they had rules and regulations, and they were always sending out notices. Later on, we wrote about the 442nd [all-Japanese Regimental Combat Team] because we would get news releases about it. Maybe people didn't like that either." Sue responded to my comment that it seemed a contradiction that the *Free Press* was perceived as being pro-administration, pro-WRA, yet some of the staff were very left-leaning and openly critical, at least orally. "They never wrote their criticism in the paper. Their critical opinions were expressed in private."

Sue concurred with other possible causes cited by the WRA, including the inaccurate translations of English into Japanese in camp procedure notices and the policy that only American citizens could work in the camouflage net factory. The WRA report also concluded that a critical factor in the unrest that led to the riot was the fact that some Manzanar internees had family members detained in other camps. "The heads of families were picked up either December 7th or shortly afterwards," Sue pointed out. "There was no information as to when they would be released or why they were being kept [in custody]. The internees wanted their families together, and they had a lot of anxiety about what was going to happen to their fathers." Yet another critical factor was uncertainty about their future in the United States. Sue remembers the stress of learning about legislation being introduced by Congressmen. "Send them all back to Japan, take away their citizenship." Anti-Japanese groups had sought to deprive Japanese Americans of their citizenship since 1921. In 1943 the Native Sons of the Golden West pushed for national legislation to achieve this goal.[34] The so-called denaturalization bill passed by Congress and signed into law on July 1, 1944, provided that an American citizen could voluntarily renounce his citizenship during time of war. The law was a compromise to more punitive bills introduced in Congress advocating the deportation of Americans of Japanese descent.[35] "These reports were very disturbing. We were just sitting there, wondering what was going to happen. How long were we going to be there? We were in terrible suspense."

A further cause cited by the WRA was the loss of property and income upon internment.

> My mother was heartbroken over losing her store. She didn't make a lot of money, but she was making some. My mother may have been afraid to get out of camp, because we didn't have a store to go back to. We didn't have a house to go back to. While we were in camp she didn't talk at all about what we were going back to.

How much impact did the unfavorable national press have? "There was always a lot of anti-Japanese [sentiment] in the newspapers. People were worried about what was going to happen if they did get out of camp in terms of prejudice, discrimination. There were stories about discrimination in the Midwest where people couldn't get jobs or housing. What would it be like on the west coast?"

Despite all the issues contributing to the Manzanar riot, Sue concluded: "Basically the riot was caused by the conditions of living so close together with no privacy, and not being able to get out. Promises were made but not kept by the government. People wanted their families reunited and they weren't able to achieve that, and they were becoming very disillusioned."

The *Manzanar Free Press*, unlike media on the outside, did not cover the riot, as it occurred.

> "They suspended the paper that day. We did not have a paper until Christmas about three weeks later. When the Christmas issue came out the main headline was that there was snow," Sue said, laughing. "There was no coverage of the violence, nothing except one little article about the funeral services [for the internees shot during the riot] being held under the trees outside of camp. But there was no mention of why there was a funeral. Somebody gave us orders not to cover the riot."

A brief article on the violence appeared, however, three months later in the March 20, 1943, issue of the paper which was surprisingly critical of the internment: "Manzanar stands, an isolated barrack town... housing 10,000 orphans of the war whose lives are controlled and limited by confining barbed-wire fences." The article concluded by quoting a letter from Shizuo Hohri, who had been given leave clearance to relocate in Chicago: "Manzanar life is easy, but it isn't living. Life out here isn't easy, but it's life in AMERICA!" [36]

Arthur A. Hansen and David A. Hacker have presented a perspective on the riot that is in contrast to that of the WRA. They maintain that the WRA viewed the riot as a local phenomenon, rather than as part of a pattern of resistance within all the camps. Replacing "riot" with "revolt," these historians argue that the violence was an intense expression of an ongoing resistance within the camps.[37]

Christmas came three weeks after the Manzanar riot. "Nobody had Christmas celebrations. Some people were making wooden toys for the kids so at least they would have something." Sue talked about her Christmas Eve in Manzanar:

> Somebody asked me to join a group that was going to sing Christmas carols. From our block we walked to the Administration area, and when we got to First Street we heard an MP shout: "Stop!" We all stopped, frozen. The minister who was head of the group stepped forward and said: "Good evening, we are Christmas carolers and we would like to sing at the Administration [building]." The MP had his gun pointed. He thought about it for a while and finally said: "Okay, you can go." We went across the road to Ralph Merritt's apartment and sang a couple of songs. Ralph Merritt opened the door and said: "Merry Christmas." His wife was with him. They stood in the doorway and we sang another song and then we turned back across the road. The MP was still there. Someone said: "Merry Christmas" and I think he was surprised. He said: "Merry Christmas to you, too," then he walked away.
>
> People were resentful that we were [caroling]. I was scared. But I love to sing carols so I went along. Nobody came out besides Ralph Merritt. None of the people in the camp. They must have been scared, too.

What about Christmas day itself?

> We had two meals that day, a late breakfast, and they were going to serve a chicken dinner. People started getting ready, getting dressed up. But I didn't feel like doing that. I felt so bad about the whole thing. The rest of my family didn't say very much, except Hideo. He kept saying: "I've got to get out of here." I didn't tell my mother, but I felt like I had to get out too.

The agitation in the camp subsided since the most dynamic leaders, both pro- and antiadministration, were removed. Although an official WRA report maintained that the riot had cleared the air of mistrust, historian Roger Daniels argues that the opposite was true.[38] Sue agreed with Daniels: "People were all so sad because of the deaths, and they were frustrated and distrustful."

Sue herself was overwhelmed. She was thinking: "They will never let us out after this riot because everybody thinks we are anti-American. They will never let us out. Ever. Ever. God, we are going to be stuck here for the rest of our lives."

CHAPTER 8

Go Forth, Seek, and Find

In the immediate aftermath of the riot Sue recognized one of the MPs who had been sent as reinforcement, her former high school teacher Paul Greene. When he asked her whether she was doing anything to get out of camp, she reaffirmed her belief that because of the riot probably no one would be allowed to leave. She remembered vividly that he responded that he had spoken to authorities advocating assistance for internees who wanted to leave the camp, and he urged her to make plans to do so. "That reinforced the idea that I needed to get out of there." During that grim December Sue came upon something further that motivated her to take action.

> One of Midori's Chinese friends had sent her a magazine, *Time* or *Look*, one of the magazines of that period. In an article about Betty Davis in a film called "Now Voyager," there was a quote: "Now voyager, go thou forth and seek and find." I thought that was a good motto. I should go out and seek and find something. I didn't know what I wanted to do; I just wanted to get out of there.[1]

Moving Japanese Americans from their homes into camps took only a few months, but getting them out again took almost four years. Contrary to popular belief, the process of leaving camp started as early as the summer of 1942.[2] In the beginning, four categories of internees were released: Those who selected repatriation to Japan, students who were allowed to attend college under the supervision of the National Student Relocation Council, agricultural workers on temporary leave, and volunteers or draftees for the MIS, using bilingual Japanese/English skills in the Pacific Theater to serve as interpreters and translators.

Jack Kunitomi participated in two of the leave programs, agricultural leave and military service.

> "We were working on the camouflage nets at Manzanar," he recalled. "What else was there to do? A call came in for farm laborers, potato picking, sugar beet

topping and thinning. We signed up and were sent to Idaho Falls, three married couples. One couple [Shizu and Lindy Uyehara] had a two- year old girl [Linda]. We worked for a Mormon family. We quit [partly] because my wife's father was now in the Heart Mountain camp [in Wyoming]. He had developed kidney stones."

Fujioka, who had been picked up by the FBI immediately after Pearl Harbor, had been taken to Fort Missoula, Montana, without his family's knowledge. When he became critically ill, he was sent to Heart Mountain.[3] Evidently Fujioka was able to determine where his family was working as farm laborers, and when he contacted them, they transferred to Heart Mountain to be with him. Although he was expected not to live, Shiro Fujioka did recover after being reunited with his family.

Like many young Nisei, Jack was recruited from Heart Mountain into the MIS, and he laughs today about how poorly qualified he was.

> At the end of our basic [training], after seventeen weeks, the Army sent recruiters from Fort Snelling in Minneapolis. All of us who had finished the basic were tested on our [Japanese language] ability. We were given a book to read which was a simple reader in Japanese. I was able to read one line. Those of us who were able to read a little bit were sent to Fort Snelling to learn [more] Japanese. The classes were broken down into strong English/strong Japanese or strong English/weak Japanese. We were strong in English and weak in Japanese. We went to the Philippines and finally ended up in Manila. Because my class was classified strong English/weak Japanese, we were given homework to brush up on, typical propaganda leaflets in Japanese, our leaflets for the Japanese soldiers to think about. Some of the words were very strange to us.[4]

When the U.S. military needed translators proficient in Japanese, they found that 90 percent of Nisei recruits tested for Japanese-language proficiency did not know enough Japanese to be considered trainable. Scholars have pointed out the irony that after the Nisei had prepared themselves to be good Americans, what America wanted of them was the language of their parents.[5]

Sue herself seriously considered joining the military. "I thought it was one way of getting out of camp, a way of showing that I was loyal, and I did want to serve my country. I didn't join mostly because of what my mother said: 'Your brothers are all going to go eventually. I don't want you to go.' "[6]

By the fall of 1943 Sue, Komika, Kinya, Midori, Tets, and Frank and his family were at Manzanar. Hideo, true to his word, had left for Chicago on work leave, followed later by Frank. Hideo had volunteered for military service. Sue remembered that he said: "When I get married and have kids, they are going to ask me what I did during World War II. I can't tell them I was languishing in camp. I'd like to let them know I was fighting for my country." When he was rejected by the military because of bad eyesight, he realized that the only way to leave the camp was on work leave.

On October 1, 1942, the WRA instituted new regulations that opened new possibilities for leave. The official policy of the WRA from the beginning of the internment was to allow Japanese Americans to relocate out of the camps to areas outside the restricted military zones. National Park Service historian Harlan Unrau characterizes this policy as "bizarre." He argues: "If the Issei and Nisei were being excluded because they threatened sabotage and espionage, why would they be left at large in the interior where there were innumerable . . . [sites] vital to the nation's security?"[7] Nevertheless, Dillon Myer, WRA director beginning in June of 1942, believed that internees should be released and relocated and made resettlement a priority.[8] The new application procedure for leave allowed both Issei and Nisei to apply for leave in one of three categories: short term leave for up to 30 days, for circumstances such as medical needs; work leave for seasonal employment; and indefinite leave for employment or education outside the restricted military zones. To be granted indefinite leave an internee was required to show a means of support, which could include sponsorship by an organization and after an FBI check, no evidence that he or she would be a national security risk.[9]

The new procedure was so mired in bureaucracy, however, that few internees left the camps under its auspices until mid-1943.[10] The leave questionnaire has been described as "fatally flawed."[11] Two questions, intended to determine the loyalty of internees, became infamous for the intense anxiety they created. Question 27: Are you willing to serve in the armed forces of the United States on combat duty wherever ordered? The country confining them and their families behind barbed wire was asking Japanese Americans to volunteer to fight for principles of liberty, justice, and equal protection under the law. Intended for Nisei men, this question was modified on another form for Nisei women: "If the opportunity presents itself and you are found qualified, would you be willing to volunteer for the Army Nurse Corps or the WAAC [Women's Auxiliary Army Corps]?"[12]

Question 28: Will you swear unqualified allegiance to the United States of America and faithfully defend the United States from any or all attack by foreign or domestic forces, and forswear any form of allegiance or obedience to the Japanese emperor, to any other foreign government, power, or organization? Issei were being asked to forswear allegiance to Japan, the country of which they were citizens and to vow allegiance to America, the country that refused them citizenship. Nisei also found Question 28 offensive because they already considered themselves loyal American citizens, and some considered it a trap, because if they answered "yes," it would imply that they had an allegiance to Japan.[13] Of the 78,000 eligible internees, approximately 75,000 took the oath. Virtually all of those who refused were internees at Tule Lake.[14]

The Kunitomis decided to respond "yes" to both questions. Sue's brothers insisted on this response because they were American citizens. Sue's mother, however, was very conflicted. If she answered yes to Question 28, it would imply that she had an allegiance to Japan. If she answered no, she would be repatriated to Japan, leaving unwilling children in the United States.[15] Either answer was a risk. Evidently internees who had responded "no" pressured Komika to the extent that she considered doing so also, making a return to Japan a real possibility. But Midori and Tets adamantly refused to go with her. Komika's anguished indecision continued for many months.

Question 27 regarding willingness to serve in the armed forces of the United States was underscored in January of 1943 when the War Department announced the formation of the segregated Japanese American 442nd Regimental Combat Team (RCT).[16] Following the attack on Pearl Harbor, Nisei had been reclassified as IV-C, enemy alien,[17] and now would be classified IV-A, eligible for military service. The segregated unit, although signifying the restoration of their rights as citizens, also maintained discrimination of Japanese Americans.[18] Many Nisei, however, were eager to join the Japanese American RCT to prove their loyalty. The 442nd became the most decorated unit for its size and length of service in American military history.[19]

However, of 74,588 respondents in all 10 camps, 11,276 answered in the negative to both questions.[20] More than 2,200 of these "no-no" internees were transferred from Manzanar to Tule Lake in late 1943 and early 1944.[21] The internees who answered "no" did so for a variety of reasons, primarily family obligations. Young men who answered yes, were faced with being drafted and leaving their parents in camp.

> "These questions concerning the loyalty of the internees were even worse than the evacuation and the internment," Sue said, "because it caused terrible conflicts that tore families apart. It separated families much more so than the initial uprooting. During the evacuation everybody tried really hard so families would not be separated but after a year in camp almost everyone was very disillusioned. No future at all. Then to be told: OK, now you serve in the Army while your family is behind barbed wire. It was a wrenching period, especially for young men. I don't think people ever got over that because we still have schisms in the community between the draft resisters and the JACL and the veterans and the 'no-no' boys. The JACL, which has a history of being in opposition to the draft resisters, finally apologized to the resisters in 2002, even though President [Harry] Truman pardoned the resisters in 1947. Now some veterans don't like the JACL because they apologized to the draft resisters."[22]

By August 1943 the leave procedure had improved. The WRA established 42 offices throughout the country to help former internees resettle. From March to September 1943 relocation teams were sent to each camp to encourage resettlement. Recruiters from private industries were encouraged to visit camps to enlist workers. Slowly the number of internees leaving the camps had increased, rising to 11,000 by

August.[23] Most of those who left the camps on leave clearance in 1943 were Nisei between the ages of 18 and 30. By that summer, the majority of those left in the camps were the oldest and the youngest internees. Sue remembered that the *Manzanar Free Press* played a significant role in encouraging internees to relocate. "We would put announcements of jobs in different cities in the *Free Press*, and we printed letters from people who had gone east encouraging others to go out."[24]

Nonetheless, many internees, especially the Issei, were apprehensive about leaving. Sue commented: "They weren't sure what kind of welcome they would get if they relocated. In camp at least their basic needs were taken care of."[25] Fear and uncertainty about the future were made worse, according to Sue, by newspapers calling for deportations of persons of Japanese ancestry and by proposed legislation to strip Japanese Americans of their citizenship. "Some of these were rumors, but some were real," she said, "and people believed them." Having roots in California was also a factor in internees' reluctance to move to the Midwest. They also worried about very limited job prospects. "I had those fears," Sue said, "but I thought I had to keep going and try to make it out there."

The WRA had established a field office in Chicago in January of 1943. With the assistance of a number of liberal and religious groups, including the American Friends Service Committee and the Pacific Coast Committee on American Principles and Fair Play, internees moved to Chicago in numbers great enough to make it the largest of the relocation cities.[26] Sue, however, decided to relocate in Madison, Wisconsin.[27] "I had friends who had gone there and they encouraged me to join them. One of the MPs working in the Manzanar post office was from a small town near Madison. He said: 'You really ought to get out of here.' He talked about how beautiful Wisconsin was."

How difficult was the decision to apply for leave?

> "I argued with my mother," Sue admitted. "She would say: 'Why do you want to go away so far? Why don't you wait until we can get back to Los Angeles? You are going to a strange city and you don't know anybody.' I argued by reminding her that she came to the United States without knowing a word of English, in an arranged marriage, and she managed quite well. When I think about it now, I really should have been more sensitive. I left her behind with two kids. Although Hideo, working in Chicago, and I were trying to save money to send back to her, I realize now that it must have really hurt her to see us go out and leave her behind."

Sue and her mother argued constantly about her leaving. "I finally told her: 'I have a date to go.' She felt pretty sad. I never did convince her that this was the right thing to do." Before she had told her mother she had a definite departure date, she had told the staff at the *Free Press*, who all told her she was brave to leave. "My younger sister didn't want me to go. She said: 'You are leaving me with Mom.'

I said: 'I know, but we can't stay here forever. I've got to get out to do something about our future. Tets was pretty discouraged, I think. He didn't say very much. He never said very much."

One area of Sue's life story that remains puzzling, but most likely is a reflection of her father's powerful influence, is that she did not apply for student relocation, despite her strong desire to go to college. The national Student Relocation Committee, formed in March 1943 at the University of California, Berkeley under the direction of university president, Robert G. Sproul, was designed to facilitate the transfer of Nisei college students to Midwestern and eastern educational institutions.[28] A representative from the Student Relocation Committee visited Manzanar, declaring that the prospect for student relocation was the brightest it had ever been. Nisei women comprised a surprising 40 percent of internees who relocated to college.[29] "I was aware of the student program," Sue acknowledged, "but I never applied. I should have thought about it, but I just never did." When asked whether she thought it was the enduring impact of her father's message not to go to college, Sue responded noncommittally: "It could be."[30]

Sue decided to apply for work leave in Madison. In regard to the leave application process, she said: "I had an interview with Mr. [Walter] Heath,[31] mostly about why I picked Madison and what I planned to do there. The YWCA had offered me a sponsorship that was minimal, one month room and board." Evidently it was enough for Sue to be granted the leave clearance.

"Mr. Heath also told me not to gather in groups of Japanese Americans of more than four or five people, and not to argue or confront people who make anti-Japanese remarks, and to try not to be conspicuous. How could we not be? I thought it was all very strange." After her application was approved by the FBI, she was issued "a little green card." She pointed out the irony: "There is a green card for people who come here from other countries and want to work. I guess I was sort of coming from another country."

As with other Nisei, Sue was a young woman who had never been anywhere but Little Tokyo and Manzanar, taking off to be completely on her own.[32] The only assistance the WRA provided was a train ticket to Madison and $25.00 in cash. "That was it." What were her apprehensions? "Mostly whether I was going to be accepted where I was going. Hideo tried to reassure me. He thought that Chicago was pretty friendly." Sue also was apprehensive about finding a job. "I had minimal sponsorship by the Madison YWCA, a room and three meals at the cafeteria for one month. But I didn't have a job."

Despite these very real uncertainties, Sue left Manzanar in October of 1943. Sue's brother Kinya was still at Manzanar when she left. "He encouraged me to go. He said: 'I'll be here to take care of Mom.' " But he was drafted around Christmas. "When the station wagon came to the door and took my baggage, my mother was crying. Kinya and Midori and my younger brother were there. I tried to tell my mother that she could join us in the east." Sue's voice became very soft. "She just didn't want me to go." Asked whether she were ever tempted not to go, Sue said "No!" revealing the determination that energized her as an activist in later years. "I'm pretty stubborn once I make up my mind."

On the train trip east she did not encounter any hostility. "That was a relief to me, because I was really worried about how I was going to be treated." Sue traveled east via Chicago, where Hideo met her. The next day he escorted her to the train to Madison, a university city that she found beautiful. "Most of us Nisei who went to Madison were young and shy," Sue said.

The WRA office in Madison helped her get a temporary job with Dane County Clerk's Office as a secretary. After that she worked for a mail-order cheese company. She continued to live in the YWCA, paying rent when her one-month stipend ended. Although they often worked with whites, the Nisei usually socialized with other Nisei, to whom they looked for emotional support.[33] Sue, however, continued her pattern of cultivating relationships with non-Japanese individuals. "[In Madison] I went around with a group of young non-Japanese who lived in the YWCA dorm. We did get a lot of stares from people. The young women knew that we had run into a lot of discrimination in California, and they knew about the camps. But they just accepted me as their friend. It really was wonderful."

Once in Madison, although she had not applied for student relocation, Sue did apply to the University of Wisconsin. Her application was rejected on the grounds that the U.S. Army was doing secret war work at the university. "I found out later that the man in charge of the secret program was a Nisei," said Sue, "in fact, my roommate's brother, who was working on his doctorate. I was shocked. How could they turn me down? I had my FBI clearance. I had my little green card." Sue did not contest her rejection. "Maybe I should have, but when they said: 'We can't have you on campus,' I said: 'Oh well, okay.' "Although Sue later grew to be outspoken, at this time when she was a 20-year-old Nisei woman, she accepted what she was told.

Sue made her first formal presentation about the camps at the Madison Y. "I didn't have reluctance at that time to talk about Manzanar, but later when I found everybody else was not talking about the camps, I began to think I shouldn't either." A survivor from a Nazi camp was also on the program at the Y, the first time Sue heard a personal account of the "death camps." Sue conjectured that one reason people of Japanese ethnicity were reluctant to talk about their camp experiences may have been what they had heard about the Nazi camps and the rescue by the 522nd Field Artillery Battalion 442nd RTC Battalion of the people imprisoned in Dachau. Their own internment would seem almost benign by comparison.

Meanwhile, Sue stayed in touch with her mother, Midori, and Tets. "I wrote letters to them a lot. I wrote in Japanese to my mother. Although I'm not that great now, at that time I was able to write in Japanese." Sue's voice became very soft when she talked about the continuing strain of internment on her family. "My mother just said that she was okay, but Midori kept writing: 'It's awful here!' Although she had finished high school and was working for Mr. Heath, being there by herself with my

Figure 8.1 Sue at Newberry Library, Chicago, Illinois, 1944 (photograph courtesy of the Embrey family)

mother and younger brother was really hard on her. Tets wrote only occasionally, but it was obvious that it was a terrible time for him too."

Komika Kunitomi also worried about her mother in Japan, from whom she had had no news because correspondence between internees and persons in Japan was restricted. She learned later that her mother had died during the war. Sue thought that one way she could help her mother was financially. "Hideo was also worried about her," she remembered.

> After talking to Hideo, I decided to leave Madison. After living a year in Madison, I hadn't found a decent job, and I wasn't able to go to the university. Hideo was working as a waiter, and he was urging me to come to Chicago because of the good jobs. Then he called to say that he was getting married to a gal who was also working in the restaurant [Ellen]. I was sorry that I couldn't get there in time for the wedding.

Was she reluctant to leave Madison?

> In a way I was, because I had a lot of good friends there and it really was a good life, especially after Manzanar. Hideo wanted me to be in Chicago. The older brother, he wanted to look after his sister. My brother Frank was also there, so I moved in with them. Later, though, I lived with Mae Ichioka, who had been in Amache camp [in Colorado]. We had been neighbors in Little Tokyo and classmates in elementary school. Mae and I got an apartment and we lived together, just the two of us for a little while.

Later when Frank was inducted Sue lived with his wife Hide and son Gene. "Frank must have been surprised to get inducted that late, almost 30." Lindy Uyehara also was in the Service, the MIS. His wife Shizu, Hide's sister, and her daughter Linda, and Tak and Florence, Lindy's niece and nephew, all lived in an apartment in Chicago with Sue. Sue remembered having to sleep on the couch in the living room.[34]

The American Friends Service Committee office in Chicago had job listings, for former internees, among them the Newberry Library. Hired to answer the phone and prepare a monthly business report for the board, Sue was greatly impressed that the staff of Newberry Library was multiethnic. "The people at the Newberry accepted you for what you were. This is where I met Mamie Jackson, a Black gal from Texas, and Dorothy [George] Westphal whom I still correspond with [in 2003]. Although most of the people I met in Chicago did not know about the camps, Dorothy knew quite a bit about them."

Sue said about Chicago: "I had a good job and was independent. I had a good life." Terrible events that occurred elsewhere, however, cast a shadow over Sue's good life in Chicago.

CHAPTER 9

The Kunitomis, Reunited, Diminished

On August 6, 1945, the United States dropped an atomic bomb on Hiroshima, Japan, bringing death and injury to more than 160,000 people. On August 9, a second bomb was dropped on Nagasaki, killing or injuring 150,000. Sue heard the news on the radio. "Although we didn't have much information, what we did hear was devastating."

Sue heard about the unconditional surrender of Japan on August 14, 1945, when the emperor's order to the military to cease combat was rebroadcast. "My mother had thought that it would be good if they could have peace without one country defeating the other, a negotiated peace. I had told her that was not going to happen, but because she had relatives in Japan and she was living in America, she continued to hope."

Both Kinya and Jack Kunitomi were with the Army of Occupation in Japan. Kinya, on furlough from the Northern Hokkaido area, was walking down the street in Tokyo when somebody called a nickname only his family and friends would know: "Kimbo! Kimbo!" In a truck passing by was Hikoji Takeuchi, the young man who had been shot in Manzanar by an MP. His mother had insisted on going back to Japan, so he went with her. Kinya recognized him and waved as the truck went by. They never saw each other again in Japan, but they did get together when Hikoji returned with his mother to America.

When Kinya and Jack visited relatives they discovered that the Kunitomi name was well known in Okayama. Sue recounted what her brothers had told her: "The villagers were very surprised to see a Japanese in an American uniform. Both Jack and Kinya had saved their ration coupons for cigarettes, Kleenex, sugar and other restricted items, and they showed up unannounced with duffel bags full of gifts."

With the surrender of Japan, Sue realized that the camps soon would be closed.[1] Despite the belief of the War Department by late 1944 that Japanese Americans were no longer a threat to the security of the West Coast, the ending of the exclusion was delayed. The exclusion of Japanese Americans from the Western Defense Command Zones one and two, born of political pressure, was sustained for political reasons. The 1944 national election campaign was in full swing, and some voters on the West Coast would be alienated by the return of Japanese Americans.[2]

Meanwhile the legal challenges to the authority of the federal government, Endo, Yasui, Korematsu, and Hirabayashi had reached the U.S. Supreme Court. The Endo *ex parte* case that became a landmark in U.S. legal history had been initiated by James Purcell, an attorney who had been recruited by Saburo Kido of the Japanese American Citizens League to work on the case. Purcell filed a habeas corpus petition on behalf of Mitsuye Endo, on the grounds that she was denied the right to work because of unlawful detention by the army. The U.S. Supreme Court on December 18, 1944, ruled in *Endo, ex parte* in Endo's favor. The decision lifted the ban on returning to the West Coast for Nisei not charged with disloyalty.[3]

The government was notified in advance about the Supreme Court ruling and one day before the court's decision was announced, General Henry Pratt, the new Western Defense commander, issued Public Proclamation #21, rescinding General John L. DeWitt's mass exclusion orders.[4] The general reaction of the evacuees to the announcement that the exclusion order had been rescinded was disbelief.[5] A storm of protest by the remaining internees greeted Dillon Myer's announcement that the camps would be closed within a year. Mess hall bells rang, summoning internees to "feverish discussions."[6]

> "They knew starting over would be a hardship for them," Sue explained. "They would have to get jobs and find houses, both critically scarce. Many at Manzanar were so fearful of leaving, that some of them even wanted to stay and have a community. Ralph Merritt wanted to establish a community at Manzanar, but there weren't that many people left, mostly older people and very young people. It's interesting that they even considered it."

A decisive impediment to creating a community, however, was the fact that The Los Angeles Department of Water and Power intended to reclaim the land on which Manzanar had been built. In observance of the lease agreement, the WRA began to remove all structures in March 1946 with the exception of the cemetery, the two guardhouses, and the auditorium.

Evidently, Komika Kunitomi, despite her anxieties about leaving, never considered becoming a resident of the proposed Manzanar community. Sue said: "She wanted to get back to L.A., especially because Choko was still in the sanitarium." Komika was not alone in wanting to return to Los Angeles. Despite efforts of the WRA to disperse the ex-internees throughout the United States, the vast majority of them returned to the West Coast. Within five years Japanese Americans in Los Angeles reached their prewar population of 37,000.[7] Newspapers and even public officials, especially in California, raised loud cries of protest, criticizing the military for permitting the internees to return to the West Coast.[8] Despite the preponderance of returnees to the Coast, internees had well-founded fears regarding returning to southern California. California had a reputation for being blatantly anti-Japanese.[9]

"We heard from people who had gone back to California," Sue remembered. "They were having trouble finding jobs; employers didn't want Japanese in jobs that were visible to the public. Hearing about this hostility affected my thinking about our family going back to Los Angeles. I was hoping they would come to Chicago, but my mother didn't want to."[10]

Komika Kunitomi moved out of the camp in September 1945, relatively late, nine months after the exclusion law was lifted. Sue thought her mother's reluctance to leave was primarily caused by not wanting to go to Chicago, as Sue was urging her to do. Between August 15 and September 15, 1945, 10 blocks in Manzanar were closed and the living quarters were consolidated.[11] Manzanar War Relocation camp closed on November 21, 1945 with the last 42 internees leaving at 11 a.m.[12]

Hideo evidently wanted to go back to Los Angeles as soon as the exclusion order was lifted. Frank stayed in Chicago, not returning to California until his son Gene was in high school. Midori and Tets returned to Los Angeles with their mother. Because of her secretarial skills Midori secured a job with Los Angeles County. Komika was enterprising, finding odd jobs, including sorting shrimp to be frozen according to shape, and grading walnuts according to size. However, their struggle to relocate was grueling.

In 1948 Midori decided to marry Phillip Iwata and live in Chicago. Iwata had been removed with the other Japanese Americans from San Fernando Valley to Manzanar, where Midori had met him. When the exclusion ended he was living and working in Chicago. Because Midori was leaving Los Angeles, her mother asked Sue to come home. Sue was extremely reluctant. "My brothers put pressure on me: 'Take care of your Mom.' " A core value among Japanese Americans that sons take care of parents had been disrupted by the dispersing of families during resettlement.[13] Nisei women found themselves in a demanding new situation with few role models. Sue's sense of duty and subsequent responsibilities for the Kunitomi family exemplified the role of Nisei women during resettlement.

The obstacles to resettling on the West Coast were formidable.[14] A primary concern was the possibility of a hostile reception by those now living in areas Japanese Americans had been forced to abandon. Sue said candidly: "We did not encounter much outright hostility, but when we came back to Little Tokyo we were all surprised, because it was mostly Black. The Blacks were feeling that they were being pushed out, so there was tension." The tension was primarily due to the postwar severe shortage of housing and jobs. African Americans, newly employed in wartime industry, had found that Little Tokyo, vacated by interned Japanese

Americans, was part of the 5 percent of the city that had no racial restrictions on housing.[15] Called "Bronzeville," Little Tokyo had been transformed. Even the Hongwanji Buddhist Temple had been converted to Providence Baptist Church.[16]

In January 1946, 6,800 African Americans were living in the Little Tokyo area. While no large-scale open conflict occurred, African Americans and Japanese Americans encountered each other through inevitable intermingling.[17] Although when Sue finally found a house to rent for her family, the neighborhood was mixed, they did not have that much contact with the blacks. "We were busy all the time and they also were all working."[18]

Takinori Yamamoto, who has been an activist cohort of Sue since 1971, had a unique experience with black residents of Little Tokyo when he was a 17-year-old. "There was an abandoned storefront next door to Toyo Hotel, and I wandered in one Sunday morning. I found the space occupied by several Black people who were singing their hearts out. It seemed like a wondrous/spiritual place. I was moved; in fact, I started to sing along. These people were accepting of me, so I stayed on for some time. I went several more Sundays to participate in the singing."[19]

While some younger Japanese Americans, like Yamamoto, were discovering enjoyable aspects of resettlement, the older ones had severe anxieties. Finding a place to live presented a formidable challenge. Former internees were housed in WRA trailers in Griffith Park, in Quonset huts in San Pedro, and hostels that the churches had established. Restrictive covenants, legally binding prohibitions against selling or renting to non-Caucasians, complicated the housing problem. "There were certain areas you simply couldn't live in," Sue remembered.

Phil Shigekuni, who later worked with Sue on the redress and reparations campaign, wrote about the restrictive covenants encountered by his family: "In 1947 we were able to move into a home on 37th Place, just east of Normandie. 37th Place at that time was on the 'color line.' Any home located south of 37th Place (Exposition Boulevard, principally), had in its deed a restrictive covenant prohibiting the sale of the home to anyone except someone of the white race. Since the lady who sold us our home violated this covenant, this middle-aged man…took it upon himself to go from door to door soliciting signatures from his neighbors demanding that we and a Negro family across the street get out. As it turned out, we didn't have to move. That year the Supreme Court ruled restrictive covenants to be unconstitutional."[20] The Supreme Court issued this decision in 1948 in *Shelley v. Kramer*.[21]

When Sue returned to Los Angeles Jack was with the Army of Occupation in Japan, and his wife Masa had left Heart Mountain and returned to Los Angeles with their son Dale. During internment her family had rented their house in Hollywood to a non-Japanese family that they were able to repossess. Sue found, however, that the other Kunitomis, were under acute duress.

> They never said anything about it while I was still in Chicago, but they were living in a terrible place. There was a house in front where one family lived. Behind this

> house there was a row of rooms with kitchenettes. Hideo, Ellen and their daughter Phyllis lived in one. Kimbo came back from the Service so he was there with us. There was no running water, just a cold faucet outside. And no bathroom. When we had to go to the bathroom or take a shower, we had to do it in the front house, while they were still awake so we could get into the house. I knew that I just had to find a different place to live and soon! After we moved out, the place was torn down. The city said it was not up to code.
>
> I went with quarters and dimes to a public phone and starting calling places to rent. As soon as they heard my name they said: "No, we don't have anything." I had an argument with one realtor about it. He said: "It's not us; it's the people who live in the community; they don't want you." But I think it was also the real estate agents. Finally, I found a house for rent on Crocker Street, near Skid Row, actually. But it was a nice block close to Little Tokyo. My mother could do her shopping and walk to the temple. I worked at the [Los Angeles County] Health Department on Spring Street, so I could take the bus and come back and pick up Phyllis, who was at the Maryknoll School and bring her home. It was convenient.

Komika, Hideo, Ellen, Phyllis, Kimbo, Tets, and Sue lived in the Crocker Street house. Choko left the sanitarium in the early 1950s and she and her husband, who was doing gardening work, came to live in an apartment next door.

Memories of the internment prevented most Japanese Americans from trusting people outside their ethnic community.[22] Their distrust was intensified when they sought employment. Gardening and landscaping became the primary livelihood for Nisei men. "This was the only way to get started," Sue explained. "They had no other jobs. There was no affirmative action at that time."

Drawing on her growing self-confidence and independence, Sue secured her first job after returning to Los Angeles with the County Department of Education, transferring shortly thereafter to the Health Department. "I did not have shorthand, but I could take dictation on the stenotype. In Chicago I had gone to school to learn stenotyping,[23] one of the big things at that time."

While employed with the Health Department Sue encountered the anti-Communist loyalty oaths. In 1948, the Los Angeles City Council and Board of Supervisors required an anti-Communist loyalty oath for all city and county employees.[24] Sue laughingly admitted being blasé about signing the loyalty oath after her experience at Manzanar. "Oh, another one of these things. I'd been there; done that."

She was not blasé, however, about two other loyalty issues that had a powerful impact on the Japanese American community. The year after Sue's return to Los Angeles, the infamous "Tokyo Rose" trial took place in Federal District Court in San Francisco.[25] Iva Toguri, raised and educated in Los Angeles, was stranded in Japan after Pearl Harbor. Conscripted by the Japanese military along with 14 other English-speaking prisoners of war, she was ordered by the Japanese government to broadcast propaganda over Radio Tokyo. "Tokyo Rose" was the term coined by

American military men for several female broadcasters heard on Japanese controlled radio.

When the war ended Iva was living in Japan with her husband Felipe d'Aquino, a Portuguese national of Japanese descent whom she had met at the radio station. She became trapped in cold war politics that led to two lengthy arrests and a "highly problematic" trial.[26] Very few Japanese Americans supported her during her trial.[27] In November 1949, d'Aquino, the only English-speaking broadcaster arrested by the FBI and tried for treason as "Tokyo Rose," was sentenced to 10 years in prison and a $10,000 fine.

Awarded time off for good behavior, she was released from prison in 1956 after serving approximately seven years. Having also lost her citizenship, the Immigration Service ordered her deported, but she successfully fought against the order with the assistance of activist attorney Wayne M. Collins. In 1975, Clifford Uyeda, the JACL, and Senator S. I. Hayakawa launched a campaign for a presidential pardon for d'Aquino. Iva Toguri d'Aquino was granted a pardon by President Gerald Ford on his last day of office, January 19, 1977.[28]

A lesser known case also occurred during the first few post-camp years. Tomoya Kawakita, a native Californian, was accused of mistreating American prisoners of war of the Japanese while working for the Japanese as an interpreter. He was given the death sentence in 1948, which was commuted to life imprisonment by President Dwight D. Eisenhower. President John F. Kennedy granted him a presidential pardon on the condition that he return to Japan and never seek entry into the United States.[29]

Japanese Americans, including the JACL, distanced themselves from both cases, which they considered much too controversial.[30] Sue vividly recalled the mood of the Japanese American community during these trials. "I was very afraid when I went out that people might connect me with Tokyo Rose. That was a bad time. I think we all felt a little guilty by association with Kawakita because he was a Nisei."[31]

While their elders were concerned about getting jobs and finding housing and fearful about being associated with Japanese Americans on trial for treason, younger ex-internees were exploring their new life in Los Angeles. Sue's niece Phyllis Kunitomi Murakawa, daughter of Hideo and Ellen, remembers suede buck shoes, 78 rpm vinyl records, felt hats and gloves, and polished wing-tip shoes. She also was aware, though, of the serious issues.

> I was very young and I overheard so much in the evening when I was supposed to be sleeping. My family members wanted to get back on track and finish college, others wanted a career, and then there were the ones that wanted to live the American Dream and have a family and own a home outside the inner city, which was gray and dismal.[32]

Tetsuo Kunitomi evidently found his new life in Little Tokyo oppressive. Sue remembered sadly:

> We learned that Tets wasn't going to school, when a probation officer came to visit us. We were shocked. We thought he got up every morning and went to [Belmont High] school. I asked him: "What are you going to do? You need to have a high school education if you want a job." He said: "Learning to speak English properly won't help me get a job. There is nothing in Little Tokyo."

When Tets was 18, he decided to join the army and signed up for a two-year stint, although all the Kunitomis tried to dissuade him. He argued that he would get to travel and also perhaps learn a skill, and that he would be safe because there were no wars going on. He went into basic training, and came home on leave "looking very strong and healthy." In 1950, he reregistered for three more years. Evidently his reasoning had proved persuasive. Sue thought at the time: "It's not such a bad idea. Jobs are hard to get for people who don't have any skills."

After the Korean War had broken out in 1950, he was sent to Japan when he was 22. He wrote often to Sue, who sent him books. "He wrote back: 'I didn't like the left-wing books you sent me; send me something else.'" Without warning the Kunitomi family received a telegram that Tets had died. "Hideo was the most anxious to find out how, so he called the Surgeon General's office. The information they had was that he died of a heart attack. He collapsed on the street in Yokohama and was taken to the Army hospital." Sue added very softly, "He died there."

Tets came home in a flag-draped coffin, with one of his buddies as military escort. Sue has written about the funeral service at the Koyosan Temple in Little Tokyo: "There was a change of guard every few minutes. Their soft-spoken orders mixed with the solemn chants. The curling incense smoke made hazy halos of the young faces who came mourning their dear friend."[33]

Throughout her narrative, Sue described Tets as deeply distraught by the evacuation and camp life. He seemed to have been an exception to the younger people in the camps who generally were not as distressed with the harsh conditions as their elders.

> He never said very much, but you could tell a lot from his attitude about school and his wondering about the Constitution and about why we were in camp. Midori said that she thought that he always wanted to serve in the Army, that he wanted to show he was an American citizen. That's contradictory to his feelings about the Constitution and being in camp. But the whole story of the camps is contradictory.

Sue knew that the death of Tets, the youngest son, was bitterly hard for her mother, but she spoke with admiration: "I think she took it better than the rest of us. As a Buddhist she believed that he would be in a better life." Reflecting the Buddhist belief that one is able to communicate with the dead, Sue said: "My mother would go and talk to them. Midori also would go to the cemetery if something was bothering her, and she would talk to my mother."

Eight years later in 1960, the Kunitomis were traumatized again when Hideo died of cancer of the pancreas with little warning. Sue remembered that, although her mother characteristically appeared stronger than others in the family, it pained her immeasurably to have two sons die. "She had a picture of her mother in Japan, one of Tets, and one of Hideo on her chest in the bedroom. [Alongside] an incense box and incense holder, she had a tiny Saki cup that she put hot rice in every night and offered to them. Choko carried it on afterwards."

In "Some Lines for a Younger Brother," Sue expressed her profound attachment to Tetsuo in a poignant essay.

> On December 27, 1969, I joined several hundred young people who made a day-long pilgrimage to the Manzanar cemetery. . . . Dedication services ended that freezing, wind-swept and emotional day. I looked beyond the monument and the crowd. Out of the painful memories my mind dusted out of the past, I saw again the blurred impressions of the barbed-wire fence, the sentry towers and the tar-papered barracks. For a moment I saw again the 12-year-old boy with his head cocked, his shoulders sagging, his eyes fighting to keep open in the sun, while the long and lonely desert stretched out behind him.[34]

CHAPTER 10

Nisei Progressives and Beyond

That bitterly cold and emotional pilgrimage in 1969 led Sue Kunitomi Embrey into a 35-year endeavor to raise awareness of the enduring consequences of Executive Order 9066. This campaign, culminating in the designation of Manzanar as a National Historic Site in 1992, had a long prelude in progressive politics for Sue. Sue's first experience with national politics was in 1947, when she joined a group supporting the third-party presidential candidacy of Henry Wallace, vice president during President Franklin D. Roosevelt's third term of office. Sue explained her attraction to liberal politics. "I had felt helpless in camp. I realized if you don't have people representing what you believe in, then you have no power."[1] She also remembered how much she had appreciated working in an integrated racial environment in the Newberry Library in Chicago. When she returned to Los Angeles, she sought organizations that worked for racial integration and found Nisei for Wallace.

Organizations such as Nisei for Wallace were manifestations of a postwar revival of progressive politics in Los Angeles. Amid the social and economic chaos of the Great Depression in the 1930s, Los Angeles had been the site of a labor movement led by the new Congress of Industrial Organizations. Despite conservative politicians' use of racial fears to divide the voters, a progressive coalition had continued to grow in strength during the 1930s. Racist politics, however, became a more commanding force during the war years, and progressive movements were further undermined by anti-Communist crusades that had developed during the 1930s. From the late 1940s through the early 1960s, Los Angeles was a volatile mix of both Communism and battles for liberal reform. Anti-Communist politics dominated. Virulent assaults on civil liberties were under the rubric of McCarthyism, after Wisconsin Senator Joseph McCarthy, who had attacked individuals as disloyal or subversive without evidence. Additionally, the Congressional House Un-American Activities Committee (HUAC) began hearings in Los Angeles in 1947 to investigate alleged Communist infiltration in Hollywood. Eventually nearly 400 individuals were blacklisted for presumed subversive activities, costing them their livelihood and careers. In spite of this environment, progressives persisted.[2]

During the early 1940s, the Nisei for Wallace group was campaigning for racial integration, redress, and civil rights. Wallace, running for president on the Progressive Party ticket, was campaigning against the cold war, the arms buildup, and racial segregation.[3] "I admired Henry Wallace," Sue said, "because he also advocated, among other policies, a discontinuance of discriminatory hiring practices, and a termination of restrictive covenants in housing, all of which were considered radical ideas in 1947. I went to the first Wallace for President meeting in Los Angeles at Sak [Sakae] and Fumi [Fumiko] Ishihara's home."[4] Ishihara, a university-educated member of the Communist Party who had served in the MIS during World War II, is credited with forming the Los Angeles Nisei for Wallace. He had joined the Communist party as a member of the Asian Commission that was part of the Black Caucus. He claimed to have no political ambition, wanting only to be part of a group or system that would help people.[5] His wife Fumiko Okanishi Ishihara, whose internment in the Poston Camp in the Arizona desert had kindled her activism, was chair of the East Los Angeles Progressives and represented Los Angeles County and the state of California in the national Progressive Party.[6]

Sak and Fumi placed an ad in the *Rafu Shimpo* announcing a meeting of Nisei for Wallace and 20 people showed up, including Sue Kunitomi and Arthur (Art) Takei. Although Takei knew the Ishiharas, Sue had never met any of them before. Takei had been incarcerated in the camp in Rohwer, Arkansas, and in a postwar interview he recalled mainly being "pissed off" and plotting how to protest the injustice.

Most of the Japanese American community, however, strongly opposed Progressive political activism.

> "1948 was the first presidential campaign following the war," Sue emphasized, "and Japanese Americans didn't want to be conspicuous. So soon after internment they were very fearful and were just trying to make a living. The Japanese American community is conservative, basically. Liberals and Communists were painted with the same brush by the general population in those days. You couldn't be anything left of center."

Many years later Sue came to sympathize with Japanese Americans who feared and censured conspicuous political campaigning by other Japanese Americans. At the time, however, she was defensive about her activism, which exposed her and other activists to severe resentment in the community. "This hostility took its toll.

People dropped out of the Nisei for Wallace campaign. Gradually we stopped having meetings. A few of us still got together, but not many." Many of the members were targets of FBI harassment, including those whose only political action was precinct walking, persuading Japanese Americans and African Americans to register to vote.[7]

Remarkably, however, in May 1948, more than 31,000 people, from a variety of progressive groups, heard Wallace speak in Gilmore Stadium in Los Angeles. Several Nisei for Wallace activists, including Sakae and Fumi Ishihara, Arthur Takei, and Sue, met with Wallace in Los Angeles during the campaign.[8] Although the Nisei for Wallace had hoped for at least 4 million votes nationwide, he received a disappointing 1,157,140. Nevertheless, on election night Sue, Sak Ishihara, and Takei, discussing how they would continue their progressive activism, decided to do so as the Nisei Progressives.[9] The founding conference of the organization, with Sak Ishihara as chair and Sue as secretary, occurred on January 26, 1949, at the First Unitarian Church on West Eighth Street in Los Angeles. The meeting had been called to "organize a new, progressive organization that will work (1) to further the economic, political and social rights of the Nisei; (2) to tackle problems relating to the Japanese American community; and (3) to pursue a program for peace, prosperity and freedom for all."[10]

Although the Nisei Progressives, which also had members in San Francisco, Chicago and New York,[11] were intent on addressing issues that specifically affected Japanese Americans, they also raised awareness of anti-miscegenation laws, unfair labor practices, housing discrimination, and the dangers of nuclear weapons, which were issues of concern to other progressives. Through their mimeographed newsletter, *The Independent*, the Nisei Progressives of Los Angeles attracted members who were not Nisei and others who were not Japanese American. Although short-lived, it attracted an assemblage of students, workers, writers, artists, teachers, Communists, Socialists, Democrats, and independents.[12] Sue has written with reverence about the role the Nisei Progressives played in the evolution of her political philosophy: "Activism is very much my lifestyle.... My most meaningful experiences came during the post-war years with the Nisei Progressives, a group who held to the vision that change was possible when enough people hope and dream and work for a better America for all."[13]

Nisei Progressives helped to elect Edward R. Roybal to the Los Angeles City Council in 1949, the first Mexican American on the Council since 1881. Sue recalled: "Roybal was an intelligent person who was looking out for not only Mexican American people, but also for the whole working class. I admired him especially for working to give minority and working class people a voice in government." After Roybal was defeated in his first run for City Council in 1947, his supporters established the Community Service Organization, which was aggressive in fighting racial discrimination.[14]

Nisei Progressives also campaigned against the 1952 Immigration and Nationality Act, commonly known as the Walter and McCarren Act. Introduced into the U.S. Congress by Representative Francis E. Walter of Pennsylvania and Senator Pat McCarran of Nevada, the bill would allow Issei to become naturalized American citizens, a right previously denied them. It would also restore a token immigration quota for Japan. Included in the Act, however, were provisions from the Internal Security Act of 1950, known, somewhat confusingly, as the McCarran Act, which provided for the detention of individuals who were suspected of engaging in acts of espionage or sabotage.

The JACL supported the Walter-McCarran bill, arguing that since the detention provisions had already been established by the 1950 Internal Security Act, the benefit of allowing Issei to become citizens outweighed the negatives of the Walter-McCarran bill.[15] Sue explained the Nisei Progressives' opposition to the Walter-McCarran bill.

> Title II of the bill gave the President authority to remove anybody from any area for national security purposes. This was only ten years after we had been sent to camp. We believed strongly that we needed to get that Title II removed from the bill. We had a lot of opposition from the JACL who did not want us to oppose the bill because it would give citizenship to our parents. It was a dilemma.

Despite opposition from Nisei Progressives, the Walter-McCarran bill was passed into law, including Title II.[16] The Act also established a national origin quota system, heavily weighted in favor of north European nations, while allowing only 185 immigrants per year from Japan. The passage of the Walter and McCarran Act, nevertheless, had a major impact on the Japanese American community with substantial numbers of Issei, including Komika Kunitomi, enrolling in citizenship classes. Komika was 70 years old and knew very little English, but she passed the citizenship test and became a citizen of the United States on September 5, 1956.[17]

Nonetheless, pervasive anti-Communism of the late 1940s, the so-called red scare, continued to cast a wide net. The political climate of fear not only affected writers, actors, and film directors, but also trade unionists, public officials, and teachers. The Nisei Progressives, like many liberal organizations, were harassed by the FBI, which claimed that the Progressive Party was a Communist front. Within this context the Nisei Progressives disbanded in the mid-1950s. In July 1958, Sakae Ishihara was issued a subpoena to appear before House Un-American Activities Committee (HUAC). When he appeared in the Federal District Court in downtown Los Angeles, he refused to testify citing the Fifth Amendment—constitutional protection against self-incrimination. From then on Ishihara was a target of the FBI who followed him everywhere into the mid-1960s. "[T]hey just wanted me to point out fellow Progressives like Art [Takei] and Sue [Embrey]."[18]

Sue described the period of Nisei Progressive activism as "scary." She remembered it was not a good time to stand up for ideas, which the majority of Americans did not embrace.

> Affirmative action, equal housing, equal jobs. We were getting a lot of opposition. We would stand in front of churches on Sunday and pass out leaflets for progressive issues. People were angry at us for even being there. They would say we were a bunch of Reds. Some people said it to my face. Nothing had prepared me for this kind of activism. I was very innocent, expecting everybody to welcome us. Even with local politics when we were walking precincts around the neighborhood in Little Tokyo and Echo Park, people wouldn't open the door.

Despite FBI harassment, Sakae Ishihara remained a Communist for a number of years, until he severed his ties in 1949 because he opposed Russia's invasion of Hungary. Thereafter, he kept a low profile, working quietly for progressive causes.[19] Arthur Takei worked in the Progressive Party and later in the labor movement. Sue continued to work in the Democratic Party, campaigning for progressive Democrats, including Edward Roybal, Richard Alatorre, Shirley Chisholm, George McGovern, Jimmy Carter, and Jessie Jackson, among others.

Sue met Garland Monroe Embrey in 1948 at a Nisei Progressive party.[20]

> A mutual friend introduced Gar to me and he asked me for my phone number. I gave it to him, even though I had a boyfriend, Clifford Barkley, a Caucasian. I had been going with him for quite a while. I first met him also at a Nisei Progressive party. Clifford never came into my house. My mother knew I was dating a Caucasian, and she didn't like it. He would park his motorcycle and wait for me, then we would go together on the motorcycle. My mother also didn't like that I rode a motorcycle, poor behavior for a Japanese.

Since intermarriage met with extensive resistance at that time, what was it that attracted Sue to Clifford?

> I found him interested in doing all kinds of things, more than Nisei men, who were very conservative, not willing to take risks. They were not interested in doing anything other than playing poker or watching football. I was more interested in things like going to the theater, and these Caucasian men were also interested in that kind of cultural activity.

Perhaps after internment, Nisei men maintained a low profile and stayed within their communities, socializing with other Nisei men. However, these are Sue's views and perhaps she eventually would have found Caucasian men who preferred football to the theater.

Garland Embrey recalled: "I met Sue at a fundraising party for Henry A. Wallace in 1950.[21] I was involved with all kinds of people like Fumi and Sakae [Ishihara] through their political work. They didn't confine themselves to Nisei groups. They participated in a lot of political activities. There was a lot of activity in Los Angeles for Wallace."

Figure 10.1 Garland Embrey, 1950 (photograph courtesy of the Embrey family)

Gar phoned Sue after meeting her at the fundraiser, asking her to go with him to the Nisei Week celebration, an annual commemoration in Little Tokyo of Japanese American culture. She said she would meet him in Little Tokyo. "He realized I didn't want him at my house." Eventually Gar insisted on coming into her house, arguing that he and Sue could not keep meeting on the street, and he was confident that he could talk to Sue's mother. Sue recalls that as she and Gar were sitting in the living room talking, "My mother came in and said to him: 'You go home.' He stood up and said: 'Oh, Mrs. Kunitomi.' She turned her back, went into her room and closed the door." Gar expressed surprised that Mrs. Kunitomi had spoken to him in English. Sue said: "I think she was practicing that a long time before she got the courage to say it."

Garland's version of this incident is very similar to Sue's.

> "She was a little old lady who couldn't speak English very much. She came into the room and said: 'You go home! I no like you.' I said: 'We should talk this over Mrs. Kunitomi.' That scared her to death, and she turned around and ran out of the room." Laughing, he added: "Shortly after that, her mother told Sueko that she had to get out of the house. And Sue had been the one to support her mother, to come back from a good job in Chicago to help her mother relocate out of the camp."

Sue's meeting with Gar's mother, who lived in Los Angeles, was less dramatic.

> She was okay with me. Gar was also close to his Aunt Kate, his father's sister. She stayed in touch with him after his mother had divorced his father. When he told her: "I don't know how you feel about it, but I'm going to marry a Japanese woman," she said: "I feel happy for you; that's fine." After we were married, we went fairly often to see them.

Her marriage to Gar may have been acceptable to Gar's mother and aunt, but it was fiercely opposed by Sue's mother. Her sister Midori and brother Hideo had complained: "Mom gets really upset when you go out with these guys." They had pressed her to find "a nice Nisei boyfriend." Sue had responded: "I can't find one that I like." After an especially heated argument about dating Gar, Sue left home abruptly.

> I had come home from a date and she had locked the bedroom door. I got some blankets from my brother and his wife and I slept on the couch. The next morning when I was getting ready to go to work, my mother came out, very mad, saying: "You know I don't want you going out with this guy!" She was so angry she was going to hit me. Hideo was there and I said: "Get her away from me." I packed my

> stuff in a suitcase and said: "I'm going to leave and I'm not coming back." My brother didn't say anything.
>
> At work our elevator operator was a wonderful African American woman. I was telling her about my problems and she said: "I own a big house. You can come live with me." That night Gar said: "I guess we'd better get married." I stayed with the elevator operator a week or so, until I got married. She was a very, very generous woman.

Garland and Sue were married in November 1950 in the First Unitarian Church in Los Angeles. Reverend Stephen Fritchman presided. A reception was held at the Graphics Art Workshop on Hollywood Boulevard. Although Sue had informed her siblings, only her brother Hideo came with his wife Ellen and daughter Phyllis. "Her mother had told Sue's relatives that they couldn't go to our wedding," Gar remembered. "But Fumi and Sakae [Ishihara] were old buddies and after the ceremony and reception we went to their apartment and had drinks."

Statistics on interracial marriage in Los Angeles County show that between 1924 and 1933 only 2 percent of the Japanese American population married non-Japanese. Between 1948 and 1951 it has risen to 12 percent. Although this increase in interracial marriage indicates cultural changes, when Sue married Gar, 88 percent of Japanese Americans married Japanese Americans.[22] I asked Sue whether her parents had been explicit when she was growing up in telling her that she could not date Caucasians. "It was just accepted, understood. We didn't have any way of socializing with them."

Although in October 1948 the California Supreme Court decision in *Perez v. Sharp* led to the termination of the state's anti-miscegenation law, Garland and Sue risked significant censure by both the Japanese American and the Caucasian communities. On the advice of one of Gar's professors at UCLA, they obtained their marriage license in Santa Monica to avoid reporters at Los Angeles City Hall seeking to write sensational stories on mixed-race couples.

Notwithstanding the repeal of the anti-miscegenation law, exogamy brought *haji* (shame) to one's family in the perception of the Japanese American community. Komika told Sue's brothers and sisters not to have anything to do with her after she married. "But they did contact me," Sue remembered gratefully. "Hideo and his wife came by with Phyllis. Midori also came, although they came to see me without my mother knowing."

> Most of my Japanese friends didn't like the fact that I was married to Gar. They would come around, but not very often. Most of them had not had contact with non-Japanese, except maybe in the workplace, so it was hard for them to be comfortable. They would be shy. The women, especially, wouldn't have anything to do with me. The men were a little more tolerant, my brothers' friends.

Figure 10.2 Sue's wedding portrait, 1950 (photograph courtesy of the Embrey family)

Sue thought her ease with Caucasians began in Manzanar. "Because of my work in the *Manzanar Free Press* office, I was in frequent contact with Robert Brown, the assistant Project Director. I also made friends with the Caucasian MPs." She admitted these contacts were not on a social basis, nor ones of equality, and that living in Madison was her first experience with having Caucasian friends since her school days.

Although she maintained that she did not think marrying Gar was anything unusual, she admitted that before getting married she had apprehensions. Sue also wondered whether his friends, and especially his relatives, who were from Texas, would accept her. She described meeting Gar's Texas relatives several years later. "Evidently they didn't tell the cousins and the kids that I was Japanese, because they were really shocked . . . not saying a word. But the kids were playing with our kids. By then we had two little boys." Sue had told me that she and Gar had explained racial segregation in the south to their kids, thinking it would be a learning experience for them. They had been told:

> "When we go to Texas we are going to find separate bathrooms and drinking fountains for colored and white people, and you can choose whichever one you want." They wanted to know: "Well, what are we anyway?" I knew, of course, that their dad was Caucasian, but Sue had to tell me that Japanese people were considered white. "But I told [the kids] they could do whatever they wanted at drinking fountains. The first time they heard the word 'Nigger' used in conversation [in Texas] my kids almost jumped out of their seats, they were so shocked."

In addition to doubts about being accepted by his family, Sue had other worries about marrying Gar. "Mostly, would we be able to find a place to live?" Even after the restrictive covenants on housing were illegal by the time Sue and Garland were married, they were rejected as tenants. "There would be a sign in the window that there was a vacancy, but the [owner] would say: 'Oh, that's been taken.' And we knew it wasn't. We knew it was because of me."

Did Gar realize at the time how unusual he and Sue were? "Her mother threw her out of the house," he said, laughing, "and told her she wasn't going to let her marry a *hakujin*.[23] But I anticipated that. Oh yes, I knew. I knew that we would face a certain amount of prejudice. I had known several Black/white marriages when I was working on the South Side of Los Angeles."

Both Sue and Gar related how they were reconciled with her mother. Sue recalled:

> I would try to call my mother, and she would hang up on me. Hideo said: "Don't call her. Leave her alone. She gets too upset." Then Midori called to tell me that they were having a memorial service for my father at the Buddhist temple. Gar and I went to the service and sat in the back. My mother's best friend was sitting behind us. When the family went up to offer incense, she pushed me and said: "You go up there; you are family." I drew back, but she insisted: "You go up there."

> I finally offered incense as part of the family. She said to me later: "I told your mother that things are changing. Young people are getting married to whomever they want and she shouldn't be so old fashioned." I guess that helped a little bit. My mother didn't say anything to me, but she told my sister later she was glad that I had come. She was surprised.

Gar's recollection complements Sue's:

> Sueko's mother had a memorial for her husband and Sue and I decided to attend. Her mother sat almost behind me, because she was with a choir group. After the Buddhist chants, each member of the family, one at a time, went forward to a huge urn and put a pinch of incense inside. An elderly lady who was in her mother's choir leaned forward and said: "You go, you go." I thought that was very nice. I was going to go anyway. I put my pinch of incense in, thinking: "She can't cause a fuss in church. She has to watch me become a part of the family." The tradition is that the family invites everyone who came to the service for a Chinese meal, at that time across the street at the Far East Café. I sat down at the table and thought it was so funny: "She is going to feed me too." She couldn't make a fuss there either.

Sue said the reconciliation was not complete until their son Gary was born in 1955. "I asked her if she would come and baby sit and she did." Sue and Gar settled in Echo Park, located a few miles north and slightly west of downtown Los Angeles. During the 1950s, Echo Park was nicknamed "Red Gulch" because of blacklisted filmmakers and leftist artists and writers who lived there. By the 1970s, it had an influx of immigrants.[24] Sue and Gar raised their children in that neighborhood.

Gary Embrey described the Echo Park of his youth.

> Some of the Chicanos in this neighborhood also were in the Laborer's Union, which was close to the Communist Party at the time. A lot of people in the neighborhood were Jewish progressives. There were a lot of leftwingers. There were a number of interracial couples. I remember as a little kid seeing Black/white couples in Echo Park, three of them in our neighborhood. At that time you didn't see them anywhere else. This neighborhood was extremely political in the 1960s and the 1970s. Most people were for George McGovern, who ran against Richard Nixon in the 1972 presidential election. There were anti-Viet Nam war signs everywhere. It was like a hotbed. We had to deal with FBI agents. Their harassment was almost normal for Echo Park.[25]

Garland Embrey's political activism had begun when he became a Socialist in high school.

> I believed that we had to change the economic system. We had to do something about the Depression. In 1935 the Roosevelt administration put through Congress

> the WPA [Work Projects Administration][26] bills, funding projects that would help unemployed. I thought that was very sensible, because the work was badly needed, and the government programs produced very good work. They created the Civilian Conservation Corps, and my cousin joined that and stopped riding on freight cars.

Garland became president of the International Relations club in high school.

> The war in Spain had broken out. We invited a professor of Spanish to speak at our school. He was a Loyalist and a Republican.[27] He gave a dynamic speech, a fantastic speech. It fired me up. For the rest of the war I was raising money in nickels and dimes and attending all the rallies for Spain, then I began to see who was supporting Spain [Fascists]. I joined the American Student Union, which had been started by Socialists and Communists. That's what made me a radical.

Since there had been gossip in the Kunitomi family about Garland being in the Communist Party, I asked him whether he were. "I was only in the Young Communist League[28] and I worked on the South Side [of Los Angeles] registering voters among the Black population." These activities evidently were enough to trigger FBI surveillance. "Actually it started around 1937 when I was active on the UCLA campus as a student, and in 1941 [when working there on an assembly line] I was fired from Lockheed[29] for being a radical. Then Joseph McCarthy came in riding high. Between 1950 and 1952 I did not apply for a teaching credential, because all my friends who applied for a credential were subpoenaed by what I call 'the little guys committee' in California, the Tenney Committee.[30] I didn't get a teaching credential until McCarthy had died in 1957."

Sue remembered being harassed by the FBI because of Garland's liberal activism.

> We had visits from them. We had phone calls from them. One time I was home with Gary, who was about two years old. Two men came—they always wore gray suits—and knocked on the door. Gary was playing on a little porch in front of our apartment. When they identified themselves and said: "We would like to come in and talk to you," I said: "No. I don't want to talk to you." People who had been followed by them, then had been subpoenaed, had told us: "Don't ever let them in. Once you let them in, you're lost because they will ask you all kinds of questions." I said: "Gary, come in the house, honey." The agent said: "Oh, his name is Gary?" Intimidation. When Gary came inside I closed the door in the face of the agent.

As an adult Gary read the FBI file on his father and said: "I was really proud that my mother slammed the door in their faces."[31] The FBI also harassed Garland at work, when he was teaching at Vista del Mar Child Care Service, a private school that had not require a teaching credential. "We used to laugh about it," Sue said, "that they were training young FBI agents with people like us because there must have been bigger fish." Garland explained:[32] "I was a little frog in a big pond, since I was a very minor leader in the progressive movement. But J. Edgar Hoover just hung in there. I would get weird telephone calls. It took Hoover a long time to let go."

When new junior colleges in Los Angeles needed teachers, Garland learned that he could get credentialed to teach because he had earned an MA degree in psychology from California State College Los Angeles. In 1959, he was hired by West Los Angeles College, where he taught for almost twenty years. "It was a perfect place to teach with my background in psychology and sociology. I could teach about racism. I enjoyed that the most of any job I ever had." In summarizing his political beliefs, Garland Embrey emphasized what "progressive" meant to him. "Mainly to work for a kind of socialism where the means of production are controlled by the people rather than by a bunch of nitwits who manage to ruin everything every 15 years with a depression."

Concluding the interview I asked Gar whether he wanted to add anything. He did. "At the same time Sueko was doing this [being involved in progressive activism], she went back to school … two years at junior college … two years at Cal State, then she got her teaching credential and a Masters Degree in English at USC." Sue had told me that when she was going to school Gar was very supportive, an attitude toward women and education that was in absolute contrast to that of Gonhichi Kunitomi, Sue's father. Gar confirmed his support:

> Sueko was a hard working gal who looked after her mother. Besides that, when I began to read the political theories of socialism and communism, they said that there should be equality between men and women. That meant that men had to help. They had to do half the work. I took it literally. When Sueko and I decided to have children, we shared the work.

Bruce was born in 1958, when Gary was three years old, and despite Gar's help with childcare and housework, Sue was limited to part-time study. She earned her bachelor's degree in English at California State College Los Angeles in 1969 and her master's degree from University of Southern California in 1972. While working toward her degrees, she held a number of teaching positions with a provisional credential, including teaching children who were "educable mentally retarded," kindergarten, and first grade for the Los Angeles Unified School District. After earning her degrees she taught courses in Asian American Studies at Harbor Community College, University of California Santa Barbara, and University of Southern California. She also worked at the University of California Los Angeles Asian American Studies Center in curriculum development.

She remembered affectionately that when she received her master's degree Gar was extremely happy and her mother was very excited. I asked Sue: "When you got your master's degree, did you think about what your father had said to you?" She responded: “Yes. A big burden had lifted off my shoulders. It was an immense relief that I had been able to finish my education. But I also felt guilty because he had said: ‘You can’t go to college because you have two strikes against you. You’re a woman and you are Japanese.’ I still think about what my father would have said if he had been alive.” What would Gonhichi Kunitomi have said about his daughter’s continuing commitment to progressive activism, despite the risk of alienation from the Japanese American community?

CHAPTER 11

The Unquiet Nisei

Nisei, including Sue's family, suffered in silence for many years. In 1987, historian Richard Drinnon, in his biography of Dillon Myer, called Sue "an unquiet Nisei."[1] Sue responded to his description. "Yes, I know he did, but for a long time I didn't talk about the camps." She described the first time she spoke about the camp to anyone outside the family, nearly twenty years after she had left Manzanar. When a Caucasian neighbor in 1961 had commented on the hot Santana winds typical in Southern California in the fall, Sue replied: "I hate the wind. It reminds me of Manzanar." Her neighbor Ellen, who did know about the internment, expressed interest in Sue's experience and later visited Manzanar with her. While the wind was constantly blowing hard, Ellen had been standing by the front entrance of the camp under the electric wires snapping in the wind. "It really scared me that the wires could snap off," she told Sue. "I can imagine now why you hated the Santana."

The majority of both Issei and Nisei did not talk about internment to anyone, even their children. Reluctant to dredge up bitter memories, those who spoke of the camps did so superficially and focused on pleasant memories, mainly of friendships established. They buried depressing camp memories because there was a feeling of shame, that they had done something wrong. Even between parent and child or husband and wife the real subject remained untouched.[2] Jeanne Watasaki Houston, coauthor with her husband James of the popular memoir *Farewell to Manzanar*, did not tell her Caucasian husband about the camps for 20 years.[3]
Sue explained her perspective on this silence.[4]

> How could we talk about it? Everybody was confused and bewildered. It took a long time to sort it out, to process it. And people are still doing that. It was a traumatic, traumatic experience. It's been very hard to get any oral histories. Even

> Hikoji [Takeuchi], the man who was shot by the MP, had never told his story to his kids. When we got him to give the Park Service an interview, the first thing he said was: "The first night at Manzanar I looked up and there was a hole in the roof and I saw those beautiful stars. The sky was so pretty." Imagine, in a place like that to look at the sky and say: "It's beautiful." That was the first time his kids heard about the camp.[5]

Amy Iwasaki Mass, who had been interned at Heart Mountain and after the war earned a DSW from the University of California Los Angeles, makes an astute distinction between repression and being "consciously aware of something we don't want to think of, deliberately putting it out of our minds." She argues that people who are betrayed by a trusted source, as were Japanese Americans by their government, develop feelings of shame and a sense that there must be something wrong with them.[6] Sue agreed:

> They felt that they did something wrong and that was why they were put in camp. What were they guilty of? They weren't guilty of anything except they looked like the Japanese enemy. It's an emotional thing, not a logical thing at all. Fred Korematzu who was the plaintiff in the Supreme Court case [*Korematsu v. United States*] did not talk about the internment. His daughter came home from school one day and said to her mother: "We are studying a case called *Koretmatsu versus the United States*. Is that a relative of ours?" Her mother told her for the first time: "It's your father."[7]

Even Sue's siblings refused to talk about the camps. Jack's daughter, Kerry Cababa, related how she came to know about the camps and her parents' feelings about the experience.[8]

> I remember hearing conversations about people: "Don't you remember them? They were in such-and-such a camp." Summer camp was all I could identify with. My younger sister Colleen was teaching at Grant High in the [San Fernando] Valley. She had a panel discussion in the late '90s and invited my dad to talk on the evacuation and camps. I went to listen. One boy asked my father: "If this happened today, what would you do differently?" He answered that he would fight like hell against it. He said it with such conviction. I had never seen that from him before. I believe it was because he was asked a direct question by that student. We kids, of course, had never asked directly any questions like that. It had been building up probably for years and years and when he was finally asked the question, he answered it with a lot of anger.
>
> He is very, very bitter. It's a sore subject with him. But he has mixed emotions. I think he is also very sad. He was an American citizen so he was very angry

> about being taken away. He has nothing good to say about Earl Warren. He talks especially about Terminal Island: "How could they do that to these people?" When he talks about harvesting sugar beets, he laughs and tells how the geese would be flying so low over the fields, they would knock them down with broomsticks, then cook and eat them. Even at that time, though, he had conflicting emotions. He thought they should be good Americans. He actually did. He was drafted into military service out of the camps.

Jack spoke about not returning to Manzanar and his maintaining silence about the camps for nearly sixty years.[9] "We hardly ever talked about camp. I was very angry because of the Constitution. Why would America do that to us citizens? That was a chip on my shoulder. Later, I thought it was time I stepped in and helped Sue by supporting her. I'm glad I did."

Kerry's mother Masa also did not talk much about the camp. "My brother Dale was born there," Kerry said, "but it was also a sad time for her because she lost a brother. He had volunteered out of Heart Mountain and became part of the 442nd RTC. He was killed in France. Her memories were painful and her emotions were embarrassing to her, so talking about camp was avoided."

How does Kerry explain that Sue spoke up about the camps when other Nisei did not even want the subject raised?

> She was considered radical in the '70's. My mother never said Sue was a bad person. She just said that she was a little bit too radical for our family. Those people who resisted her, who did not want her to talk about the camps, haven't all gone away. It may be cultural because [Japanese Americans] are not supposed to speak out.

I asked Nancy Iwata, Midori's daughter, what she had heard from her mother about the camps.

> I remember doing a high school report on the camps. It wasn't that my mother was embarrassed; she just didn't want to talk about it. I wanted to interview Grandma and of course my mother said: "No, Grandma doesn't want to talk about it." She was adamant about that. She said: "You need to talk to Sue." I knew a little about camp from talking about how Mom and Dad met. My mother did say that the internment was wrong. Of course, Sue took it further and devoted her entire life to the cause.[10]

Sue's commitment to the cause began when Warren Furutani and other young activists at UCLA invited her to join them on the first Manzanar Pilgrimage, December 27, 1969. She was impressed that Furutani and Victor Shibata had been looking for a cause for Japanese Americans, had thought of the camps, and had come up with the term Manzanar Pilgrimage.

On an exploratory trip Warren and Victor had found the camp site totally overgrown, but saw in the distance "this white monument[11] jutting up out of the tumbleweeds. It was a phenomenal site." Recognizing that the monument marked the site of the camp cemetery, they understood that the Manzanar Pilgrimage would be not only an historical pilgrimage, "but also a pilgrimage to pay our respects for the people who had died in camp. That's why we have a religious ceremony as part of the pilgrimage."

Furutani acknowledged that the Sansei's ignorance of the camp was revealed by their planning the Pilgrimage for late December. "The wind blowing off the Sierras screamed down the valley.... The weather was bitterly cold. And we got our first lesson on how life must have been in camp. The experience humbled us."[12]

When Garland and Sue attended the 1969 Pilgrimage, it was the first time Sue had been back since October 1943. "I thought it would be just a return trip, an adventure." She could not remember exactly where the camp was until somebody flagged them down and directed them to parking. She recognized a couple parked next to them as Karl and Elaine Yoneda, Communist activists, who had driven from San Francisco to attend the Pilgrimage. Elaine, a Caucasian had accompanied her husband to Manzanar during internment. Although the Yonedas had lived near Sue's family in the camp, Sue first met Elaine at the Pilgrimage.

While the young people were passing out shovels and other tools to clean the areas around the cemetery and the entrance, Warren asked Sue and Elaine to talk to the media. Sue remembered: The media people asked us: "'Was it always this cold?' They had all gone to Lone Pine to buy mufflers and gloves and knitted hats. I was prepared. I knew it would be cold. It turned out to be the coldest day in Owens Valley that year and people got a better understanding of what camp life was like."

When questioned about food, living quarters, and employment in the camp Elaine and Sue both talked about how dreadful conditions had been. Tricia Toyota, who had been recently hired as a television news reporter, interviewed Sue, and the interview was broadcast on the 6 o'clock news. Sue was confronted later by angry members of the community who complained: "How come you are still talking about the camps? Don't bring up the past."

One reporter asked Jim Matsuoka how many people were buried in the cemetery. Jim's response was later amplified in a poem : "A whole generation, inheritors of this legacy of fear never left this place, but lie buried here.... These quiet Americans who spoke not, who objected not, who will not rock the boat in order to be model citizens, their souls lie buried here at Manzanar."[13] Matsuoka's assertion, also broadcast on national television, created a predominantly negative response from the Japanese American community. Sue recalled, however, that the television coverage also showed young people cleaning and painting the cemetery monument. "That had some positive effect in the community."[14]

The 1969 Pilgrimage had a much larger attendance than expected, about 250, mostly young people. It was not, however, the first Pilgrimage for every participant.

Two Issei ministers, Sentoku Mayeda and Shoichi Wakahiro, both of whom had been interned at Manzanar, had been coming by themselves annually for 25 years since the closure of the camp to pray for those who had died at Manzanar. Sue related: "Reverend Mayeda told us: 'When we were inside, they had machine guns to keep us in, then [after the war] they put locks and guards to keep us out.'" The second Pilgrimage was in May 1970, organized by the Sansei in response to a request by Reverend Mayeda, who took a busload of people who had not been in camp, but wanted to see the cemetery.[15] The next pilgrimage was in 1971.

Sue did not begin to speak in the public arena about the camps until after her first Pilgrimage in 1969. "Subsequent pilgrimages and interviews always stirred up a lot of memories for me. I was remembering things, not all of them bad. I had made friends [in camp], and I had worked on the paper, which I had loved to do, but before the pilgrimages I had a couple of nightmares, really bad dreams." Later she wrote: "The trauma of that first return to Manzanar, the nightmares that disturbed my nightly sleep, the tears that fell unchecked, sent me on a search from which I have never returned ... there is a need to know about the pain, the psychological effects, the human struggles, the battle for survival."[16]

Richard Drinnon contends that Sansei activists during the 1960s and 1970s "reopened old questions and old wounds...and joined by a few exceptional Nisei, such as Sue Kunitomi Embrey of the Manzanar Committee, became the driving force for raising awareness of the camps."[17] Sue confirmed Drinnon's claim. "It was the Sansei who got me started talking about camp. They were activists on the [university] campuses with the Free Speech Movement. When they became aware of the history of the internment, Asian Americans had an issue they could rally around."

Michi Weglyn has called Warren Furutani, the "spiritual head" of Sansei and Yonsei activists."[18] He was working for the JACL as a youth director in the late 1960s and early 1970s, encountering students who wanted to interview people about the camps and had difficulty finding anyone willing to talk. Sue agreed to talk to the students and tried to get other people to participate. Most people refused. Amy Ishii was one who was willing to talk. She had been at Heart Mountain with her mother and eight siblings, while her father was at Crystal City, Texas, after being picked up by the FBI. Sue and Amy created a slide program of the different camps for presentations at schools. Estelle Peck Ishigo, a Caucasian, who went to Heart Mountain with her husband Arthur, was also willing to talk about the camps.[19]

"But Amy and Estelle were exceptional," Sue declared. "There was a photographic exhibit of E.O. 9066 in Pasadena. We tried very hard to get volunteers as docents, but people turned us down. A man said to me: 'I know if I start talking, I'll start crying. I'll get very angry and I don't want people to see me angry.'"

At the time I interviewed Furutani in 2003 he was president of the Los Angeles Community College Board of Trustees and a senior consultant on Politics and Education for Speaker of the California State Assembly, Herb Wesson. He spoke with intensity about his relationship with Sue and their activism regarding the internment.[20] I asked him when he learned what the camps really were?

> Camp was always in the backdrop. I was aware of the fact that my mother and father met in camp, but it had the characteristic of summer camp. They played baseball and they ate in a big mess hall. Most of the stories were [in the context of] this interesting phenomenon called camp. Sue had a different view, much more open. She started filling in the empty blanks [in the history] for us. She became critical to us along with Edison Uno, Edison's sister, Amy Uno, Jim Matsuoka, and other younger Nisei who were in Manzanar. They became invaluable resources because there were no books.

Warren admitted that he was confronted by people who were very angry that he was raising the issue.

> People in the JACL felt it was better left forgotten. The Sansei, though, had curiosity about the camps. It was like something buried in a shallow grave that the winds of time had blown away and you saw a face sticking up. The more they didn't want us to talk about camp, the more we wanted to do it. That was our mode, to challenge things, to question things, to look beyond the surface. Sue was one of our most important guides.
>
> Of course, a lot of us younger people said: "We never would have gone. Why did you go?" Sue gave us a reality check: "If your family was from Terminal Island, what would you have done if in 48 hours after the attack on Pearl Harbor they told you to get out? How would you have dealt with the reality that within the first twenty-four hours the leaders of your community were arrested by the FBI?" This was the first time we'd heard some of those things, because there were no books to read. It was quite a leap from summer camp, where your mom and dad met and enjoyed dances and the guys played baseball with their buddies everyday.

How does Furutani explain that Sue, a Nisei woman, spoke up when most Nisei were infuriated by that behavior? "She was politically different. At her age and during that time, having an interracial marriage was unique. Her politics were leftist without a doubt." Warren stressed that Manzanar was only one of Sue's myriad involvements.

I asked other interviewees the same question: "How do you explain that Sue launched campaigns to remember the camps while most of the Nisei wouldn't even approach the subject?" Sue's older son Gary, who followed his parents in activism and politics, including advocacy for United Farm Workers, situated his mother's efforts to raise awareness of the internment within a larger political context.[21] "Coming out of Manzanar, she went to Chicago for a couple of years and became independent. She created a political environment for her life, working for the United Farm Workers, Nisei for Wallace. My dad encouraged her a lot, too. She had already been in the anti-[Viet Nam] war movement." Sue worked on a number of progressives issues, including affirmative action, equal housing, equal jobs, and was a staunch supporter of Tom Bradley, who served on the Los Angeles City Council from 1961 to 1969, and later became the first black mayor of the city, 1973 to1993.

Gary spoke with great animation about a memorable speech his mother made.

> After the invasion of Cambodia,[22] my mother spoke at an anti-war rally at MacArthur Park. I was in high school and went to this massive rally. There was my mother up on the bandstand, speaking. I remember watching her from the audience and looking around and seeing 50,000 people and thinking: "Wow! This is big!" My mother made a pretty militant speech. I remember that.

Sue's younger son Bruce also emulated his parents' activism, leaving high school after three years to become an organizer for United Farm Workers. In her poem "Just the Way I Hoped" Sue described Bruce as "a fierce and angry protector of the *campesinos* (farm workers.)" Bruce also situated his mother's speaking out about the internment in the larger milieu of the progressive movement.[23]

> I'm not sure what made her radical. Certainly the camps played a role. But *shikata ga nai*, it can't be helped, may be why [other] people didn't take this on. They came out of that experience shocked and full of self-blame. I think her taking it up was liberating. She changed. She went through a conscious or unconscious—but I think it was partly conscious—transformation where she became more outspoken, more resolute and wiser. She assumed the role of counselor and educator and organizer, not just for Japanese or Asians, but for everyone who was looking for an answer to what was wrong with society and how they could make it better. I think the camp story transformed her as much as she transformed it.

Bruce spoke admiringly about his mother's patient and reasoned approach, which was emotional but not angry. "What was amazing to me is that I would be steaming, fuming. We watched the [Commission on Wartime Relocation and Internment of Civilians][24] testimony on TV for the redress and people would break down in tears. But she would be very patient and forgiving and nonjudgmental." Bruce vividly remembers the first Pilgrimage in 1969, although he did not attend. "I was about 11. My mother and father went to Manzanar, and my brother and I went to Aunt Choko's house to sleep. We heard them when they came back that night, quite late. My mother was elated, very animated and happy."

Bruce's earliest memories, however, are those in which his mother was involved in anti-Vietnam War activism and campaigning for fair wages and improved working and living conditions for the United Farm Workers. "I remember walking picket lines with her at Safeway [Market.]" His memory of her speaking at MacArthur Park differs somewhat from that of his brother. "I remember being on stage with her, and the young people were telling her to be militant and dramatic. She was more patient and expository. She was not the rabble-rousing type."

Bruce articulated with considerable sensitivity and insight the development of his mother into an effective leader. "She channeled her energies for years into protest movements, but I watched her grappling with the appropriate responses to racism, and how she could become more effective." Although he realizes that Sue sometimes derived satisfaction from being recognized, he is impressed by her lack of ego. "One of the things I'm trying to teach my kids is that the satisfaction you get from doing what you need to do shouldn't be derived from ego, but from your own assessment of the role you have played in helping something come into being. My mother has always led by example."

Garland Embrey was modest about his influence on Sue's activism: "When I met her, she was already politically aware and active, very much so. When I introduced her to people like [liberal activists] Fumi and Sakae [Ishihara] she naturally agreed with them because being in camp was, of course, one of the main things that happened to her. She was going to fight that injustice."[25]

When I interviewed Takinori Yamamoto, who is a member of the Manzanar Committee and had known Sue for over 30 years, he referred to Garland's influence. "The fact that she was married to a non-Japanese person who didn't put her in a position of having to be compliant, made a difference." Yamamoto has tremendous admiration for Sue. "Speaking with conviction and knowledge, Sue has been the one that people respond to. She taught us that you can't be complacent about the camp experience."[26]

Several interviewees referred to Sue's educational and political background. Paul Tsuneishi, who worked with Sue on the redress and reparations campaign, said: "It's her academic background. She is a teacher. Also, she had very liberal leanings. Her education and political activism formed the background of what she was able to do. She made sure that the framework was there. She was the backbone of that whole thing."[27] Phil Shigekuni spoke for many who appreciate Sue's passionate dedication to forcing public recognition of the injustice of the internment. "How could you not accept leadership and follow somebody who had that kind of dedication and that kind of vision?"[28]

A close friend and colleague since 1973, Arthur A. Hansen, stressed Sue's

> natural dignity and her sense of self, a good sense of proportion and perspective, in every way a healthy human being. She was schooled in a principled ideological movement for a long time. [Membership in] the Nisei Progressives caused her go against family and community. She also had to go against her family when she married outside of the community. But she felt comfortable with herself, comfortable in Japanese culture, comfortable in non-Japanese culture. She could be an unquiet Nisei because she wasn't a loudmouth Nisei. She was unquiet in a sense that she just didn't shut up.[29]

Figure 11.1 Sue in 1978 at the Seattle Washington Day of Remembrance, a commemoration of the day President Franklin Roosevelt issued Executive Order #9066 (photograph by L. Hga, courtesy of the Embrey family)

Perhaps the efforts of Sue and others to break the silence about the camps is evident in the experiences of her grandchildren, Monica and Michael Embrey, Bruce's children.[30] Monica thinks she was eight or nine when she first heard about the camps. Michael said: "I was probably a little younger. The first Manzanar Pilgrimage I didn't know why we were going to this deserted place. My dad told me: 'It's to learn about your history.'" Around the same time as his first Manzanar Pilgrimage Michael recognized he was part Japanese. "Our first Manzanar attendance made me realize that we have a lot to learn about."

Sue herself situated her work for the Manzanar site within the larger context of her progressive politics. She called attention to the fact that she had steadfastly supported Tom Bradley. In 1974, Bradley appointed her to the City Commission on the Status of Women. During her 10 years of service, the commission endorsed the hiring of more women in city departments, worked to ensure that female city employees were covered adequately by Social Security and Medicare, advocated a living wage for domestic help, and campaigned for equal pay for equal work.

While Sue was president of the Los Angeles Commission in 1980, President Jimmy Carter selected her as a delegate to the National Women's Commission Conference in New York, then as 1 of 35 U.S. delegates to the UN Conference on Women in Copenhagen. An important experience for Sue was hearing forthright opinions of delegates from other countries about what America should be doing to counteract anti-American feelings. "The American delegates were taken by surprise," Sue concluded, "but I think we need to be more sensitive to the needs of women in developing countries."[31]

Her far-reaching activism had extracted a toll, however. Alisa Lynch, Chief of Interpretation and Cultural Resources Management, Manzanar National Historic Site, stated: "It takes individual courage to tell the story. Sue was willing to take the hits. She has paid, I think, a high price, politically and personally, for her work at Manzanar."[32] In an interview conducted by Arthur Hansen and David J. Bertagnoli in 1973, Sue admitted that her family was "fed up" with their home life being continually disrupted by the demands on her time and attention, meals being interrupted, phone calls that had to be answered, and perhaps the perception that Manzanar was her highest priority. Sue and Garland divorced in 1978. Although he was gallant and affectionate toward Sue in my interview in 2004, Sue wondered whether her activism had been the cause of the divorce.

In the 1973 interview Hansen suggested that, although Sue perhaps would disavow the label "radical," her participation on the Manzanar Committee had succeeded in radicalizing her. The "unquiet Nisei" responded: "I've reached the point where I don't even care what anybody calls me. Progressive activism has now become part of my life. I've spoken out much more strongly on issues since I've been working with the Manzanar Committee."[33]

CHAPTER 12

The Manzanar Committee

The Manzanar Committee is rarely mentioned in the secondary literature. Since Sue Embrey has been considered *The* Manzanar Committee, once even being called the "Messiah of Manzanar,"[1] I have relied on Sue to recount its history in obtaining both state landmark and national historical site recognition.[2] Her account is augmented by comments of others who were involved with the Manzanar Committee.

The beginning of the Manzanar Committee, following the 1969 Pilgrimage, was tentative, an ad hoc group originally called the Manzanar Project. Sue attributed the idea of forming a committee to Warren Furutani, who was working for the JACL and attempting to disseminate information about the camps to students. The Los Angeles Department of Water and Power (DWP) had reclaimed the Manzanar property, according to the lease negotiated with the federal government. The DWP inquired whether the JACL would like to obtain the cemetery area and the front entrance of Manzanar. Furutani presented the offer to the emerging Manzanar Committee. "We didn't know what to do with the offer," Sue admitted, "but we accepted it and cleaned up the cemetery and the front entrance."

"We had two purposes in forming the committee," Sue stated. "The first was education, informing people about the camps. The second was to file an application to designate Manzanar as a California State Landmark." The Committee had become a cohesive group by the time we started [that process] in [19]'71. Members, in addition to Sue and Warren Furutani, were Don and Susan Rundstrom, Ron and Pat Rundstrom, Amy Ishii, Rex Takahashi, Jim and Faye Matsuoka, Bill Leong, Henry Matsumura, and Ryozo Kado.

These members of the Manzanar Committee wrote the story of Manzanar, documenting its significance in California history, a requirement for State Historical

Landmark status. The Committee cited three justifications for being granted the status: Manzanar was the first WRA camp constructed; it was the camp nearest to Los Angeles, which has the largest population of Japanese Americans; and the cemetery with the *I Rei To* tower was a site of considerable historical and archeological significance and should be preserved as a landmark.

Rex Takahashi composed the original draft:

> In the early part of World War II, 120,000 persons of Japanese Ancestry were interned in relocation centers by Executive Order 9066, issued on February 19, 1942, by President Franklin D. Roosevelt. Manzanar, the first of ten such concentration camps, was bounded by barbed wire and guard towers, confining 10,000 persons, the majority being American citizens. May the injustices and the humiliation suffered here as a result of racism and economic greed never emerge again.

The committee had added the Japanese phrase *ton de mo nai*, "It's Incredible."

Members initially disagreed about the wording, some thinking it too strong, but the Committee ultimately submitted that version. Manzanar was awarded the provisional designation of California State Landmark by the Department of Parks and Recreation on the condition that there be fewer words for the plaque, which had to be hand-cast in bronze. The Committee learned through the JACL, however, that it was not the number of words, but certain terminology that was considered objectionable: concentration camp, racism, and economic greed.[3]

Sue, Warren Furutani, and Amy Ishii met first with the State Department of Parks and Recreation. In addition to objecting to the Committee's terminology, the State wanted to include hysteria as a cause. A compromise was effected: "hysteria" was included, and "economic exploitation" replaced "economic greed." To no one's surprise there was no agreement on "concentration camp."

Alex Garcia, California Assemblyman whose district included Little Tokyo, was supportive of the Manzanar Committee's work. He and Dennis Nishikawa, his aide, who had been the president of the Sacramento Chapter of the JACL, arranged for the Committee to meet with William Penn Mott, the director of the Department of Parks and Recreation.

During the meeting the Parks and Recreation representatives argued that there was not enough evidence that the relocation centers were concentration camps. The Manzanar Committee argued that they had submitted ample historical evidence. The Committee stressed that the wording should reflect the views of the people who were inside the camp, and not the people who were looking in from the outside. Finally, Director Penn-Mott stated that he could not accept the wording and excused himself from the meeting. As Sue and Warren both remembered the incident, there were angry exchanges between Warren and Penn Mott, as the director was leaving. Penn Mott finally stormed out of the room, declaring: "You can have it all!"[4]

The designation of California State Landmark 850 was approved in January 1972. "It was a very short time for us to have accomplished that," Sue said. "The final wording on the plaque of the State Historical Site is as follows:

> In the early part of World War II, 120,000 persons of Japanese ancestry were interned in relocation centers by Executive Order 9066, issued on February 19, 1942. Manzanar, the first of such concentration camps, was bounded by barbed wire and guard towers, confining 10,000 persons, the majority being American citizens. May the injustices and humiliation suffered here as a result of hysteria, racism, and economic exploitation never emerge again.

The attendance of Nisei at the annual Pilgrimages, which had been disappointing to the organizers, began to increase in 1973 when the State Landmark plaque was dedicated. About 1,500 people, many of them Nisei, attended that pilgrimage. "It was amazing!" said Sue. "They came on motorcycles, in Mercedes Benz' and junky little cars."

Penn Mott, who was later appointed as head of the National Park Service (NPS) by President Ronald Reagan, spoke at The Manzanar Pilgrimage of April 14, 1973, during which the state plaque was dedicated. Penn Mott graciously admitted that he had done a lot of reading since the tumultuous meeting with the Manzanar Committee and that he had changed his mind: Manzanar was a concentration camp. Ryozo Kado cemented the plaque in place, aided by the former internees who had been teenagers when they helped him build the original stone guardhouse and the obelisk at the cemetery. The cemetery and obelisk were sacred to many in the Japanese American community, including Sue's mother. The last time she went to Manzanar was 1980, when she was 90 years old. Sue expressed sadness, remembering her mother's apologizing at that time: "I want to pay my respects, but I just can't go anymore."

Following the dedication of Manzanar as a California State Landmark, the Manzanar Committee began working on having it designated a National Historic Landmark. Efforts during the 1970s by the California Department of Parks and Recreation to establish a state park at Manzanar drew considerable opposition from several groups. The opinion of residents of Owens Valley was expressed in a letter to California Governor Edmund G. Brown, Jr. by the Lone Pine Chamber of Commerce. The "pioneer history of the Manzanar area speaks for itself and does not require keying in on three and a half short years for its claim to fame or infamy." On a similar note, the Owens Valley Native American groups reminded Inyo County supervisors that "Indians have a definite history in this valley."[5] The Manzanar Committee was especially concerned about the cemetery. In a letter dated February 9, 1974 to the Chalfant Press in Lone Pine Sue wrote: "The cemetery area represents living history. It also represents a very strong and important concept in the Japanese American culture: *haka mairi*, which means pilgrimage to the cemetery." She

Figure 12.1 Sue, the Unquiet Nisei, at the Manzanar Pilgrimage, 2000 (photograph by Mario Gershom Reyes)

concluded that the Manzanar Committee would oppose any plan by any agency that “would make Manzanar a tourist attraction.”[6]

While the annual pilgrimages grew in attendance during the 1970s and 1980s, and the Manzanar Committee expanded its educational outreach to community groups and schools, Manzanar was gaining recognition as a historic site deserving preservation and interpretation.[7] While the land at Manzanar, owned by the

Los Angeles Department of Water and Power, was largely neglected, the Manzanar Committee endeavored to maintain the area around the cemetery.

Congress authorized a study of sites that had been important in the Pacific area of World War II. Primarily through the efforts of the Manzanar Committee, breaking the silence about the internment camps, Manzanar was designated a National Historic Landmark in 1985. The Manzanar Committee then campaigned for a bill to establish Manzanar as a National Historic Site. Rose Ochi of the Manzanar Committee and Mel Levine, a Congressman from West Los Angeles, worked on the wording for the National Historic Site bill, House Resolution 543.[8]

Many of the citizens of Owens Valley, however, were opposed to any preservation of Manzanar. They argued that the Manzanar camp was not something they asked for but had been imposed on their community during World War II by the federal government. The State plaque with the term "concentration camp" intensified the opposition.

Bill Michael, director of the Eastern California Museum in Independence for 19 years and a strong advocate for the Manzanar Committee, said:

> The way we dealt with that over time was education. One key factor we stressed was that two-thirds of the people in the camp were American citizens, born in this country and guaranteed certain rights. They were not in the Japanese Emperor's army. We had to talk about that repeatedly, because there are individuals who were not able to distinguish between the Japanese military in World War II and the Japanese Americans at Manzanar.

Michael recalled recurrent intimidation:

> There were threats to burn down the auditorium of the camp before they would allow it to be a "Jap museum." Ross Hopkins [the first Superintendent of Manzanar National Historic Site] took those [threats] seriously, [installing] a fire suppression system and exterior lighting. Ross also received threats on his life. I had people yelling at me. I had a gentleman in the museum one day who was a World War II veteran. You have to excuse the language, but I'm going to quote him directly. He was in here with a woman. After they viewed our exhibit they came up to the desk and he said: "This is a nice museum but I've got to tell you that fucking Jap exhibit is wrong. If it takes me every day of the rest of my life I will see that exhibit out of here and I will see you fired." I said: "We believe the exhibit belongs here. It is part of our history." The woman who was with him was ready to swing at me. He actually had to wrap his arms around her and take her outside while she was yelling at us.

Where does this intense anger come from? Michael responded:

> My interpretation is that there are two components, both shocking. One is that racism is alive and well in America, and it's passed from parents to children strongly. The other component is what we refer to as post-traumatic stress syndrome. There are people still fighting World War II. A lot of these World War II vets had appalling experiences. We had one veteran who had been on the Bataan Death March and had horrible experiences as a prisoner of war in Japan. Someone with that experience and that service to our country—it was difficult opposing him. I started realizing that there are a number of people who came home from World War II as heroes, but there was no recognition really of the trauma they had been through. They won the war. But some of these guys 50 years later had trouble packing up their personal experience in the war. Out of that came some of the hatred and the resistance to recognizing the [Manzanar camp] history because to them these [internees] were still Japanese.

Los Angeles Mayor Tom Bradley, who was a strong advocate of the National Historic Site bill, appointed Rose Ochi, director of Criminal Justice Planning in the mayor's office, as a liaison to the Inyo County Board of Supervisors and to the NPS. Sue expressed great admiration for the way in which Rose Ochi helped persuade the residents of Owens Valley to support preservation of Manzanar. "She invited the Supervisors of Inyo County to lunch in Independence. Rather than telling them what we wanted Manzanar to be, she asked them what they wanted." To the locals Manzanar was always about someone else, the Japanese people who were there during the war, then were gone, then returned to visit now and then. They did not see the camp as part of their own history. Acknowledging their position as valid, Ochi also was able to present the positive aspect of economic development that would result from having a National Historic Site in the community, which has a scarcity of jobs. "I don't think those guys were prepared for Rose Ochi!" Sue said.

In May 1991, Sue, Rose, and Hiro Takusagawa, a 442nd Regimental Combat Team veteran, who represented the National Japanese American Historical Society, testified before the House Subcommittee on Public Lands and National Parks. Sue presented evidence about the significance of the remaining features of the camp: the cemetery, the gardens, the rocks, and the stone walls, which could help educate Americans about what happened there. She stressed that it was important to preserve our history even though it may not be positive. The bill was passed by voice vote.[9]

Meanwhile, a companion bill had been introduced in the Senate by Alan Cranston of California.[10] The bill was stalled in subcommittee because of the powerful opposition of the Los Angeles Department of Water and Power Commission, which wanted something in return for giving the land to the Park Service for development as a historic site. A complex compromise was worked out by which the Bureau of Land Management would find land of equal value and size to Manzanar, transfer that land to the DWP, which would then transfer Manzanar property to the Interior Department of the federal government.

Sue laughed when she remembered Mayor Tom Bradley's impatience with the memos Ochi sent him complaining about the delays with the National Historic Site bill. "No more memos!" he ordered. He asked Senator Dale Bumpers, the subcommittee chair, to send the bill to the Senate floor for a vote. Rose and Sue testified for the Senate bill. "The legislative aides for Mel Levine and Bob Matsui, U.S. Representative from California, were very, very supportive," Sue said with profound appreciation. The bill to designate Manzanar as a National Historic Site passed on November 26, 1991, with 400 yes votes to 13 no votes.[11] Manzanar was officially designated a National Historic Site on March 3, 1992.

Arthur Hansen gives Sue, supported by the practical work of the Manzanar Committee, significant credit for Manzanar being designated a National Historic Site. "It wasn't strictly a Nisei/Sansei cadre, either," he said. "There were also non-Japanese involved. The effort cut across groups and generations. Clearly, though, the moving force was Sue and a small cadre of dedicated people."[12] Sue thoughtfully gave credit to Rose Ochi and Bill Michael. "I don't think we would have been able to turn the local people around without Bill Michael's steady support for Manzanar."

In an interview Michael described the campaign to preserve Manzanar in a manner both perceptive and thoughtful.[13]

> I wasn't just another government representative telling people what needed to be done. I was a local, very involved in the communities. Also we had been growing professionally at the museum, continuing to raise our standards. I think the main thing I contributed was continuity. As committees formed and disbanded or another government agency got involved, I had some collective memory of what had been committed to or done. Year after year I could carry that forward.

He believes that public meetings with Owens Valley residents and Japanese Americans, person to person, were significant.

Michael does admit to being apprehensive when he received phone calls from the chairman of the Inyo County Supervisors, impatient about the complaints he was getting from residents, especially about the phrase "concentration camps" on the historic plaque. Bill Michael's narration underscores the reality that there is still considerable controversy over the use of the term "concentration camp." Historian Greg Robinson censures Franklin Roosevelt for presiding over "a joint army-WRA policy of denial and euphemism" in which "camps with armed guards and barbed wire were officially named 'relocation centers.'"[14] Richard Drinnon contends that Milton Eisenhower, the original director of the WRA, later tried to shield himself "from the simple truth that enclosures where people, most of them citizens, have been penned without being charged with crimes and without being processed by ordinary process of law, and shot if they try to leave, are enclosures correctly called concentration camps."[15] Michi Weglyn points out that Harold Ickes, secretary of the interior, called the camps "fancy-named concentration camps."[16] Harry Truman, vice president during the forced removal, stated: "They called it relocation, but they put them in concentration camps, and I was against it. We were in a period of emergency, but it was still the wrong thing to do."[17]

Sue's daughter-in-law Barbara Becker speaks for many in the Japanese American community who now approve the use of the term.

> Yes, people were not exterminated in this country, but there was a plan to destroy their pride in their culture and heritage. This happened in a democracy. I think it was as much a denial of human rights as this country could have gotten away with. What happened in Germany happened under fascism. I use the term "concentration camp" to make people think.[18]

Jack Kunitomi has a different view: "Because I had known about Dachau[19] and those Nazi camps in Europe, I couldn't imagine using that term. We were more or less treated like human beings in our camps. I know it's a sore point with many people. I'm still debating it."[20]

Warren Furutani, intimately involved in the conflict over the inclusion of "concentration camp" on the State Historical Landmark plaque, stated:

> The idea of putting it in bronze was an indelible statement. [Using] concentration camp was critical, the most important thing for all of us is to have the power to define ourselves for ourselves and by ourselves. Our definition of the camp experience was not a relocation center. That was the outside-looking-in perspective. From the inside-looking-out perspective it was a concentration camp.

Echoing Hansen, he concluded: "When people argued that the Jews were put in concentration camps, my argument was: 'Those weren't concentration camps; they were death camps.' It's a matter of perspective."[21]

Bill Michael asserts:

> The most important thing we can do at Manzanar is educate people and give them a chance to experience some of the emotional content of that site. If you put the term "concentration camp" at the highway signpost, there is a segment of the public who will not enter that site and we will never have the chance to educate them. If we make that term a barrier, educational opportunity is lost.[22]

The Manzanar Committee, with Sue Embrey as chairperson, issued a statement that its definition of "concentration camp" is that of Webster's New World Dictionary. "A prison camp in which political dissidents, members of minority ethnic groups, etc. are confined." Further, the Committee asserted: "The Manzanar Committee has never compared the WRA camps to those in Nazi Germany at any time."[23]

Sue admitted her own early hesitation. "When Rex [Takahashi] suggested the words 'concentration camp,' I was feeling very uncomfortable with it. I began to change my mind after reading a lot of materials. The term 'relocation camp' is not appropriate, because relocation actually means something temporary, and it means that you can always go home." She praised the NPS for reaching out to all groups, including those who are opposed to the use of "concentration camp." She credited the NPS for helping convince opponents that Manzanar National Historic Site is an appropriate commemoration of the camps. Sue concluded: "We've made our point and I just call it Manzanar National Historic Site because that is the formal name now."[24]

Now that Manzanar is a National Historic Site, how has the attitude of the Japanese American community changed since the first pilgrimage? "In the beginning people were always asking me: 'Why are you bringing up the past? We had enough exposure during the war. There is still a lot of anti-Japanese feeling.' I think some of them feel they now have permission to talk about it. If they don't, that history is going to die with them."

About the residents of Owens Valley, she said: "Last year [2002] the Dow Villa Motel [in Lone Pine] had a big sign saying: 'Welcome Manzanar Pilgrimage.' And their local television station has announced the dates of the pilgrimage every year for quite a few years. Maybe they think we are not quite as radical as they once thought we were."

When asked about the lasting contributions of the pilgrimages, Sue replied: "Because the Pilgrimages led to the creation of the National Historic Site, our history is going to be documented. The most important contribution was that we kept the issue alive, not only with the mainstream public, but also with Japanese Americans. In this way the Pilgrimages helped the redress effort."[25]

CHAPTER 13

Redress and Reparations

Sue testified before the Commission on Wartime Relocation and Internment of Civilians (CWRIC) in 1981 that the education campaign of the Manzanar Committee "was instrumental in bringing about the movement for redress and reparations."[1] The redress movement was organized by Japanese Americans to obtain an apology and compensation for their wrongful detention during World War II. Sue's involvement in the campaign demonstrated how her activism had matured and accentuated her enduring commitment to justice for the Japanese American community, despite the risk of further alienation. Although reparations from the federal government had been discussed as early as 1946 at the first postwar convention of the JACL,[2] the concept of *shikata ga nai* (it can't be helped), caused many Japanese Americans to oppose redress and reparations, much as they had resisted the campaign to raise awareness of the camps. Although throughout three decades following the internment various groups attempted to pursue redress, the issue was ignored or opposed by the majority of Japanese Americans.

Edison Uno, a member of the faculty of San Francisco State University and an active and influential advocate for redress, introduced a resolution calling for redress at the 1970 JACL convention, but no action was taken.[3] Sue expressed high regard for Uno.[4]

> Edison was in the forefront of the redress campaign. Every time the JACL had a convention, Edison would try to get a resolution passed that would commit the JACL to redress. Tragically, midway in the redress movement, he died of a heart attack in 1976. He was only 47. I think that in the short time he had, he kept the redress issue alive.

In April 1975, Uno came to Los Angeles for a meeting with the San Fernando Chapter of JACL at the invitation of Phil Shigekuni and Paul Tsuneishi, who sought his advice about forming a redress group. Impatient with the JACL's inaction on redress, Tsuneishi reasoned that the San Fernando JACL Chapter could establish a separate corporation to campaign for redress and reparations. E. O. 9066 Inc. was founded on April 26, 1975 with Paul Tsuneishi as president, Phil Shigekuni as vice president, and Sue Embrey as secretary. "We asked Sue to be involved," Paul explained, "because of her work with Manzanar." Sue joined because she supported the concept of redress and liked the group's political views. Although there were many supporters, the core group was small and included Lyle Asaoka, Ken Honji, Amy Ishii, Joan Lang, Tomoo Ogita, Hana Shephard, and Richard Yamauchi."

The threefold purpose of E. O. 9066 was defined in a position paper:[5]

> (1) To educate the public concerning the evacuation of persons of Japanese ancestry at the start of World War II, (2) to formulate and propose legislation to compensate those affected by Executive Order 9066, (3) to seek executive, congressional or judicial authority for the Supreme Court to review the constitutionality of the evacuation order (Executive Order 9066). This would include a review of such landmark [Supreme Court] cases as the Korematsu and Hirabayashi decisions.

Expressing concern for aging Issei, the paper stressed the need to move swiftly to get legislation introduced and to actively solicit support from all sectors of the Asian community, including the JACL, as well as from other concerned Americans. The concluding sentence stated the philosophy of the newly formed E. O. 9066: "We love our country enough to believe part of its greatness lies in its willingness not only to admit when it is wrong, but then to take positive steps in making amends for its mistakes."

The involvement of Paul Tsuneishi, a Nisei, in the Japanese American redress movement was a natural progression from his earlier activism in the civil rights movement. He had been a member of the San Fernando Valley National Association for the Advancement of Colored People (NAACP) and had created the Sunland-Tujunga Fair Housing Council, which fought discrimination in housing. Tsuneishi's family had been sent to the Pomona Assembly Center in 1942, where he stayed only a few months because he volunteered to help get Heart Mountain ready for internees. He was then drafted into an all-Nisei unit, becoming the fourth member of his family to join the MIS.

Paul joined the San Fernando Valley Chapter of JACL in 1972 and became district governor of the Southern Chapters in 1978. Despite his activism, Paul was doubtful about the success of the redress campaign. "We thought the best thing that could happen would be an educational focus. I don't think any of us really believed redress would happen. I know Phil was as doubtful as I was."

Phil Shigekuni is a yonsei (fourth generation) although he was born in 1934, atypical as an older fourth-generation person. His mother's grandfather had come to America in the early twentieth century, one of the first émigrés from Japan.[6] When he was in the second grade his family was sent from Los Angeles to Santa Anita assembly

Center for six months, then to the WRA camp in Amache, Colorado. Despite his camp experience and the politically liberal inclination of his family, he was not politically active until he was persuaded to join the San Fernando Valley Chapter of JACL in the early 1970s. His political awareness grew as he became acquainted with Paul. Subsequently Phil was elected president of the San Fernando Chapter.

Phil recalled how he and Sue had helped Paul Tsuneishi organize E. O. 9066, Inc. as a result of the meeting with Edison Uno in April 1975. "We knew we needed to be independent. We got people who were not the accommodating type. They provided the passion that we needed for the movement."

To build support for their redress E. O. 9066 surveyed Japanese Americans throughout southern California asking about their internment in a WRA camp, their opinions about seeking reparations, and, assuming they favored reparations, who should be entitled to reparation payment. The majority of respondents strongly favored redress in the form of individual payments to all persons who had been incarcerated as the result of the presidential Executive Order 9066.

Despite the results of the survey Phil recalls: "The most difficult part of the whole redress process was changing people's minds. It was frustrating. *Shikata ga nai*: to endure is a virtue. After being virtuous by enduring you can't go back to the government and say: 'Hey, you've done us wrong. We want money from you.' That is why it was hard."

Like Paul, Phil doubted that redress would actually be achieved. "Frankly, I felt that the whole idea that the government would apologize and come up with compensation was just far fetched. It was something we had to do and it was a kind of catharsis for us, feeling that we were doing something positive, but *never* thinking it was ever going to happen."

It was not until its convention in 1978 that the JACL, yielding to growing pressure from E. O. 9066 and other Japanese Americans who were frustrated about the redress movement, adopted a proposal put forth by Dr. Clifford Uyeda of San Francisco. To make redress and reparations the priority issue, Uyeda, who had been elected president of the national JACL, appointed John Tateishi, also of San Francisco, to chair the National Committee for redress. JACL's strategy at that time was three fold: (1) to move the redress issue into the public arena by launching a media campaign; (2) to seek the drafting of legislation for redress and reparations; and (3) to get the legislation introduced in Congress. Tateishi's tactic was to persuade Congress to authorize a commission to study the redress issue.[7] As many Nisei feared, the backlash began immediately.[8]

U.S. Senator S. I. Hayakawa, interviewed by local newspapers, at the 1978 JACL convention in Salt Lake City, asserted that the JACL should stop seeking compensation for the past wrongs, that the campaign was "absurd and ridiculous."[9] The *shikata ga nai* faction criticized Tateishi for even raising the issue.

E. O. 9066 was not the only group pressing for redress. The Seattle Evacuation Redress Committee was formed in the early 1970s and, like E. O. 9066, conducted polls among Japanese Americans soliciting their opinion about the redress campaign.

An action-oriented group, the Chicago-based National Council for Japanese American redress (NCJAR) created by William Hohri, condemned Tateishi's idea of a congressional commission as an indication of weakness and confusion.[10] "Tateishi was trying to create a climate for debate," Sue reasoned, "but he couldn't win either way."[11] Despite the conflict within the Japanese American community, the members of E. O. 9066 Inc. were convinced that JACL had made a national campaign for redress a priority, in large part due to the efforts of their group to keep the issue alive by surveys, presentations at civic groups and churches, and letters to the editors of Japanese American newspapers. Merging its program with JACL, E. O. 9066 Inc. was formally dissolved on January 14, 1980.

In 1983, NCJAR, under the direction of Hohri, filed a class action suit in federal court seeking redress in the form of direct payments, $210,000 for each former internee.[12]

> "It was a real grass-roots action," Sue commented. "He wanted 100,000 *ronins,* (originally the term for Samurai who avenged the death or dishonor of their lord). These were plaintiffs who would donate $1,000 each in the class action suit for redress. Ralph Lazo, the Mexican American who was at Manzanar, was one of those *ronins*. I gave William Hohri quite a bit of money too."

The lawsuit, after five years of delays and appeals, finally was disallowed by the Supreme Court in 1988. Hohri expressed his enduring faith in campaigning for redress in an eloquent statement: "We believe that a small group with little more than its remembered pain and desire to have its grievances addressed can act to repair a breach in our democratic society, despite the best efforts of our government to intimidate and silence us. Our movement has become part of our legacy to America, our contribution to American democracy."[13]

Meanwhile, continuing to believe that there was little chance of getting monetary reparations, the JACL pressed forward on the campaign for a congressional study.[14] Sue explained: "The JACL thought that Congress was not ready for reparations. I, myself, was very pessimistic. There were too many other big issues that Congress had to deal with, and this was something that affected just a small number of people. We didn't have political clout."[15]

The JACL enlisted the aid of members of Congress they believed would be sympathetic to the issue of redress. A small JACL group, including John Tateishi, met with Daniel Inouye and Spark Matsunaga, both of Hawaii, and California Congressmen Norman Mineta and Robert Matsui. The senators advised them that before Congress would consider any legislation to seek compensation, JACL had to establish an official determination of wrongful action by the government, because the American public was not convinced that an injustice had occurred. The JACL voted to seek legislation to create a congressional commission to investigate the internment. Tateishi has written: "We knew that our position would be unpopular in the Japanese American community, and we would be harshly criticized . . . [but] It made sense to us that an official investigation . . . would eliminate the myth of military necessity."[16]

In August 1979, Inouye, Matsunaga, S. I. Hayakawa (apparently having changed his perspective on redress,) and Senator Ted Stevens of Alaska introduced S. 1647. In September House Majority Leader James Wright of Texas, Congressmen Matsui and Mineta, and 114 cosponsors introduced H. R. 5499. On May 22, 1980, S. 1647 was unanimously approved by the Senate, and on July 21, the House of Representatives approved H. R. 5499 by a vote of 279 to 109.[17] On July 31, 1980, President Jimmy Carter signed Public Law 96-317, which created the Commission on Wartime Relocation and Internment of Civilians, which would investigate the facts and circumstances of the internment.[18]

Commission members were Joan Bernstein, former general counsel of the Department of Health and Human Services, chair; Congressman Daniel Lungren of California, vice-chair; former senator Edward Brooke of Massachusetts; former Massachusetts Congressman Father Robert Drinnan, SJ; Dr. Arthur Flemming, chair of the U.S. Commission on Civil Rights; Arthur Goldberg, former Justice of the U.S. Supreme Court and a former ambassador to the United Nations; Father Ishmael Gromoff of the Pribilof Islands in Alaska; Hugh B. Mitchell, former senator and representative for the state of Washington, and Judge William Marutani of Pennsylvania, the only Japanese American on the commission.[19]

For 20 days in 1981,the Commission heard testimony from 720 former internees. For most of them this was the first time they openly expressed pain and anger about the internment. Sue remembered her reaction to the testimony of former internees: "I sat spellbound and listened as one person after another spoke of heartbreaking events." Reports on the hearings characterized the testimony as extremely emotional, even traumatic. Sue agreed:

> It was very unusual for the Japanese community to express that kind of feeling. It was almost as if they had been given permission to talk. It wasn't their fault that it happened, although they blamed themselves. It was a tremendous breakthrough for Japanese Americans. They talked in front of the Commission, so I'm sure they felt that now they could talk with their family and their friends. I would imagine that this caused a lot of discussion within families. I know some Sansei sat down with their parents with a tape recorder.

Sue recalled testifying before the CWRIC.[20] Excerpts from her testimony demonstrate her maturity as an activist.

> The period I spent in Manzanar was the most traumatic experience of my life. It has influenced my perspective as well as my continuing efforts to educate, persuade and encourage others of my generation to speak out about the unspeakable

> crime. While speaking out has been a cathartic experience for me, I have found that it has not been the same for other former internees.

Sue also spoke as the representative of the Manzanar Committee:

> The investigation that this commission conducts must surely address the serious issues that the Japanese American experience presents to the American people—the violation of human rights guaranteed by the United States Constitution, the stripping of our human dignity, and the destruction of our community. If we do not all stand in support of the Bill of Rights, can we honestly say that it will not happen again?

Nevertheless, many Japanese Americans were hostile to the idea of redress, some to the point of writing letters to newspapers, and openly opposing redress in JACL meetings.

The Commission's report to Congress in December 1982 was contained in a volume of 467 pages, entitled *Personal Justice Denied*. The final sentence of the report states: "It is our belief that, though history cannot be unmade, it is well within our power to offer help and to acknowledge error."[21] Sue appraised the Commission's report: "Their conclusion was that the internment was the result of race prejudice, wartime hysteria, and lack of political leadership. That was the conclusion we had back in 1972 when we put up the plaque at Manzanar. So what's new? I was glad, though, that they came to that conclusion, because before they hadn't admitted that it was racism."

The Commission followed its report in June 1983 with five recommendations: (1) Congressional passage of a joint resolution, signed by the president, offering the nation's apology; (2) issuance of a presidential pardon for individuals convicted of violating statutes pertaining to the removal and detention; (3) provision of restitution of "positions, status or entitlements" lost as a consequence of E. O. 9066, including review of "less than honorable" discharges of Japanese Americans from military service; (4) provision of congressional funding for a foundation to sponsor research and education about the removal and internment; (5) appropriation of $1.5 billion in federal funding for reparations of $20,000 to each of an estimated 60,000 survivors of the removal.[22] Despite earlier opposition to redress, most Japanese Americans supported the recommendations. "They were more interested in getting the letter of apology, though," Sue said. "That was my reaction, too. I could use $20,000, but oh, that letter of apology really lifted the burden off their shoulders, and they could talk about what happened to them."

There was intense opposition to the congressional recommendations within the Caucasian community, including, not surprisingly, some key members of the Franklin Roosevelt administration. John J. McCloy, assistant secretary of war during the incarceration of Japanese Americans, argued that the Japanese Americans "benefited from the relocation rather than suffered." He claimed: "The relocation method against the Japanese was a good reason why serious acts of sabotage did not occur on the West Coast after the President's order was given." McCloy criticized the congressional hearings as "outrageous and a disgrace to our Congressional Investigating Legislative System."[23]

Karl R. Bendetsen, architect of the removal and incarceration policy, justified his actions as proper, asserting that if the circumstances were repeated he would respond in the same manner. "If a major attack had come and if there had been no evacuation, most Japanese residents along the Western Sea Frontier, whether U.S. or Japanese born, would have supported the invading forces." He argued that the term "internment" was false, that people of Japanese ancestry were merely excluded from the "military frontier, families were not separated, Japanese American property was protected, and essentially, life in the WRA camps was advantageous."[24]

The most virulent opposition was voiced by Lillian Baker, a prolific writer who fought tenaciously for more than 30 years to refute the facts of the internment camps. In *The Japanning of America: Redress and Repatriation* she contends: "The Japanese Americans who rolled along with the movement for 'redress and reparations' are either filled with self-pity or have empty pockets, or both.... The U.S. is, indeed, paying former disloyal Americans—traitors—who renounced their citizenship and is also paying former *Japanese* nationals who were enemies in World War II."[25]

Lillian Baker became infamous in the Japanese American community for her disruptive behavior during the congressional hearings on redress and reparations. Sue remembered the incident vividly.

> A veteran of the 442nd was testifying about his experiences, and right in the middle of his testimony, Baker got up and tried to grab his paper away from him. She was sitting in front near the TV cameras. The audience starting yelling: "Throw her out! Throw her out!" Two security officers grabbed her and walked her out. That night, she was on the news, as an opponent of redress, so she made her point.

Baker targeted Sue as cofounder with Warren Furutani of the Manzanar Committee. "She was sending me copies of stuff, big packages. At first I used to open them. Then I thought: 'This is ridiculous.' So I just wrote on them: 'Return to sender.'" Sue recalled Lillian Baker with residual frustration.[26]

> Originally she was trying to express her point of view about the camps, then she got into redress and the Manzanar Site. She would use quotes from the Supreme Court or even things that I or Edison Uno had written and take them out of context to prove her points that Manzanar never had any barbed wire, that people were free to come and go, and they were never actually confined. She always made

> a big point that there were no guard towers at Manzanar. She said there was a fire tower with a big sign that said: "Ring this bell like hell when there's a fire." Sue laughed. "I never saw a sign like that."

Bill Michael related his experiences with Lillian Baker and one of her supporters. W.W. Hastings.[27] "Never in the years I've been here [in Owens Valley] has Lillian Baker been here. However, a couple of her friends had relocated to Bishop. They appeared at public meetings and wrote letters that were strongly shaped by Lillian's point of view. Their opposition was more strident when it became apparent that something was going to happen at Manzanar with the NPS.

At the opposite end of the spectrum from Baker was Aiko Yoshinaga Herzig, Warren Furutani's mother-in-law, who has been called an "unsung hero of the redress movement."[28] She had been recruited by William Hohri to act as a lobbyist for NCJAR. In conjunction with that job and out of curiosity, she began researching the records on the internment in the National Archives. Because of this experience she was offered a job as a research associate with the CWRIC. Plodding through countless documents, Aiko Herzig uncovered a "smoking gun." a report by John L. DeWitt, head of the Western Defense Command, which was thought to have been destroyed. The report stated in part: "It was impossible to establish the identity of the loyal and the disloyal. It was not that there was insufficient time in which to make such a determination; it was simply a matter of facing the realities that an exact separation of 'sheep from goats' was unfeasible." Herzig's discovery destroyed military necessity of swift action, as the rationale for the internment and substantiated the racism driving DeWitt's belief that all Japanese Americans were potentially disloyal.[29]

The redress movement gained significant momentum in 1983 when members of the Bay Area Attorneys for Redress, led by Peter Irons, Dale Minami, Rod Kawakami, and Peggy Nagae, reopened the 40-year-old Supreme Court cases of *Fred Korematsu v. United States, Gordon Hirabayashi v. United States,* and *Min Yasui v. United States*. These legal proceedings are popularly known as the *coram nobis* ("error before us") cases. The attorneys sought to overturn the convictions of these Japanese Americans by using the obscure legal procedure, writ of error, which can be used only when a defendant has been convicted and released from custody, and only to raise errors of fact that were knowingly suppressed by the prosecution.[30]

Irons, attorney and professor of political science at University of California, San Diego, had found documents from government lawyers dated 1943 and 1944, complaining that evidence had been suppressed by their superiors in these cases. This evidence revealed a pattern of ethical violations, manipulation of the judicial process, and violation of individuals' rights to fair and impartial trials.[31]

In legal hearings between 1983 and 1988 Federal District Court judges vacated the convictions of Koretmatsu and Hirabayashi, who had been found guilty of violating the exclusion order. Min Yasui died before a decision could be made, and his case was abandoned.[32]

> "When I first met Gordon [Hirabayashi] I talked to him about his case," Sue remembered. "I asked him if he thought that it could ever be set aside. He said: 'I sure wish it could be, but I don't know how to do it.' When the Supreme Court decisions were overturned, I thought it was amazing. The Supreme Court is the highest court in the land. How can you appeal their decisions?"

The evidence discrediting the legal basis for the exclusion and detention coincided with the redress efforts, augmenting the educational potential and strengthening the legal arguments for redress.[33] In 1987, Sue was in Washington, D.C. speaking at the opening of the Smithsonian Institution exhibit on the removal and internment. "I was quoting something in the newspaper from that day about Gordon Hirbayashi's case. One of the government's arguments was that suppression of evidence had been a mistake. I said to the audience: 'I leave you with a question: Did the government really make a mistake?' " I asked Sue: "What is your answer to your own question?" She said emphatically: "It was not a mistake. It was racism."[34]

Congress finally acted on the Congressional Commission's recommendations, signing all five of them into law in Civil Rights Act of 1988. Phil Shigekuni spoke poignantly of the Act. "I remember the day it was signed, August 10, 1988. I said a few words on the plaza next to the community center in Little Tokyo. I remember just breaking down emotionally." He paused, then said very softly: "It was really quite an emotional experience."[35]

On November 21, 1989 President George H. Bush signed the bill appropriating funds for reparation payments to former internees. A letter of apology signed by the president accompanied the checks:

> A monetary sum and words alone cannot restore lost years or erase painful memories; neither can they fully convey our Nation's resolve to rectify injustice and to uphold the rights of individuals. We can never fully right the wrongs of the past. But we can take a clear stand for justice and recognize that serious injustices were done to Japanese Americans during World War II. In enacting a law calling for restitution and offering a sincere apology, your fellow Americans have, in a very real sense, renewed their traditional commitment to the ideal of freedom, equality, and justice. You and your family have our best wishes for the future.[36]

In an article in the *Rafu Shimpo* Sue wrote:

> The question is inappropriate and impertinent, but it is inevitable given the press corps' pursuit of sensationalism. "What will you do with your $20,000?" I don't know what I'm going to do with my $20,000 ... I won't believe it until I have the

> check in my hands.... Let each of us ordinary people accept the U.S. government's apology and the check the same way our Issei generation endured the internment—with grace and dignity.... We are participants in an historic moment in America. At long last, we hold justice in our hands. I will savor this moment and remember those who are no longer with us.[37]

The first checks were issued in 1990 to nine of the oldest internees, one of whom Sue knew, Sugi Kiriyama. "She was 100 years old and had been at Manzanar. After the ceremony at the Department of Justice that commemorated the issuance of the reparations checks, Sugi, despite her age, went with her daughter touring all over Washington."[38]

In addition to Sue, members of the Kunitomi family who received reparation checks were Frank, Gene, Jack, Kinya, and Midori. Choko had died three months before the checks were issued. Komika Kunitomi had died on June 4, 1983, seven years before she would have received reparation for the loss of her store and her freedom. Sue remembered sadly: "My mother did not live long enough to even know what the Commission's recommendations were, although we talked about the redress movement. She would say: 'All those people lost so much money. They really should get reimbursed.'"[39]

The property loss that Komika Kunitomi and others sustained was one of the compelling arguments for the redress movement. Virtually every family suffered crushing economic damage, and the loss of personal and family possessions inflicted inexpressible mental and emotional harm. The Issei, stripped of their property and traumatized by their confinement, were generally unable to start again from scratch and rebuild their businesses or farms.[40] Sue summarized the losses other than property: "It destroyed the whole community, not just in Los Angeles. Although segregated, we had a very strong base to keep people together as a community. We had churches, temples, social groups and women's groups. [The internment] disrupted everything. We had to completely rebuild after the camps."[41]

The destruction of the Japanese American community was the direct result of the violation of their civil rights. Although the Supreme Court never ruled that the removal and incarceration of Japanese Americans was unconstitutional, historians have identified constitutional infringements that they believe occurred.[42] The violations include those that have been discussed in Sue Embrey's narration: freedom of speech, freedom of press, right to assemble, freedom from unreasonable searches and seizures, right to an indictment or to be informed of the charges against one, right to life, liberty and property, right to be confronted with accusatory witnesses, right to call favorable witnesses, right to legal counsel, right to a speedy and public trial, right to reasonable bail, freedom from cruel and unusual punishment, right to habeas corpus (to be brought before a court), and right to equal protection under the law. Two violations not addressed in Sue's chronicle are the right to vote and freedom from bills of attainder and *ex post facto* laws, legislative acts that inflict punishment without trial.

Erica Harth, professor of humanities and women's studies at Brandeis University, who spent a year of her childhood at Manzanar while her mother was teaching in the camp, argues that certain conditions within the United States facilitated the myth of Japanese American disloyalty.[43] "The number of ethnic Japanese living in the continental United States before removal to the camps was miniscule—barely two-tenths of one percent of the total population." Similar to Sue's frequent references to Japanese American "lack of clout," Harth argues that their small population resulted in their being regarded by the general population with indifference and ignorance. Even those who were acquainted with Japanese Americans often expressed a naïve unawareness of and blithe lack of sympathy for Japanese Americans. This perspective is unmistakable in a letter the parents of a high school friend sent Paul Tsuneishi while he was interned at the Heart Mountain camp in Wyoming.

"Now Paul you know that you are an American Citizen, so why don't you serve your country without question or demands, and you will see that you will be treated fine. Don't question—just be what you are—an American. We are sure that Uncle Sam will not mistreat you, but will restore your rights and the rights of your people. So be of good heart and serve your country."[44] Paul maintains: "It is a fair statement, I think, to say that the Kaestners' letter reflected the consensus of most citizens at that time."[45]

Foremost among the conditions identified by the CWRIC that permitted the removal and incarceration of Japanese Americans was the sanctioning of Executive Order 9066 by President Franklin D. Roosevelt.[46] Scholars differ about Roosevelt's motivation for the mass incarceration. Greg Robinson argues that Executive Order 9066 and the consequent forced removal of Japanese Americans was "a pragmatic decision, made by a practical-minded President in a time of crisis." However, he goes on to argue: "Although the President may have seen the evacuation as entirely a matter of military judgment, underlying his approval of that plan was a carelessness toward innocent people that was born of prejudice."[47] Historian Roger Daniels states unequivocally: "The leader of the nation was, in the final analysis, responsible." As with Robinson, Daniels attributes Roosevelt's action to two motives: it was expedient and the president himself harbored anti-Japanese prejudices.[48]

Sue's comments about Roosevelt illustrate the growth of her political consciousness. When Chiye Mori on the staff of the *Manzanar Free Press* criticized Roosevelt, Sue was shocked and thought Chiye's remarks were "terrible." In February 2003, Howard Coble, chairman of the House Subcommittee that oversees security legislation, said that he believed President Roosevelt was justified in sending 110,000 people of Japanese descent to internment camps, in part for their own protection from potentially hostile citizens. Sue's comment: "This wrong-headed thinking is still present today. Roosevelt's administration conducted an anti-Japanese campaign because he wanted to win the war. We got caught in that propaganda and people looked on us as being the same as the Japanese enemy."[49]

The scholarly literature suggests that the responsibility was systemic with innumerable individuals and agencies, both state and federal, contributing to the decision to incarcerate Japanese Americans. Perhaps no leader has come under more scrutiny for his advocacy for removal and incarceration of Japanese Americans than Earl Warren, then attorney general of California, who later became, as a justice of the Supreme Court, a resolute defender of individual freedom and a crusader for social justice. Scholars recount Warren's racist testimony before the Tolan Committee in 1942: "When we are dealing with the Caucasian race we have methods that will test the loyalty of them, but when we deal with the Japanese we are in an entirely different field and we cannot form any opinion that we believe to be sound." The very fact that there had been no reported cases of sabotage or espionage by Japanese Americans was evidence of their guilt, Warren testified, since such acts had been organized for some future time.[50]

Warren did come to regret his decision. He later wrote:

> I have since deeply regretted the removal order and my own testimony advocating it, because it was not in keeping with our American concept of freedom and the rights of citizens. . . . It was wrong to react so impulsively without positive evidence of disloyalty. It demonstrates the cruelty of war when fear, get-tough military psychology, propaganda and racial antagonism combine with one's responsibility for public security to produce such acts.[51]

Nonetheless, Sue, speaking for many Japanese Americans, could not forget Warren's actions during the war: "Political leaders were all against us, especially Earl Warren."[52]

Partially because an individual such as Warren was prominently involved in the removal and incarceration, the Japanese American community remains uneasy that such violations of civil rights could happen again in America. Sue voiced the concerns of many about the repercussions following the attack on the World Trade Center Towers in New York City on September 11, 2001: "Right after 9/11 they started talking about who was responsible. I worry about Arab Americans. They are keeping a lot of them without any charges, without a trial or a hearing. That is what happened to the Issei." Many whom I interviewed for this book stressed that in times of peril, under the guise of national security, violation of civil rights is allowed. As Warren Furutani put it: "People need to stand up now to determine what's right rather than wait until 40 or 50 years from now and have [another] *coram nobis* case." [53]

The interviewees have also repeatedly emphasized the enduring impact of the internment that even redress could not eradicate. Playwright Rosanna Yamagiwa Alfaro stresses: "Healing and redemption always come at a price; it's not easy to put together a cloth once it's torn, a vase once it's shattered. Things can never go back to life as usual; there is no closure."[54] Sue expressed her thoughts about closure: "Time changes an individual's response to the experience, but I was always pensive and sad when I visited Manzanar. Despite redress, for many people the wounds will never heal." [55]

CONCLUSION

The Legacy of Sue Kunitomi Embrey

"We never thought we would get so far," Garland Embrey said, referring to the campaign to raise awareness of the internment. One step after the other, Sue kept going and going. That's quite a legacy."[1] Sue acknowledged: "I am happy that the [Manzanar National Historic Site] Interpretive Center is open," "but when people congratulate me, I feel at a loss for words. I am proud of what I did, but not sure what kept me going." When I asked what had enabled her to persevere against sometime bitter opposition for more than three decades, she responded:

> I'm not sure. Many times, I'd get so discouraged, but I just kept thinking that maybe something hopeful would happen. Most of the Issei had *gaman,* a philosophy to endure silently. What's happened has happene d. Let's not talk about it, but I thought that talking about it could be a catharsis for people, that it would help heal the wounds. Keeping it inside just made it worse. I think it has held some people back because they haven't been able to really free themselves of that experience. Now that the Manzanar National Historic Site has been established, more and more are speaking out. Alisa [Lynch] has a list of people who are willing to be interviewed [by the National Park Service,] which we couldn't get ten years ago. I think the Manzanar National Historic Site gave them permission.[2]

Her belief that the Manzanar campaign would give people permission to talk about the camps and be a catharsis does not completely explain her persistence when confronted with the reality that many Japanese Americans rejected her efforts. To the question: "What kept you going?" Sue consistently responded that she really did not know, until one day she gave a surprising reply. "My mother's strong Buddhist faith and her support of the Pilgrimages may have been one of the strongest influences."[3] Komika Kunitomi's devout Buddhism was apparent when she attended the pilgrimages at Manzanar until age 90. "Every time we would go, she would offer incense at the cemetery," Sue remembered. "She also would leave a cup of water, saying: 'Those people buried there are probably dry and hot.' " An intrinsic value of the Issei was being very close to the deceased.[4] Sue's mother was expressing a traditional Buddhist value in a cemetery in Owens Valley. Sue may have been sustained by the belief that she and her mother were continuing to honor their culture, and undoubtedly recalling the painful estrangement when she married Garland, she deeply appreciated Komika's support.

While it may not be possible to determine definitively the influences that mold an individual, the indications in Sue's narrative are revealing. The profound, abiding authority of Sue's father is unmistakable in her not applying for college through the National Student Relocation Council, in her passive acceptance of rejection by the University of Wisconsin, and most movingly when she experienced feelings of guilt, thinking of her father, when she earned her master's degree at the University of Southern California. However, she prevailed over her hesitations and feelings of guilt. With the support of her egalitarian husband Garland Embrey, she successfully pursued a higher education. Ultimately she defied the "two strikes against you" edict of Gonhichi Kunitomi.[5]

Although internment at Manzanar was not of her choosing, her experience on the *Manzanar Free Press,* where she associated with liberal thinkers such as Chiye Mori and listened to leftist political views, was a significant turning point in her life. She realized for the first time that she could voice her own opinions and even criticize the government. Although she was not immediately converted to liberal, independent values, the *Free Press* associations planted the seeds that grew into decades of activism.

In her job at the Newberry Library, Sue learned firsthand that "People are not always focused on racial issues."[6] When Sue described her residence in Madison, Wisconsin, and Chicago, Illinois, she identified the elements of a good life: "I had a good job. I was independent."[7] This good life, with the freedom to shape her own history, was disrupted when she was obliged to return to Los Angeles to help her mother, but she took with her a self-sufficiency far greater than she had when she had left Little Tokyo.

During the postwar resettlement, responsibilities were thrust upon Nisei women, who had no role models to guide them in these extraordinary circumstances.[8] Finding her family in acute distress, Sue took charge, locating a comfortable and convenient place to live, despite encountering landlords who refused to rent to people of Japanese descent. In a city of blatant anti-Japanese bias, she secured employment despite a severe lack of jobs.

The traditional family structure had broken down during internment, and in postwar years Nisei had increased exposure to Caucasians.[9] Yet marriage between races remained a formidable barrier. Japanese marriage was still considered to be rooted in *giri,* obligation to parents and family.[10] Riding a motorcycle with the

Caucasian Clifford Barkley was one of the most dramatic expressions possible of independence and boldness. It was an obvious rebellion against everything Sue had been taught about not bringing *haji* to her family and community.[11]

Marrying the philosophically progressive Garland Embrey was the most provocative decision of Sue's adult life. While many Nisei women of Sue's age were spending more time with their mothers and sisters than with friends,[12] Sue was estranged from her family by the shame and guilt imposed by her mother. The estrangement took years to resolve. Sue had already become involved with progressive politics when she met Garland. Their marriage was a fundamental factor in the continuing growth of her progressive ideology and activism.

Taking an active role in the Nisei for Wallace campaign and later in the Nisei Progressives was in distinct contrast to the majority of Japanese Americans who maintained a low political profile after internment.[13] Sue described her activism as "scary." Her husband was under surveillance by the FBI and most of her friends deserted for fear of being tainted by the couple's liberalism. The Japanese American community was even more hostile than the mainstream. It was the wrong time, Sue pointed out, to promote affirmative action, unrestricted housing, and equal employment opportunities.

Despite her marked individuality, Sue's political growth had factors in common with other Nisei who became politically aware, notably in her involvement in protesting American involvement in the Viet Nam war. Sansei also perceived opportunities for social change during the late 1960s and early 1970s, when political movements for civil rights motivated them to unite with progressive Nisei.[14] Warren Furutani spoke of younger activists being drawn to Sue. "More than the Manzanar Committee, although that will be her most enduring reference, what made Sue unique to us, was that she had a progressive political perspective. Whether it was an issue like the camps, or education, or the Viet-Nam war, or civil rights issues, she was a progressive."[15] Equally, the awareness and energy of the Sansei provided a platform for Sue's activism. She frequently said: "It was the Sansei who got me started talking about the camps."

When she began talking about the camps in the late 1960s, Sue engaged with the course of history at a time when change was possible. Phil Shigikuni, however, viewed Sue's accomplishments as more than establishing a link between her activism and the civil right movements. He perceived her as being "ahead of her time, out front with social issues."[16] His perception may be due, in part, to Sue's being a Nisei. As Gary Embrey emphasized: "There weren't a lot of Nisei in the farm workers protests or the anti-war movement. Nisei tend to be very conservative."[17] Bruce Embrey's earliest memories are walking picket lines with his mother at Safeway for the United Farm Workers and her speaking at MacArthur Park in 1972. "I remember those things as vividly as the camp experiences."[18]

Both her sons referred to Sue's ability to maintain dignity despite hostility from her community. Avishai Margalit, professor of philosophy, University of Jerusalem,

Figure C.1 Sue with sons Gary (left) and Bruce, at a 1999 event during which Sue was honored by the Los Angeles city council for her work on the commission on the status of women and the Manzanar committee, as well as other community-based activism (photograph courtesy of the Embrey family)

states: "We recognize dignity by the way we react to humiliation."[19] Sue considered the Issei as role models in this respect. "The Issei dressed up when the day came to be removed. The women wore hats and gloves and the men wore suits and hats. The Issei never lost their dignity while they were in camp. I never heard my mother say anything about not being proud of being Japanese. I was never ashamed of being Japanese."[20]

Sue remembered one time when she did not react with dignity. She was watching the televised trial of the soldiers who were involved in the My Lai massacre in Vietnam. "I just blew up. I said to my husband: 'Dammit! We were lucky to get out of Manzanar!'" As she later reflected on this incident she revealed the growth in her political philosophy. "I was wrong to think that." She explained that the more she learned about history, the more she believed that America is strong and can make amends for the injustices it had committed.[21]

Admiration for Sue's fortitude is a salient characteristic of the memories of Sue's colleagues and family. Art Hansen used the metaphor of moving mountains. "Sue Embrey has been a conscience that spurred meaningful public action against widespread ignorance of the Japanese American evacuation and also [against] oppression of the civil rights of other marginalized groups based on gender, race, sexual preference."[22] Rose Ochi believes that Sue will be remembered as a person with passion and tenacity and purpose.[23] Takinori Yamamoto, a Manzanar Committee colleague, declared: "Sue is the epitome of what it means to be a Nisei woman trying to make a difference."[24] Paul Tsuneishi considers Sue "one of the treasures of the Nisei generation."[25]

Sue's niece, Nancy Iwata regards Sue as a role model, especially for Japanese American women.[26] Kerry Cababa, another niece, declared emphatically: "She is a hero."[27] Sue paid a price, however, for her heroic stance. To Kerry's portrayal she responded poignantly: "There are a lot of people in the community who don't think I'm a hero, who don't approve of what I did."[28] Despite a lingering sorrow caused by the opposition of her community, Sue was never apologetic. She drew strength from her Japanese heritage. In a resolute speech at the 1972 pilgrimage, she declared: "We are not here to argue with those who believe that the evacuation should be forgotten.... Neither are we here to defend ourselves against those who hold our generation accountable for compliance with executive orders and military regulations."[29]

Sue's observations demonstrate her keen awareness of being witness to nine decades of Japanese American history. She has written:

> The 150 year history of the Japanese in America... is one of triumph and tragedy. It is the story of an immigrant group that helped to build America, and after suffering the indignities of forced removal and incarceration, rose to recoup their lives and rebuild their communities. ...It is a legacy of the undaunted courage and indomitable spirit of Americans of Japanese ancestry, a legacy of which all who believe in a democratic society can be proud.[30]

Professor Margalit discusses individuals whom he considers "moral witnesses." Sue Embrey embodies his description: "Among the self-defining features is the mission of telling your story, of living with a sense of being a witness."[31] Margalit believes that moral witnesses are hopeful in their belief that if not in the present, at some time there will be a community that will listen to their testimony.[32] Sue actually was able to create a community that would listen to her story. A particularly powerful confirmation of these triumphs occurred on September 17, 2005 when Guard Tower #8 was dedicated at Manzanar.

The erection of the guard tower had been particularly controversial for more than 30 years. Although Lillian Baker had insisted that the towers were for fire prevention, much of the opposition was residual aversion to admitting that guard towers were used to confine American citizens, who had not been convicted of any crime.[33] Sue, who was honored during the dedication for her decades of perseverance in raising awareness of the internment camps, referred to the tower as an icon of "what the whole thing was about: imprisonment, loss of civil liberties, loss of identity."[34] Or as Jack Kunitomi said: "They had weapons up there, and they were pointed in at the camp."[35] Alisa Lynch declared: "It is this tower that most distinguishes Manzanar for what it was from 1942 to '45, a place of confinement. For those who were here, who can forget the guard towers, the searchlights or the armed military police?"[36]

Members of the community who are perhaps aware of Sue's story for the first time are those who have written their observations in the Manzanar National Historic Site guest book. "I didn't know." ... "I could not help but cry at some of the exhibits."—"No dust storm can sweep away the lasting effects."—"When will we ever learn?"—"The exhibit has totally changed my mind about the relocation of Japanese Americans."—And the straightforward, all embracing: "I'm sorry."[37]

Sue firmly believed that raising awareness of the camps would help former internees heal their enduring wounds. While the healing of an individual may be a psychological process, Sue's mission, helping Japanese Americans heal, became a political movement. The triumph of that movement, driven by her powerful sense of justice, was confirmed at the Grand Opening of the Interpretive Center of Manzanar National Historic Site, on April 24, 2004, when more than 2,500 people rose in unison to give her a standing ovation. This acclamation was not only a profound expression of gratitude by her community, but it was also a powerful acknowledgment of the fortitude of Sue Kunitomi Embrey that enabled her to refocus a community and reshape history.

Afterword

Jack Kunitomi has characterized his sister's legacy as being that of a fighter: *Yamato damachii.* "That means valiant spirit!"[1]

Sue Embrey's *yamato damachii* was powerfully tested in 2005 when Garland Embrey died on March 18. Despite her divorce Sue remembered with great affection the years of love, admiration, and political activism she shared with Garland. Her courageous spirit endured a further and devastating shock in 2006 when her son Gary was killed in a hiking accident on February 5. She found some consolation in her grief by remembering that Gary had appeared on her behalf at the 36th annual Manzanar Pilgrimage on April 29, 2005, when she was too ill to attend. After many years of avoiding the Pilgrimages, preferring to visit Manzanar in solitude, Gary spoke with pride about his mother and the Manzanar Committee. Speaking directly to his colleagues, the teachers present, he stressed: "We have a special responsibility to teach American history not as people might prefer it, but as it really was."

Sue Kunitomi Embrey never recovered from the ills that prevented her from attending the Pilgrimage in 2005. Her body, exhausted by grief and illnesses, including those that originated in the dust of Manzanar, surrendered on May 15, 2006.

A Buddhist memorial ceremony for close family and friends was held in Koyasan Temple, Little Tokyo, on May 20. A public memorial service was held at Higashai Honganji Temple on June 17. In a private ceremony the bishop of Koyasan Temple gave Sue the Buddhist name *Manzanar Henro Suei Daishi,* meaning "enhancing her own nature and singing the teaching of the Dharma and entering into Nirvana through the Manzanar Pilgrimage."

Sue's daughter-in-law Barbara Becker had expressed Sue's legacy in personal terms: what she would want her children to learn from her. "I don't want that legacy to be lost when people who were at Manzanar are gone. It's amazing how little people do know [about the internment]."[2] Sue had a similar wish for her own legacy. During our last interview, when Sue was in relatively good health, she said: "Looking back on my life I think I have accomplished what I wanted to do. I hope I have established a direction for young people to follow."

Figure A.1 Sue Kunitomi Embrey, *yamato damachii*, Valiant Spirit (photograph by David Fujioka; courtesy of the Embrey family)

A speech given by Monica and Michael Embrey at the 37th Annual Pilgrimage on April 29, 2006, provides the evidence that her valiant spirit lives on and that Sue's own wish for her legacy has been fulfilled.

> "In the early days of the Manzanar Pilgrimage," Monica said, "our grandmother often spoke of how gratifying it was to have so many Sansei and young people of all races coming and struggling to understand how and why this happened. More importantly, she always said how essential it was that so many people came forward pledging to fight against something like this ever happening again. Unfortunately, it has happened again. Following 9-11, there was an illegal detainment of 1200 Arab and Muslim Americans.... [I]f we don't know our history, it can repeat itself."
>
> Michael stressed:
>
> Everything that happened here deserves more than just a paragraph in an American history textbook. While growing up, going to the Pilgrimage every year opened my eyes and made me less tolerant of different types of oppression, such as racism, sexism, homophobia, classism and ageism.
>
> Monica concluded:
>
> In the fighting spirit of my grandmother, I want to say we young people must learn from the commitment of our grandparents, learn from their perseverance, their strength, and their courage in this great injustice. We must learn not only to endure but also learn that through dedication and determination, injustice can be made right. Our grandmother never said *Shikata ga nai.* She says *Nidoto nai yoni,* let it never happen again.

Appendix I

The Ten War Relocation Authority Camps

Shortly after Franklin D. Roosevelt issued Executive Order 9066 on February 19, 1942, the federal government had notified the city of Los Angeles that 4,725 acres of land owned by the city's Department of Water and Power at Manzanar, California would be appropriated for an assembly center, which would be converted to the first War Relocation Authority (WRA) camp.[1]

The other nine camps were Topaz, officially Central Utah Relocation Center, Poston in western Arizona, Gila River in central Arizona, officially Colorado River Relocation Center, Amache in southeastern Colorado, Heart Mountain in northwestern Wyoming, Jerome and Rohwer, both in southeastern Arkansas, Tule Lake in north-central California, and Minidoka in south-central Idaho.

National Park Service Historian Harlan D. Unrau quotes from the War Relocation Authority's own reports to describe the "inhospitable" characteristics of the sites. Manzanar and Poston were in the desert and internees in these camps suffered extreme temperatures and dust storms in both summer and winter. Poston's desert climate was extremely harsh, its land completely undeveloped. Gila River had extreme summer temperatures, while Heart Mountain had temperature ranging from 30 degrees below to more than 100 above zero. Conditions at the two most northern camps, Minidoka and Heart Mountain, were characterized by painfully harsh winters and severe dust storms. Minidoka's land was covered with lava outcroppings. Tule Lake was located in a dry lake bed, predominantly covered with greasewood. Amache had been the site of a former stock ranch. Jerome and Rohwer were on swampy ground, with excessive humidity and mosquito infestations.[2]

These WRA centers were separate from internment camps set up by the Justice Department for Japanese Americans who had been arrested immediately following Pearl Harbor. Those were located in Santa Fe, New Mexico; Bismarck, North Dakota; Missoula, Montana; and Crystal City, Texas. Isolation camps for "trouble makers" were later established in Moab, Utah, and Leupp, Arizona.

Appendix II

Conditions that Allowed the Internment[1]

(1) General John L. DeWitt, head of the Western Defense Command believed that ethnicity determined loyalty.
(2) The administration of FDR ignored the FBI and Naval Intelligence when they advised that nothing more than careful watching of suspicious individuals was needed.
(3) General Dewitt relied heavily on civilian politicians to reach his decisions, and politicians repeated the "prejudiced, unfounded themes of anti-Japanese factions on the West Coast."
(4) President Roosevelt took no effective measures to calm the West Coast and refute rumors of sabotage and espionage.
(5) General DeWitt was temperamentally disposed to exaggerate the measures necessary to maintain security. Moreover, he gave priority to security while disregarding civil rights of the internees.
(6) Secretary of War Henry L. Stimson and John J. McCloy, Assistant Secretary of War, whose views on race mirrored those of DeWitt, failed to insist on a clear military justification for the measures undertaken by DeWitt.
(7) Attorney General Francis Biddle, while contending that exclusion was unnecessary, did not argue to the President that failure to make a case of military necessity would render the exclusion unconstitutional or that the Constitution prohibited exclusion on the basis of ethnicity.
(8) There was no effective opposition to the removal and incarceration because those representing civil rights in Congress, the press and other public forums were silent or even in support of the exclusion.
(9) President Roosevelt, without raising the issue to Cabinet level discussion or requiring a careful review of the situation, sanctioned the implementation of Executive Order 9066.

Notes

Introduction

1. Nisei are the second generation of Japanese in America, the children of the immigrant Issei. The Sansei are the third generation, the Yonsei, the fourth, and Gonsei, the fifth. The definitions of generations can be expanded to mean historical cohorts, individuals with affinities in concerns and experiences, despite belonging to different conventionally defined generations.
2. The founding and evolution of the Manzanar Committee is explored in chapter 12.
3. Frank Hays transferred to the post of Pacific Area Director for the Pacific West Region, stationed in Honolulu. He was replaced at Manzanar by Thomas Leatherman in September 2005.
4. The sources for the ensuing brief history of Owens Valley are Bahr, *Viola Martinez, California Paiute, Living in Two Worlds,* 18–26; Wehrey, *Voices from This Long Brown Land,* 211–214.
5. Sahagun, "Judge Threatens DWP Sanctions," June 25, 2006; "In Owens Valley Water Runs Again," December 7, 2006.
6. Unrau, *The Evacuation and Relocation,* 100.
7. Weglyn, *Years of Infamy,* 56–60. Around 110,00 Japanese Americans were removed from the West Coast and a segment of Arizona. By the end of the war the total numbered over 120,000 internees, including people of Japanese descent from Alaska and those from Latin American countries, notably Peru, who were sent to U.S. Department of Justice camps as forced participants in possible exchange arrangements for American prisoners of war.
8. Yamano, "Brooding Silence," x, xi, 18, 29. Confirms the research of Nagata 1993 and Mass in Daniels, Taylor, and Kitano, eds., 1991 that the internment was rarely discussed in Japanese American families.
9. Nikkei is a term generally used in the same way as Japanese American. It is also used to identify all persons of Japanese descent who had immigrated or who are descendents of immigrants.
10. Asakawa, March 10, 2003, nikkeiview.com/archives/03/03/2003.htm; see also Yamano 1994.
11. The redress movement is discussed in chapter 13.
12. Hansen, email correspondence with author, April 12, 2002. The redress movement was a campaign to convince the federal government to apologize for the internment and to award reparations to former internees.
13. Hansen, interview, June 25, 2003, 39.

14. Sue Embrey, correspondence with author, April 19 and 22, 2002.
15. Fujino, *Heartbeat of Struggle,* xxix.
16. The audiotapes and transcripts will be archived at the Manzanar National Historic Site, Independence, California, available to all interested persons.
17. The Manzanar riot is explored in chapter 7.
18. Yamashita, "Little Tokyo Eons Ago," 31.

Chapter 1 Growing Up in Little Tokyo

1. Niiya, ed., *Encyclopedia*, 214.
2. Ibid.
3. Midori, n.d. "Family History," 1. Sue thought her father immigrated to the mainland around 1905–06.
4. Daniels, *Prisoners without Trial,* 6; Modell, *The Economics and Politics of Racial Accomodation,* 19, 98.
5. Sue's accounts of her parents' immigration to the United States are related in interview 1, November 3, 2002, 6–8.
6. Most early immigrants were men who planned to return to Japan within four or five years. Yanagisako, *Transforming the Past*, 27–28.
7. Interview 1, November 13, 2001, 6–10.
8. Kitano, *Japanese Americans,* 39–40; Nakano, *Japanese American Women,* 24–29.
9. Interview, May 12, 2004, 12, 5.
10. Ibid.
11. Gonhichi Kunitomi's passport and the marriage license of Gonhichi and Komika are in the Embrey family files.
12. Hosokawa, *Nisei,* 120.
13. Niiya, ed., *Nanka Nikkei Voices, Vol. III,* "Turning Points," 1.
14. *Nanka Nikkei Voices,* "Little Tokyo: Changing Times, Changing Faces," Vol. III, 16–17.
15. Miyatake assumed a significant responsibility in Manzanar Internment Camp by secretly photographing camp activities in violation of military regulations. The Tokyo Miyatake Collection is the preeminent source for photographic documentation of Manzanar. See Unrau, *The Evacuation and Relocation,* 535; Cooper, *Remembering Manzanar,* x, xi, 28, 39, 44, 54; Niiya, ed., *Encyclopedia,* 280–281.
16. Lon Kurahsige, *Japanese American Celebration and Conflict,* 19.
17. Modell, *The Economics and Politics of Racial Accomodation,* 71; Niiya, ed., *Encyclopedia,* 238. Precise data are not available prior to 1940. There were 35,000 Japanese Americans in Los Angeles, the majority of whom lived in Little Tokyo. Of this population in 1940 18% was races other than Japanese.
18. Modell, *The Economics and Politics of Racial Accommodation,* 71.
19. Ibid.; Hosokawa, *Nisei,* 164–165.
20. Nakano, *Japanese American Women,* 40.
21. Interview 1, November 13, 2002, 2.
22. Interview 1, November 13, 2002, 6.
23. *Nanka Nikkei Voices III* 2004, 16–17.
24. Interview 19, March 19, 2002.

25. Niiya, ed., *Encyclopedia,* 387.
26. Jack Kunitomi, interview by author, August 8, 2003, 14.
27. Niiya, ed., *Encyclopedia,* 8.
28. Nakano, *Japanese American Women,* 36; Yanagisako, *Transforming the Past,* 28–29.
29. Interview 1, November 13, 2002, 6.
30. Nakano, *Japanese American Women,*54; Modell, *The Economics and Politics of Racial Accommodation,* 90; Hosokawa, *Nisei,* 155–156; Takezawa, *Breaking the Silence,* 62; Niiya, ed., *Encyclopedia,* 242; Kitano, *Japanese Americans,* 66; Yanagisako, *Transforming the Past,* 1985, 202, 227–228.
31. Interview 14, February 12, 2003, 14–15.
32. Modell, *The Economics and Politics of Racial Accomodation,* 86; Matsumoto, *Farming the Home Place,* 65; Kitano, *Japanese Americans,* 152.
33. Interview 14, February 12, 2003, 16.
34. Ibid., 158.
35. Interview 1, November 13, 2002, 27.
36. Takezawa, *Breaking the Silence,* 65.
37. Lon Kurashige, *Japanese American Celebration and Conflict,* 40: a study in the 1930s showed the percentage of juvenile delinquents in Little Tokyo to be significantly less than any other ethnic population, including native-born whites. Kitano, *Japanese Americans,* 146, has also noted the lower rate of juvenile delinquency of Japanese Americans.
38. Interview 2, November 20, 2002, 37–38.
39. Ibid.
40. Interview 1, November 13, 2002, 50–51.
41. Embrey, "Some Lines for a Younger Brother," 1.
42. Kitano, *Japanese Americans,* 62–66.
43. Sue Embrey, conversation with author, January 7, 2005.
44. The author is indebted to Nakano, *Japanese American Women*; Matsumoto, *Farming the Home Place*; Takahashi, *Nisei/Sansei*; Yanagisako, *Transforming the Past*; and Kitano, *Japanese Americans;* for constructive discussions of Japanese American family life.

Chapter 2 Old Values in a New Home

1. Interview 2, November 20, 2002, 65.
2. Interview 1, November 13, 2002, 28–29.
3. Jack Kunitomi, interview, August 8, 2003, 11–12.
4. http://www.geocities.com/CapeCanaveral/853/moxaing.html20057.
5. Matsumoto, *Farming the Home Place,* 64
6. Interview 1, November 2002, 29.
7. Jack Kunitomi, interview, August 8, 2002, 7–8.
8. Ibid.
9. Ibid.
10. Ibid., 7. Jack began expressing his musical talents in ballroom dancing while in high school and was still actively engaged in dancing in 2006.
11. Kim, "Processes of Asian American Development," 71.

12. Interview 4, December 11, 2002, 17, 21.
13. Matsumoto, *Farming the Home Place,* 190.
14. Interview 2, November 20, 2002, 31–32.
15. Jack Kunitomi, interview, August 8, 2003, 15–16.
16. Interview 2, November 20, 2002, 23–24.
17. Matsumoto, *Farming the Home Place,* 84; Yanagisako, *Transforming the Past,* 68–69.
18. Interview 2, November 20, 2002, 45–46.
19. Matsumoto 1993, *Farming the Home Place,*180; Nakano, *Japanese American Women,* 106.
20. Interview 2, November 20, 2002, 45.
21. Ibid., 50.
22. Ibid., 20.
23. Interview 1, November 13, 2002, 47–50.
24. Interview 2, November 20, 2002, 57.
25. Interview 1, November 13, 2002, 19.
26. Nakano, *Japanese American Women,* 37; Yanagisako, *Transforming the Past,* 19, 166, 248–249; Kitano, *Japanese Americans,* 44.
27. Matsumoto, *Farming the Home Place,* 65; Kitano, *Japanese Americans,* 124, 129, 130, 134; Takezawa, *Breaking the Silence,* 64; Nakano, *Japanese American Women,* 105–106; Takahashi, *Shifting Japanese American Identities,* 152, 153; Fugita and O'Brien, *Japanese American Ethnicity,* 37, 45–46.
28. Hoobler, *The Japanese American Family,* 73; Modell, *The Economics and Politics of Racial Accommodation,* 78–79; Hosokawa, *Nisei: The Quiet Americans,* 131.
29. Interview 2, November 20, 2002, 27.
30. Matsumoto, *Farming the Home Place,* 78; Yanagisako, *Transforming the Past,* 217–218.
31. Fugita and O'Brien, *Japanese American Identity,* 84; Takezawa, *Breaking the Silence,* 1995, 68; Yoo, *Growing Up Nisei,* 18, 38.
32. Matsumoto, *Farming the Home Place,* 72.

Chapter 3 A Father's Shadow

1. Interview 1, November 13, 2002, 31
2. Nakano, *Japanese American Women,* 110; Matsumoto, *Farming the Home Place,* 71.
3. Interview 1, November 13, 2002, 34–35. The La Brea Tar Pits, a 32-acre site located on Wilshire Boulevard in Los Angeles, has been excavated for Ice Age animal remains since 1875.
4. Interview 1, November 13, 2002, 32.
5. Matsumoto, *Farming the Home Place,* 93; Takesawa, *Breaking the Silence,* 70; Fugita and O'Brien, *Japanese American Ethnicity,* 1991, 77.
6. Interview 1, November 13, 2002, 32.
7. Ibid., 36–37.
8. Takesawa, *Breaking the Silence;* 68; Matsumoto, *Farming the Home Place,* 69.
9. Interview 1, November 13, 2002, 35.

10. Yoo, *Growing Up Nisei,* 31; Matsumoto, *Farming the Home Place,* 70; Takahashi, *Shifting Japanese American Identities,* 32–33; Fugita and O'Brien, *Japanese American Ethnicity,* 85–88.
11. Quoted in Modell, *The Economics and Politics of Racial Accommodation,* 160.
12. Ibid.
13. Matsumoto, *Farming the Home Place,* 70.
14. Interview 1, November 13, 2002, 25, 27.
15. Jack Kunitomi, interview, August 8, 2003, 13.
16. Waugh, *Hidden Crime and Deviance,* 154; Takahashi, *Shifting Japanese American Identities,* 46.
17. Niiya, ed., *Encyclopedia,* 228. The Japanese language schools were temporarily closed during World War II. Eventually reopened, they were never as influential as they had been prior to the war.
18. Yoo, *Growing Up Nisei,* 95.
19. Matsumoto, *Farming the Home Place,* 192; Fugita and O'Brien, *Japanese American Ethnicity,* 84–88; Kitano, *Japanese Americans,* 25–26, 52; Nakano, *Japanese American Women,* 110.
20. Jack Kunitomi, interview, August 8, 2002, 24–26.
21. Yoo, *Growing Up Nisei,* 79; Nakano, *Japanese American Women,* 112, 117; Modell, *The Economics and Politics of Racial Accommodation,* 133.
22. Interview 2, November 20, 2002, 8.
23. Sue's account of her father's death and funeral are presented in interview 2, November 20, 2002, 65–69.
24. Interview 3, December 4, 2002, 7.
25. Interview 4, December 11, 2002, 11, 19.
26. Interview 2, November 20, 2002, 65–69.
27. Interview 14, February 12, 2003, 15.
28. Interview 3, December 4, 2002, 8–10.
29. Jack Kunitomi, interview, August 8, 2003, 26–27.
30. Interview 3, December 4, 2002, 12.
31. Ibid., 4.
32. Ibid., 12–13.
33. Yanagisako, *Transforming the Past,* 171.
34. Interview 4, December 11, 2002, 12–13.
35. Ibid.
36. Ibid., 8–9.
37. Ibid., 64.
38. Ibid.

Chapter 4 The Impact of the Attack on Pearl Harbor

1. Fugita and O'Brien, *Japanese American Ethnicity,* 53–60; Lon Kurashige, *Japanese American Celebration and Conflict,* 19.
2. Burton, et al., *Confinement and Ethnicity,* 27; Kitano, *Japanese Americans,* 18–20.

3. Hosokawa, *Nisei,* 96; Niiya, ed., *Encyclopedia,* 117.
4. Unrau, *Evacuation and Relocation,* 9.
5. Hosokawa, *Nisei,* 122.
6. Schlesinger, Jr., ed., *Almanac,* 486.
7. Jack Kunitomi, interview, August 8, 2003, 34–42.
8. Schlesinger, Jr., ed., *Almanac,* 481, 485: On September 26, 1940, President Roosevelt announced an embargo on the export of scrap steel and iron outside the Western Hemisphere, intending to deprive Japan of essential materiel. The Japanese ambassador to the U.S. Kichisaburo Nomura and special envoy Saburo Kurusu had been negotiating with the U.S. State department.
9. Robinson, *By Order of the President,* 75; Niiya, ed., *Encyclopedia,* 11; Burton et al., *Confinement and Ethnicity,* 28; Hosokawa, *Nisei,* 237; Yoo, *Growing Up Nisei,* 95.
10. Hosokawa, *Nisei,* 217.
11. Ibid., 236. For a comprehensive discussion of Tanaka's prewar political activity see Scott Kurashige, *Transforming Los Angeles,* 226–249.
12. Jack Kunitomi, interview, August 8, 2003, 36–37.
13. For comprehensive discussions of the JACL, see Weglyn, *Years of Infamy;* Muller, *Free to Die for Their Country;* Drinnon, *Keeper of Concentration Camps;* Myer, *Uprooted Americans*; Takahashi, *Nisei/Sansei;* CWRIC, *Personal Justice Denied.*
14. Hosokawa, *Nisei,* 250; Modell , *Economics and Politics,* 83.
15. Kim, "Processes," 85, 90, 96, 199.
16. Modell, *Economics and Politics,* 183.
17. Niiya, ed., *Encyclopedia,* 298; Muller, *Free to Die for Their Country,* 11, 24; Weglyn, *Years of Infamy,* 38; Modell, *Economics and Politics,* 39–43.
18. Niiya, ed., *Encyclopedia,* 409–411; Hosokawa, *Nisei,* 287–288; Daniels, *Prisoners without Trial,* 37.
19. Weglyn, *Years of Infamy,* 49; Niiya, ed., *Encyclopedia,* 349–350; Daniels, *Concentration Camps,* 49–50.
20. Interview 3, December 4, 2002, 39.
21. Daniels, *Prisoners without Trial,* 50.
22. Robinson, *By Order of the President,* 96; Weglyn, *Years of Infamy,* 93; Daniels, *Concentration Camps,* 42–43.
23. Daniels, *Politics of Prejudice,* 15–18; *Concentration Camps,* 32–34.
24. Robinson, *By Order of the President,* 89.
25. *Los Angeles Examiner,* December 8, 1941, 1.
26. Hosokawa, *Nisei,* 310–311. For other accounts of the Terminal Island mass departure see Modell, *Economics and Politics,* 70; Daniels, *Concentration Camps,* 50; Weglyn, *Years of Infamy,* 122; Robinson, *By Order of the President,* 106–107; Niiya, ed., *Encyclopedia,* 385–386.
27. Weglyn, *Years of Infamy,* 122.
28. Interview 3, December 4, 2002, 41–44.
29. Takezawa, *Breaking the Silence,* 76; Hosokawa, *Nisei,* 24; Robinson, *By Order of the President,* 75.
30. Interview 3, December 4, 2002, 50.
31. Unrau, *Evacuation and Relocation,* 861.
32. Daniels, *Politics of Prejudice,* 25.
33. Robinson, *By Order of the President,* 108.

34. Starr, *Embattled Dreams,* 34, 36, 64; Unrau, *Evacuation and Relocation,* 39–40.
35. Hosokawa, *Nisei,* 284.
36. Ibid., 285.
37. Weglyn, *Years of Infamy,* 37.
38. Ibid., 38.
39. Muller, *Free to Die for Their Country,* 24.
40. Hosokawa, *Nisei,* 290.
41. Weglyn, *Years of Infamy,* 284; Hosokawa, *Nisei,* 191.
42. Hosokawa, *Nisei,* 260.
43. Robinson, *By Order of the President,* 128.
44. Jack Kunitomi, interview, August 8, 2003, 41.
45. Hosokawa, *Nisei,* 259.
46. Robinson, *By Order of the President,* 131.
47. Hosokawa, *Nisei,* 259. Ironically, because Hawaii's economy was heavily dependent upon their labor, only 1,250 Japanese Hawaiians were interned, less than one percent of Hawaii's total population. 110,00 Japanese Americans were removed from the west coast and Arizona. By the end of the war the total of internees was more than 120,000, including people of Japanese descent from Alaska and from thirteen Latin America countries, who were incarcerated in U. S. Department of Justice camps in the United States to be exchanged for American military captured by the Japanese.
48. Interview 4, December 11, 2002, 49–50.
49. Ibid., 42.
50. Ibid., 44.
51. Muller, *Free to Die,* 26.
52. Smith, *Democracy on Trial,* 162.
53. Weglyn, *Years of Infamy,* 21.
54. Interview, December 11, 2002, 49.
55. Smith, *Democracy on Trial,* 134–136; Robinson, *By Order of the President,* 129; Takesawa, *Breaking the Silence,* 79; CWRIC, *Personal Justice Denied,* 121–122.
56. Jack Kunitomi, interview, August 8, 2003, 43.
57. Interview 4, December 11, 2002, 70.
58. Ibid., 44.
59. Ibid., 49.
60. Ibid., 74.
61. Smith, *Democracy on Trial,* 162.
62. Jack Kunitomi, interview, August 8, 2003, 43.

Chapter 5 Manzanar: Weeping under the Apple Trees

1. Unrau, *Evacuation and Relocation,* 77.
2. Interview 6, December 18, 2002, 8–9.
3. Interview 6, December 18, 2002, 17, 19; interview 7, January 9, 2003, 1–3.
4. Takeuchi recovered and later had a chance meeting with Kinya Kunitomi in Japan.

5. Unrau, *Evacuation and Relocation, Vol. I,* 230; Burton, *Confinement and Ethnicity*, 43.
6. For a description of the 10 camps see appendix I.
7. Hosokawa, *Nisei,* 346; Robinson, *By Order of the President,* 132; Weglyn, *Years of Infamy,* 29, n.9; Drinnon, *Keeper of Concentration Camps,* 7–8.
8. Unrau, *Evacuation and Relocation,* 293, 295.
9. Ibid., 247.
10. Ibid., 40–48.
11. Sister and brother-in-law of Sue's brother Frank.
12. See Unrau, *Evacuation and Relocation*, 438–439 for a discussion of internees' mistrust of the co-op.
13. Ibid., 465–467.
14. Interview 6, December 18, 2002, 32–35.
15. Sue was hospitalized April 16–28, 2005, with a severe bronchial infection complicated by sarcoidosis and bronchiectasis.
16. Interview 6, December 18, 2002, 19–26.
17. Ibid., 40.
18. Ibid., 41–42, 53; interview 7, January 9, 2003, 17–18.
19. Unrau, *Evacuation and Relocation,* 399.
20. Interview 6, December 18, 2002, 46–48; 51–52.
21. Smith. *Democracy on Trial,* 186–187.
22. Interview, January 9, 2003, 55.
23. Garrett and Larson, eds., *Camp and Community,* 116.
24. Interview 7, January 9, 2003, 55.
25. Unrau, *Evacuation and Relocation,* 418: The Maryknoll Home and the Japanese American Children's Home, as well as foster homes in Los Angeles; The Salvation Army's Children's Home in San Francisco.
26. Paul Spickard, History Department, University of California Santa Barbara, states: " I went through all the documents I could find in the National Archives. I don't recall any of them indicating a rule about blood quantum requirements. There hadn't been all that many generations of mixing. Most of the small number of biracial people were half-Japanese." Email to author, February 9, 2007.
27. Interview 8, January 15, 2003, 37–39.
28. Interview 6, December 18, 2002, 56–57; interview 7, January 9, 2003, 5–6.
29. For a thorough depiction of WRA camp hospitals see Hirahara and Jense, *Silent Scars.*
30. Unrau, *Evacuation and Relocation,* 456.
31. Ibid., 457–458.
32. Ibid., 458–463, 539, 540; for a comprehensive discussion of .schools in the internment camps, See Riley, *Schools behind Barbed Wire.*
33. The significant Owens Valley hostility to Manzanar is documented in Garrett and Larson, *Camp and Community.*
34. Interview 13, February5, 2003, 4, 11–14.
35. Japanese American Historical Society of Southern California V. XXV, no. 7, July/ August 2005. Although approximately 500 high school students were graduated from Manzanar, many internees believed these students had been deprived by not receiving diplomas from their original schools. On January 1, 2004 AB 781 became California state law, authorizing high school districts, unified schools districts, and county offices of education to retroactively grant high school diplomas to anyone of

Japanese descent who was interned during World War II; these diplomas can be awarded posthumously.

36. Unrau, *Evacuation and Relocation,* 432.
37. Ibid., 432–433 .
38. Ibid.
39. Interview 7, January 9, 2003, 40–41.
40. Yamano, *Brooding Silence,* 12.
41. Interview, January 9, 2003, 37–38.
42. Interview 6, December 18, 2002, 50; interview, January 9, 2003, 42–45.
43. Unrau, *Evacuation and Relocation,* 419
44. Interview 7, January 9, 2003, 49–51.

Chapter 6 Manzanar: A Community of Contradictions

1. Sue's comments in this chapter are excerpted from Interview 7, January 9, 2003.
2. *Our World,* "Foreword," n.p.
3. Interview 13, February 5, 2003, 7–9.
4. Unrau, *Evacuation and Relocation,* 436–437.
5. Interview 6, December 18, 2002, 49.
6. Interview 8, January 15, 2003, 27.
7. Interview 14, February 12, 2003, 28–29.
8. Unrau, *Evacuation and Relocation*, 445.
9. Interview, January 9, 2003, 64–68.
10. Interview 6, December 18, 2002, 54–56.
11. Wehrey, *Voices from This Long Brown Land,* 174–178. Nomura performed at the opening of MNHS Interpretive Center, singing the same songs she had sung during her days in camp under the tutelage of Louis Frizell.
12. Unrau, *Evacuation and Relocation,* 450.
13. Interview 8, January 15, 2003, 48–50.
14. Manzanar Committee, *Reflections,* 19.
15. Interview 7, January 9, 2003, 60.
16. Unrau, *Evacuation and Relocation,* 276–78.
17. Ibid., 450.
18. Ibid.
19. Garrett and Larson, *Camp and Community,* 40.
20. Unrau, *Evacuation and Relocation,* 394.
21. Interview 8, January 15, 2003, 53–71; interview 9, January 15, 2003, 1–12.
22. See Scott Kurashige, "Transforming Los Angeles," 271–327, for a detailed discussion of Japanese American Communists in Los Angeles.
23. Yoneda, *Ganbatte,* 145.
24. *Manzanar Free Press,* June 9, 1942, 2.
25. Takahashi, *Nisei/Sansei,* 105.
26. Unrau, *Evacuation and Relocation,* 395.
27. "Japanese American Citizens League Southern District, May 26, 1942, Report of Conditions at Manzanar Relocation Center." Copy in files of Sue Embrey.
28. Interview 11, January 29, 2003, 1–3.

Chapter 7 Violence and Desolation

1. Niiya, ed., *Encyclopedia,* 145–146.
2. Daniels, *Concentration Camps,* 105, 107.
3. Unrau, *Evacuation and Relocation,* 477.
4. Ibid., 411
5. Quoted in Lim, *Lim Report,* 113.
6. CWRIC, *Personal Justice,* 177.
7. Scott Kurashige, "Transforming Los Angeles," 263.
8. Yoneda, *Ganbatte,* 130.
9. Lim. *Lim Report,* 113.
10. Niiya, ed., *Encyclopedia,* 219.
11. Hansen and Hacker, "The Manzanar Riot," 87; Weglyn, *Years of Infamy,"* 300–301, n.19.
12. Unrau, *Evacuation and Relocation,* 479.
13. Ibid., Lon Kurashige, *Japanese American,* 99.
14. Ibid., 480. Committee members were Joseph Kurihara, Gengi Yamaguchi, Shigetoshi Tateishi, Sakichi Hashimoto, and Kazuo Suzukawa.
15. Unrau , *Evacuation and Relocation,*, 480; Lon Kurashige , *Japanese American,* 87–88; Weglyn, *Years of Infamy,* 122–123.
16. Sue's account of the riot, expressing her personal trauma, is a fusion of her memories, her contact with former Manzanar internees, including an interview with Harry Ueno, and her own research on the topic. Her account is excerpted from interviews 11 and 12, January 29, 2003, and interview 13, February 5, 2003.
17. Unrau, *Evacuation and Relocation,* 483–484; Cooper, *Remembering Manzanar,* 36–38; Weglyn , *Years of Infamy,* 123–124.
18. Unrau, *Evacuation and Relocation,* 484–487; Hirahara and Jensen, *Silent Scars,* 94.
19. Unrau, *Evacuation and Relocation, Vol. 2,* 478.
20. Ibid.
21. Lim, *Lim Report,* 116–117.
22. Quoted in ibid., 117.
23. Sue Embrey, email to author, July 18, 2005.
24. Unrau, *Evacuation and Relocation,* 492.
25. Tule Lake became a national historic land mark in February 2006.
26. Unrau, *Evacuation and Relocation,* 490–491; for the most comprehensive analysis of the Manzanar Riot, see Hansen and Hacker, "The Manzanar Riot."
27. Embrey, Hansen, and Mitson, *Manzanar Martyr;* Tateishi, *And Justice for All.*
28. Tateishi, *And Justice for All,* 206.
29. Ibid., 207.
30. Oliver, "Harry Ueno 97," December 21, 2004.
31. Lynch, email to author, December 16, 2004.
32. Lynch, emails to author, December 16, 2004, February 22, 2007.
33. "Project Director's Report," *Final Report Manzanar, Vol. 1,* 39–40, quoted in Unrau, *Evacuation and Relocation,* 499–506.
34. Niiya, ed., *Encyclopedia,* 345–347.
35. Weglyn, *Years of Infamy,* 229–230.
36. "The Riot and After." *Manzanar Free Press.* March 20, 1943, 15.

37. Hansen and Hacker, "The Manzanar Riot."
38. Daniels, *Concentration Camps,* 108, 110.

Chapter 8 Go Forth, Seek, and Find

1. Interview 7, January 9, 2003, 8–9.
2. Daniels, *Concentration Camps,* 72.
3. Cababa, interview, January 17, 2003, 38.
4. Jack Kunitomi, interview, August 8, 2003, 21–22; 55–56.
5. Niija, ed., 2001, *Encyclopedia,* 229; Nakano, *Japanese American Women,* 115.
6. Interview 14, February 12, 2003, 55–56.
7. Unrau, *Evacuation and Relocation,* 37.
8. CWRIC, *Personal Justice,* 183.
9. Ibid.
10. Niija, "Introduction," 6; Unrau, *Evacuation and Relocation,* 767; CWRIC, *Personal Justice,* 183; Matsumoto, *Farming the Home Place,* 133.
11. Daniels, *Concentration Camps,* 83.
12. Drinnon, *Keeper of Concentration Camps,* 78.
13. Niiya, "Introduction," 3–4; Lon Kurashige, *Japanese American Celebration and Conflict,*, 102–103; Niiya, ed., *Encyclopedia,* 260–261; Cooper, *Remembering Manzanar,* 39–40; Daniels, *Concentration Camps,* 82–83; Weglyn, *Years of Infamy,* 136–139; Drinnon, *Keeper of Concentration Camps,* 78–80, 83–97.
14. Drinnon, *Keeper of Concentration Camps,* 80.
15. Interview 14, February 12, 2003, 34–54.
16. Unrau, *Evacuation and Relocation,* 678.
17. Ibid., 667: On September 14, 1942 the War Department prohibited Nisei induction, classifying them as IV-C, the same status as that for enemy aliens.
18. CWRIC, *Personal Justice,* 193.
19. Niiya, ed., *Encyclopedia,* 163–164.
20. Ibid., 261.
21. Unrau, *Evacuation and Relocation,* 709. The Tule Lake "segregation center" was the most turbulent of the WRA camps.
22. Interview, February 12, 2003, 48–52.
23. Niiya, "Introduction," 6.
24. Interview, February 12, 2003, 61.
25. Interview 15, February 19, 2002, 11–15.
26. Unrau, *Evacuation and Relocation*, 770–771; Yoo, *Growing Up Nisei*, 154–155.
27. Sue's account of her leaving Manzanar is excerpted from interview 14, February 12, 2003, 60–74.
28. Unrau, *Evacuation and Relocation,* 743.
29. Matsumoto, *Farming the Home Place*, 141–142.
30. Interview, February 12, 2003, 62.
31. Director of the re-relocation program during its entire existence.
32. Sue's accounts of her leaving Manzanar and living in Madison and Chicago are excerpted from interview 15, February 19, 2003, 16–76.

33. Matsumoto, *Farming the Home Place*, 146.
34. Interview 15, February 19, 2003, 73.

Chapter 9 The Kunitomis, Reunited, Diminished

1. Sue's account of the closing of the camps is excerpted from interview 16, February 26, 2003, 19–25.
2. CWRIC, *Personal Justice*, 215, 239.
3. Daniels, *Prisoners without Trial*, 63; Niiya, ed., *Encyclopedia*, 145; CWRIC, *Personal Justice*, 239–240; Drinnon, *Keeper of Concentration Camps*, 60; Weglyn, *Years of Infamy*, 96, 227–228; Robinson *By Order of the President*, 229; Hosokawa, *Nisei*, 427.
4. Robinson, *By Order of the President*, 235.
5. Unrau, *Evacuation and Relocation*, 787.
6. Smith, *Democracy on Trial*, 372.
7. Robinson, *By Order of the President*, 231; Lon Kurashige, *Japanese American Celebration and Conflict*, 110.
8. Unrau, *Evacuation and Relocation*, 788.
9. Lon Kurashige, *Japanese American Celebration and Conflict*, 109; Fujino, *Heartbeat of Struggle*, 77–79.
10. Sue's account of the resettlement is excerpted from interview 16, February 26, 2003, 25–71.
11. Unrau, *Evacuation and Relocation*, 794.
12. Embrey, ed., *The Lost Years*, 13; Unrau, *Evacuation and Relocation*, 795.
13. Yanagisako, *Transforming the Past*, 75.
14. Ibid., 158; CWRIC, *Personal Justice*, 241.
15. Scott Kurashige, "Transforming Los Angeles," 344.
16. Ibid., 469–470.
17. Ibid., 345, 470.
18. Ibid., 483–484, 493. Although over the next two decades both Japanese Americans and African Americans moved to the suburbs, the persistence of racial inequality in employment led to a concentration of impoverished African Americans in South Los Angeles, while racism against Japanese Americans became more subtle and less pervasive.
19. Yamamoto, "Coming to Los Angeles," 40–41.
20. Shigekuni, "Resettlement Years," 72.
21. http://www.encyclopedia.chicagohistory.org/pages/1067.html.
22. Niiya, "Introduction," 9; Lon Kurashige, *Japanese American Celebration and Conflict*, 112.
23. Recording dictation on a keyboard machine using a phonetic system.
24. In 1950, the California Legislature passed the Levering Act, which withheld the salaries of all state employees who refused to swear that they had never been members of subversive organizations. In 1950, Congress passed the Internal Security Act that required Communists to register with the government and to be detained in the event of a national emergency. Ceplair and Englund, *The Inquisition in Hollywood*, 362–63; Schlesinger, Jr., ed., *The Almanac of American History*, 525.
25. Daniels, *Prisoners without Trial*, 91; Fujino, *Heartbeat of Struggle*, 33.

26. Yoo, *Growing Up Nisei,* 174–179.
27. Ibid., 177; Takahishi, *Nisei/Sansei,* 204.
28. Ibid. Niiya, ed., *Encyclopedia,* 148–149; Nakano, *Japanese American Women,* 183–186.
29. Niiya, *Encyclopedia,* 238.
30. Takahashi, *Nisei/Sansei,* 204.
31. Interview 16, February 26, 2003, 49–53.
32. Murakawa, "Baachan," 78–80.
33. Excerpted from Embrey, "Some Lines for a Younger brother."
34. Ibid.

Chapter 10 Nisei Progressives and Beyond

1. Interview 17, March 5, 2003, 5.
2. Gottleib and Dreier, "From Liberty Hill to Living Wage," 3–4.
3. www.progressivela.org/history/forties.htm, January 20, 2004.
4. Sue's account of her participation in Nisei for Wallace is excerpted from interview 17, March 5, 2003, 1–6; 12–16.
5. Nakagawa, "Rebels with a Just Cause, Sakae Ishihara," 1.
6. Ibid., 3.
7. U.S. Department of Justice, FBI, "Nisei Progressives," FOIPA No. 1057925.
8. Carpenter, "Nisei Progressives," 193. Since there is very little discussion of Nisei for Wallace and the Nisei Progressives in the literature, I have relied substantially on Martha Nakagawa's 1997 articles in the *Rafu Shimpo* and on Tim Carpenter's master thesis "Nisei Progressives: A Link in the Chain of Democratic Social Movements in Twentieth Century America," completed in 1998, for which he interviewed Sue Embrey, Sakae Ishihara, and Arthur Takei.
9. Carpenter, "Nisei Progressives," 31.
10. Ibid.
11. Chiye Mori, editor of the *Manzanar Free Press* during the internment, became a member of New York Nisei Progressives for a short while before relocating to Hawaii.
12. Sato, n.d., "Nisei Progressives: A Perspective," 1.
13. Embrey, "Call Back Yesterday," 1.
14. Interview 17, March 5, 2003, 17–18; Pitt and Pitt, Los Angeles, 102, 442.
15. Hosokawa, *Nisei,* 453–455.
16. In 1968, a National JACL Committee to Repeal the Emergency Detention Act was formed to campaign for the repeal of Title II. With the assistance of Senator Daniel K. Inouye and Congressman Spark M. Matsunaga, Title II was finally repealed in 1971.
17. Interview 18, March 12, 2003, 40–41.
18. Nakagawa, "Sakae Ishihara," 3.
19. Ibid., 6.
20. Sue's account of her dating and marrying Garland Embrey against her mother's opposition is excerpted from interview 17, March 5, 2003, 19–38; interview 18, March 12, 2003, 20–26, 29, 43–47.

21. Garland Embrey died on March 18, 2005. His memories of dating and marrying Sue are excerpted from an interview on January 26, 2004. He misremembered the year he met Sue, since the Wallace campaign was in 1948.
22. Niiya, ed., *Encyclopedia*, 211.
23. A relatively neutral term literally meaning "white person."
24. Pool, "A Working-Class Neighborhood," November 6, 2002, B2.
25. Gary Embrey, interview, June 10, 2003, 57–58.
26. The name was changed in 1939 to Works Progress Administration.
27. In 1936, civil war broke out in Spain between the "loyalists," who were defenders of the newly formed republic and the national fascist forces under General Francisco Franco. Loyalists, known as The Popular Front, were a coalition of Communists, Socialists, Republicans, and Syndicalists, the latter being aggressively pro-labor. The Franco government was victorious and was recognized in 1939 by Britain, France, and the United States.
28. The Young Communist League is the youth wing of the Communist Party, but does not require members to join the Party. Since Garland stated he was involved with "only" the Young Communist League, it is reasonable to assume he did not join the Communist Party.
29. An aircraft manufacturing corporation relying on contracts with the U.S. military.
30. Garland is satirizing the Tenney Committee, created by California state senator Jack B. Tenney, and nicknamed "Little Dies Committee" because of its resemblance to the Dies Committee, formed by Congressman Martin Dies. Both committees investigated groups and individuals they deemed un-American, harassing those that protested the persecution of Japanese Americans.
31. Gary Embrey, interview, June 10, 2003, 54–55.
32. Garland Embrey's discussion of his political activism and its impact on his teaching career is excerpted from Garland Embrey, 2004, interview, January 26, 2004, 10, 20–40.

Chapter 11 The Unquiet Nisei

1. Drinnon, *Keeper of Concentrations Camps,* 307.
2. Takezawa, *Breaking the Silence,* 123.
3. Houston made this statement in a discussion at UCLA, June 2, 2005.
4. Sue's discussion of the silence about the camps is excerpted from interview 7, January 9, 2003, 9, 15; interview 13, February 5, 2003; interview 18, March 12, 2003; interview 21, March 26, 2003; and interview 50, May 5, 2004.
5. Interview 50, May 5, 2004, 25.
6. In Daniels, Taylor, and Kitano, eds., *Japanese Americans*, 160–161.
7. Interview 7, January 9, 2003, 56–57.
8. Cababa, interview, June 17, 2003, 22, 32–36, 39–40, 44–50, 52, 56.
9. Jack Kunitomi, interview, August 8, 2003, 13–14.
10. Iwata, interview, July 8, 2003, 11–12, 14.
11. The monument, *I Rei To,* was constructed by internees in 1943.
12. Furutani, interview, July 8, 2003; "Beginnings," 8–9.
13. Matsuoka, "Untitled," 22–24.
14. Interview, March 26, 2003, 12–13.

15. Ibid.
16. Embrey, "Call Back Yesterday," 2.
17. Drinnon, *Keeper of Concentration Camps,* 251.
18. Weglyn, *Years of Infamy,* 278.
19. Ishigo published a book of her camp drawings entitled *Lone Heart Mountain* in 1972.
20. Furutani, interview, July 8, 2003, 23, 30–32, 36, 42–44, 46.
21. Gary Embrey, interview, June 10, 2003.
22. After promising de-escalation of the war in Viet Nam, President Richard Nixon announced in 1970 that U. S. troops were invading Cambodia. Protests erupted throughout the country.
23. Bruce Embrey, interview, April 24, 2003.
24. The Congressional Commission, created on July 31, 1980, investigated the internment, hearing testimony from more than 750 witnesses.
25. Garland Embrey, interview, January 26, 2004.
26. Yamamoto, interview, July 15, 2003, 16, 40–42.
27. Tsuneishi, interview, July 1, 2003, 34.
28. Shigekuni, interview, July 16, 2003, 41, 24.
29. Hansen, interview, June 25, 2003, 33, 38–39.
30. Michael and Monica Embrey, interview, April 24, 2003, 27.
31. Sue Embrey, email to author, September 1, 2003.
32. Alisa Lynch, interview, November 19, 2003, 28, 47.
33. Hansen and Mitson, 1974, 187.

Chapter 12 The Manzanar Committee

1. Nakayama, "The 'Messiah of Manzanar,'"1.
2. Interviews, January 22; March 19 and 26, 2003.
3. Interview 19, March 19, 2003, 73.
4. Furutani, interview, July 8, 2003, 34.
5. Quoted in Unrau, *Evacuation and Relocation,* 824.
6. Manzanar Committee, letter February 9, 1974. In file of Sue Embrey.
7. Unrau, *Evacuation and Relocation,* 825.
8. H.R. 543, introduced on January 16, 1991; cosponsors were California Congressmen William M. Thomas, Norman Y. Mineta, and Robert T. Matsui.
9. H.R. 543 was brought to the floor of the House of Representatives on June 24, 1991 by Bruce F. Vento, chairman of the House Subcommittee on National Parks and Public Lands.
10. S. 621 was introduced on March 12, 1991 by Cranston and Paul Seymour of California and Daniel Akaka of Hawaii.
11. There were 21 abstentions.
12. Hansen, interview, June 25, 2003, 18.
13. Michael, interview, June 30, 2004, 1–30.
14. Robinson, *By Order of the President,* 134.
15. Drinnon, *Keeper of Concentration Camps,* 6.
16. Weglyn, *Years of Infamy,* 218; see also Yamano, "Brooding Silence," 4.
17. Miller, *Plain Speaking,* 404.

18. Becker, interview, April 24, 2003, 26–27.
19. Nazi Concentration Camp in Germany, which the 522nd Field Artillery Battalion, 442nd Japanese American Regimental Combat Team helped to liberate in April 1945.
20. Jack Kunitomi, interview, August 8, 2003, 14.
21. Furutani, interview, July 8, 2003, 33–36.
22. Michael, interview, June 30, 2004, 35–36.
23. Manzanar Committee, *Reflections*, iv.
24. Interview 30, May 28, 2003, 52–54.
25. Interview 21, March 26, 2003, 1–7.

Chapter 13 Redress and Reparations

1. Herzig, email to author, April 18, 2003.
2. Hosokawa, *Nisei,* 510.
3. Ibid.; Daniels, Taylor, Kitano, eds., *Japanese Americans,* 188, 191, 197.
4. Interview 23, April 9, 2003, 8–10.
5. E. O. 9066, Inc., "Position Paper."
6. Shigekuni, interview, July 16, 2003.
7. Daniels, Taylor, Kitano, eds., *Japanese Americans,* 191.
8. Fugita and O'Brien, *Japanese American Ethnicity,* 148.
9. Ibid., 191–192.
10. Hosokawa, *Nisei,* 513–514.
11. Interview 23, April 9, 2003, 14.
12. Hosokawa, *Nisei,* 513–514.
13. Hohri, *Repairing America,* 225.
14. Ibid., 213; Daniels, Taylor, and Kitano, eds. *Japanese Americans,* 190.
15. Interview, April 9, 2003, 12–13.
16. Daniels, Taylor, and Kitano, eds., *Japanese Americans,* 192.
17. Robert T. Matsui died on January 1, 2005. In an email to the author, dated January 3, 2005, Sue Embrey stated: "I am devastated by the news of the passing of Bob Matsui. I just received a holiday greeting card from him, something he did every year. Best of all, I remember his personally calling me when the redress bill passed. It was so dear of him to do that. I will surely miss him."
18. Daniels, Taylor, and Kitano, eds., *Japanese Americans,* 192–193.
19. Ibid., 194–195.
20. Interview, April 9, 2003, 24–33.
21. CWRIC, *Personal Justice,* 467.
22. Ibid., 462–464; Hosokawa, *Nisei,* 515–16.
23. Daniels, Taylor, and Kitano, eds., *Japanese Americans,* 213–214.
24. Ibid., 214–215.
25. Baker, *Japanning,* 97, 22.
26. Interview, March 26, 2003, 41–46.
27. Michael, interview, June 30, 2004, 17–21.
28. Nakano, *Japanese American Women,* 206.
29. Ibid., 205–206.
30. Niiya, ed., *Encyclopedia,* 146.
31. Ibid.

32. Niiya, ed., *Encyclopedia,* 145–146; Robinson , *By Order of the President,* 251.
33. Robinson, *By Order of the President,* 251.
34. Interview, April 9, 2003, 52–53.
35. Shigekuni, interview, July 16, 2003, 32.
36. Daniels, Taylor, and Kitano, eds., *Japanese Americans,* 222.
37. Embrey, "With Grace and Dignity," 3.
38. Interview, April 9, 2003, 58.
39. Ibid, 47.
40. Robinson, *By Order of the President,* 144, 249, 250.
41. Interview, 28 May, 2003, 34–35.
42. Japanese American Citizens League, *Japanese American Experience,* May 2, 2000.
43. Harth, *Last Witnesses,* 2–5.
44. Kaestner, March 2, 1943, letter in Paul Tsuneishi files.
45. Tsuneishi, email to author, January 17, 2005.
46. CWCRIC 1997, 8–9. See appendix for all nine conditions.
47. Robinson, *By Order of the President,* 123.
48. Daniels, *Prisoners without Trial,* 72.
49. Interview, February 12, 2003, 1–3.
50. Weglyn, *Years of Infamy,* 37–38; Daniels, *Prisoners without Trial,* 37; Drinnon, *Keeper of Concentration Camps,*31–32; Hosokawa, *Nisei,* 287–288; Robinson, *By Order of the President,* 126–127.
51. Warren, *Memoirs,* quoted in CWRIC, *Personal Justice, 375–376;* Grodzins, 44–47.
52. Interview, February 12, 2003, 6.
53. Ochi, interview, July 5, 2003, 37; Furutani, interview, July 8, 2003, 39; Michael, interview, June 30, 2003, 42, 43.
54. Alfaro, in Harth, 214.
55. Embrey, email to author, January 17, 2005.

Conclusion: The Legacy of Sue Kunitomi Embrey

1. Garland Embrey, interview, January 26, 2004, 53.
2. Interview, May 5, 2004, 22.
3. Interview, 49, April 1, 2004, 11.
4. Hoobler and Hoobler, *The Japanese American Family,* 115.
5. Yanagisako, *Transforming the Past,* 78.
6. Interview, March 19, 2003, 74.
7. Interview, February 19, 2003, 75.
8. Matsumoto, *Farming the Home Place,* 162.
9. Kim, "Processes," 68; Matsumoto, *Farming the Home Place,* 13.
10. Kitano, *Japanese Americans,* 106–107; Matsumoto, *Farming the Home Place,* 85, 160, 193, 199; Yanagisako, *Transforming the Past,* 76, 105; Fujino, *Heartbeat of Struggle,* 33.
11. Takemoto, "Family Environment," 5; Matsumoto, *Farming the Home Place,* 65; Kitano, *Japanese Americans,* 158; Fugita and O'Brien, *Japanese American Ethnicity,* 37.
12. Kim, "Processes," 71.
13. Takahashi, *Nisei/Sansei,* 152–153; Nakano, *Japanese American Women,*108–109, 111; Drinnon, *Keeper of Concentration Camps,* 251, 307.

14. Takahashi, *Nisei/Sansei,* 160; Fugita and O'Brien, *Japanese American Ethnicity,* 140–141.
15. Furutani, interview, July 8, 2003, 46.
16. Shigekuni, interview, July 16, 2003, 45.
17. Gary Embrey, interview, June 10, 2003, 37–40.
18. Bruce Embrey, interview, April 24, 2003, 2.
19. Margalit, *Ethics of Memory,* 115.
20. Interview, February 19, 2003, 24.
21. Interview, February 12, 2003, 3–4.
22. Hansen, letter to Civil Liberties Public Education Fund, December 10, 1996, archived in the Arthur Hansen files.
23. Ochi, interview, July 5, 2003, 47.
24. Yamamoto, interview, July 15, 2003, 43–44.
25. Tsuneishi, interview, July 1, 2003, 42.
26. Iwata, interview, July 8, 2003, 32, 33.
27. Cababa, interview, June 17, 2003, 65.
28. Interview, May 5, 2004, 11.
29. Manzanar Committee, *The Manzanar Pilgrimage,* 17.
30. Manzanar Committee, *Reflections,* 14.
31. Margalit, *Ethics of Memory,* 171.
32. Ibid., 155.
33. Stewart, "Manzanar Icon," September, 2005.
34. Ibid.
35. Ibid.
36. Ibid.
37. Manzanar National Historic Site Guest Book, June 30, 2004.

Afterword

1. Jack Kunitomi, interview, August 8, 2003, 16.
2. Becker, interview, April 24, 2003, 15–16.

Appendix I

1. Unrau, *Evacuation and Relocation*, 98.
2. Ibid., 100.

Appendix II

1. This chronicle of conditions is excerpted from the report, issued in 1982, of the Congressional Commission on Wartime Relocation and Internment of Civilians, 8–9.

Bibliography

Primary Sources: Interviews*

Becker, Barbara. Interview by the author, Los Angeles. April 24, 2003.
Cababa, Kerry. Interview by the author. June 17, 2003.
Embrey, Bruce. Interview by the author. April 24, 2003.
Embrey, Garland. Interview by the author. January 26, 2004.
Embrey, Gary. Interview by the author. June 10, 2003.
Embrey, Michael. Interview by the author. April 24, 2003.
Embrey, Monica. Interview by the author. April 24, 2003.
Embrey, Sue Kunitomi. Interviews by the author. November 13, 20, December 4, 11, 18, 2002; January 9, 15, 22, 29, February 5, 12, 15, 26, March 5, 12, 19, 26, April 2, 9, May 7, 21, 28, June 4 , August 27, October 29, 2003; May 5, 2004.
Furutani, Warren. Interview by the author. July 8, 2003.
Hansen, Arthur A. Interview by the author. June 25, 2003.
Iwata, Nancy. Interview by the author. July 8, 2003.
Kunitomi, Yoshisuke Jack. Interview by the author. August 8, 2003.
Lynch, Alisa. Interview by the author. November 19, 2003.
Michael, Bill. Interview by the author, Independence, California. June 30, 2004.
Ochi, Rose. Interview by the author. July 5, 2003.
Shigekuni, Phillip. Interview by the author, Northridge, California. July 16, 2003.
Tsuneishi, Paul. Interview by the author, Sunland, California. July 1, 2003.
Yamamoto, Takinori. Interview by the author, Arleta, California. July 15, 2003.

Primary Sources: Documents

Embrey, Sue Kunitomi. No title. Speech at the Grand Opening of the Interpretive Center and Park Headquarters, Manzanar Historic Site. April 24, 2004.
——. "Call Back Yesterday." Speech given at symposium "A View from the Inside, Art and Literature of the Camps." Oakland, CA. October 15–17, 1976.
——. "Just the Way I Hoped." 1980. Copy in files of author.
——. "With Grace and Dignity." *Rafu Shimpo*, August 17, 1988.

*All interviews, except otherwise noted, were tape recorded in Los Angeles, California. Interview tapes and transcripts will be archived with National Park Service Manzanar National Historic Site, Independence, California.

E. O. 9066, Inc. "Brief Chronology on Redress and E. O. 9066 Inc." Files of Paul Tsuneishi, Sunland, California. n.d.

——. "Position Paper." Files of Paul Tsuneishi. Sunland, California. 1975.

——. "Reparations Questionnaire." Files of Paul Tsuneishi, Sunland, California. n.d.

——. "Status Report." Files of Paul Tsuneishi. Sunland, California. n.d.

Hansen, Arthur A. Letter to Civil Liberties Public Education Fund. December 10, 1996. Files of Arthur A. Hansen. Fullerton, California.

Japanese American Citizens League Southern District Council. "Report of Conditions at Manzanar Relocation Center." Unpublished paper. May 26, 1942. Files of Sue Kunitomi Embrey, Los Angeles, California.

Kaestner (no first name). Letter to Paul Tsuneishi. March 2, 1943. Files of Paul Tsuneishi. Sunland, California.

Kunitomi, [Iwata] Midori. "Family History." Unpublished paper. n.d. Files of Sue Kunitomi Embrey. Los Angeles.

Kunitomi, Yoshisuke Jack. "The Oliver Story." Unpublished paper. n.d. Files of Jack Kunitomi, Los Angeles.

Lofton, Shizu [Sue]. Letters from Manzanar and Minidoka Camps. Files of Sue Kunitomi Embrey, Los Angeles, California, 1942–43.

Manzanar Committee. "Keep It Going, Pass It On." 35th Annual Manzanar Pilgrimage. April 24, 2004.

Manzanar Committee. "Manzanar Committee Issues Apology for Chin's Remarks." May 9, 2006.

Manzanar National Historic Site Interpretive Center Guest Book. Visitors' comments. April 24, 2004.

Matsui, Robert T. Letter to Aiko and Paul Tsuneishi regarding President Ronald Reagan signing H. R. 442, The Civil Liberties Act of 1988. Washington, D. C., September 7, 1988. Files of Paul Tsuneishi, Sunland, California.

Mineta, Norman. Letter to Mr. and Mrs. Paul Tsuneishi regarding President Ronald Reagan's signing of H. R. 442, the Civil Liberties Act of 1988. Washington, D. C., September 1, 1988. Files of Paul Tsuneishi, Sunland, California.

Myer, Dillon S. "The Facts about the War Relocation Authority," Speech, Los Angeles Town Hall. January 21, 1944. Files of Sue Kunitomi Embrey, Los Angeles.

San Fernando Valley JACC. "Redress Celebration Program," October 1, 1988.

Sato, Wilbur. "Nisei Progressives, a Perspective," unpublished paper. n.d. Files of Sue Kunitomi Embrey. Los Angeles.

Statement of United States Citizens of Japanese Ancestry, U. S. Selective Service System. [Application for leave clearance.] 1943. Files of Sue Kunitomi Embrey. Los Angeles.

Tsuneishi, Sartoro. Testimony before Congressional Commission on Wartime Relocation and Internment of Civilians. July 20, 1981. Los Angeles, California.

Secondary Sources

Armor, John and Peter Wright. *Manzanar: Photographs by Ansel Adams*. Commentary by John Hersey. New York: Vintage Books, 1988.

Asakawa, Gil. "Patriotism, Civil Rights and Media," *Nikkei View,* March 21, 2003. http://nikkeiview.com/archives03/03/2003.htm.

——. "Personal Perspectives on the Past." *Nikkei View,* March 10, 2003. http://nikkeiview.com/archives03/03/2003.htm.

——. "Roots and Branches: Who's Japanese American?" *Nikkei View,* April 28, 2003. http://nikkeiview.com/archives03/03/2003.htm.

Bahr, Diana Meyers. *Viola Martinez, California Paiute, Living in Two Worlds.* Norman: University of Oklahoma Press, 2003.

Baker, Lillian . *The Concentration Camp Conspiracy: A Second Pearl Harbor.* Lawndale, CA: AFHA Publications, 1981.

——. *The Japanning of America: Redress and Reparations Demands by Japanese Americans.* Medford, Oregon: Webb Research Group, 1991.

——. *Dishonoring America: The Falsification of WWII History.* Medford, OR: Webb Research Group, 1994.

Barna, Mark. "Manzanar." *The Bakersfield Californian.* April 23, 2004.

Benti, Wynne, ed. *Born Free and Equal: The Story of Loyal Japanese Americans.* Manzanar Relocation Center, Inyo County, CA. Based on the book published in 1944 with photos and text by Ansel Adams. Bishop, CA: Spotted Press, Inc. 2002.

Boxall, Bettina. "Reassembling a Sad Chapter of History." *Los Angeles Times,* December 11, 2002.

Burton, Jeffery F., Jeremy D. Haines, and Mary M. Farrell. *I Rei To: Archeological Investigations at the Manzanar Relocation Center Cemetery, Manzanar National Historic Site, California.* Washington, D.C.: Western Archeological and Conservation Center, National Park Service, U.S. Department of the Interior: Publications in Anthropology 79, 2001.

Burton, Jeffrey F. and Mary M. Farrell, Florence B. Lord, and Richard W. Lord. *Confinement and Ethnicity: An Overview of World War II Japanese Relocation Sites.* With an essay by Eleanor Roosevelt, cartography by Ronald J. Beckwith, and a contribution by Irene J. Cohen. Washington, D.C.: Western Archeological and Conservation Center, National Park Service, U.S. Department of the Interior, Publications in Anthropology, 74, 1999.

Carpenter, Timothy Dennis. "Nisei Progressives: A Link in the Chain of Democratic Movements in Twentieth-Century America." California State University Fullerton: Master of Arts Thesis, 1998.

Ceplair, Larry and Steven Englund. *The Inquisition in Hollywood: Politics in the Film Industry, 1930–1960.* Berkeley: University of California Press, 1983.

Conrat, Maisie and Richard. *Executive Order 9066: The Internment of 100,000 Japanese Americans.* University of California, Los Angeles Asian American Studies Center, 1992.

Commission on Wartime Relocation and Internment of Civilians (CWRIC). *Personal Justice Denied: The Report of the Commission on Wartime Relocation and Internment of Civilians.* Washington, D.C.: The Civil Liberties Public Education Fund and Seattle: University of Washington Press, 1997.

Cooper, Michael L. *Remembering Manzanar: Life in a Japanese Relocation Camp.* New York: Clarion Books, 2002.

Daniels, Roger. *The Politics of Prejudice: The Anti-Japanese Movement in California and the Struggle for Japanese Exclusion.* 2d. rev. ed. Berkeley: University of California Press, 1977.

——. "The Japanese." In Higham, ed., *Ethnic Leadership in America.* Baltimore: John Hopkins Press, 1978, 36–63.

Daniels, Roger. *Concentration Camps: North America, Japanese in the United States and Canada During World War II.* Malabar, FL: Krieger Publishing Co., 1993.

——. *Prisoners without Trial: Japanese Americans in World War II.* New York: Hill and Wang, 1993.

Daniels, Roger, Sandra C. Taylor, and H. L. Kitano, eds. *Japanese Americans from Relocation to Redress.* Seattle and London: University of Washington Press, rev. ed., 1991.

De Vos, George A. *Acculturation and Personality Structure: A Rorschach Study of Japanese Americans.* Chicago: University of Chicago Press, 1951.

Drinnon, Richard. *Keeper of Concentration Camps: Dillon S. Myer and American Racism.* Berkeley and Los Angeles: University of California Press, 1987.

Embrey, Sue Kunitomi, "Call Back Yesterday: Our Family's Story of Resettlement." In *Nanka Nikkei Voices, Vol. I, Resettlement Years, 1945–1955.* Los Angeles: Japanese American Historical Society of Southern California, 1998, 107–109.

——, ed. *The Lost Years, 1942–46.* Los Angeles: Moonlight Publications, Gidra, Inc., 1972.

——. "Some Lines for a Younger Brother." In *Ayumi Journey, A Japanese American Anthology.* San Francisco: Japanese American Anthology Committee, 1980.

——. "With Grace and Dignity." Los Angeles: *Rafu Shimpo,* August 17, 1988.

Embrey, Sue Kunitomi, Arthur A. Hansen, and Betty Kuhlberg Mitson. *Manzanar Martyr: An Interview with Harry Y. Ueno.* California State University Fullerton Oral History Program, 1986.

"Forgotten Internees." *Los Angeles Times,* March 18, 2007.

Fugita, Stephen S. and David J. O'Brien. *Japanese American Ethnicity, the Persistence of Community.* Seattle: University of Washington Press. 1991.

Fujino, Diane C. *Heartbeat of Struggle: The Revolutionary Life of Yuri Kochiyama.* (Critical American Studies) Minneapolis: University of Minnesota Press, 2005.

Garrett, Jessie A. and Ronald C. Larson, eds. *Camp and Community: Manzanar and the Owens Valley.* California State University Fullerton, Japanese American Oral History Project, 2004.

Gerhard, Paul F. *The Plight of the Japanese Americans during World War II: A Study of a Group Prejudice: Its History and Manifestations.* Wichita, KN: University of Wichita, 1963.

Gottleib, Robert and Peter Dreier. "From Liberty Hill to the Living Wage: A Brief History of Progressives in Los Angeles." *LA Weekly,* October 2–8, 1998.

Grodzins, Morton. *Americans Betrayed.* Chicago: University of Chicago Press, 1949.

Hansen, Arthur A. and Betty E. Mitson, eds. *Voices Long Silent: An Oral Inquiry into the Japanese American Evacuation.* California State University Fullerton, Japanese American Oral History Project, 1974.

Hansen, Arthur A. and David A. Hacker. "The Manzanar Riot: An Ethnic Perspective." *Amerasia Journal* 2 (Fall 1974): 112–157.

Harth, Erica, ed. *Last Witnesses: Reflections on the Wartime Internment of Japanese Americans.* New York: Palgrave Macmillan, 2001.

Hayashi, Brian Masaru. *Democratizing the Enemy: The Japanese American Internment.* Princeton: Princeton University Press, 2004.

Hennessey, Kathleen. "Former Detainees and Other Friends of the Court Cheer." *Los Angeles Times,* June 29, 2004.

Hirabayashi, Lane, Akemi Kikumura-Yano, and James Hirabayashi, eds. *New Worlds, New Lives, Globalization and People of Japanese Descent in the Americas and from Latin America in Japan.* Stanford: Stanford University Press, 2002.

Hirahara, Naomi and Gwenn M. Jensen. *Silent Scars of Healing Hands: Oral Histories of Japanese American Doctors in WWII Detention Camps.* California State University, Fullerton: Center for Oral and Public History, 2004.

"History of The Progressive Movement in Los Angeles: The Forties." *Progressive Los Angeles Network.* http://progressivela,org/history/forties.htm.

Hoobler, Dorothy and Thomas. *The Japanese American Family Album.* New York: Oxford University Press, 1995.

Hohri, William Minoru. *Repairing America: An Account of the Movement for Japanese American Redress.* Pullman, Washington, D.C.: Washington State University Press, 1988.

Hosokawa, Bill. *Nisei: The Quiet Americans.* Boulder, CO: University Press of Colorado. rev. ed., 2002.

Houston, Jeanne Watasuki and James D. Houston. *Farewell to Manzanar: A True Story of Japanese American Experience during and after the World War II Internment.* Boston: Houghton Mifflin, 1973.

"Hahn's Pre-Owned Vision," *Los Angeles Times,* July 8, 2004.

"Involuntary Relocation to Start at Manzanar in Mid-October." *Manzanar Free Press,* September 28, 1945.

Ishigo, Estelle. *Lone Heart Mountain.* Los Angeles: Anderson, Ritchie & Simon, 1972.

"It's Official! Reagan Signs Bill." *Rafu Shimpo,* August 10, 1988.

Iwata, Masakazu. *Planted in Good Soil: A History of the Issei in the United States Agriculture.* New York: Peter Lang Publishing, Inc. American University Series IX, History,Vols., 1992, 57–58.

James, Thomas. 1987. *Exile Within: The Schooling of Japanese Americans, 1942–1945.* Cambridge: Harvard University Press.

Japanese American Citizens League National Education Committee. *The Japanese American Experience: A Lesson in American History.* Sacramento, California State Capitol: The LegiSchool Project. May 2, 2000.

Kim, Jean. "Processes of Asian American Identity Development: A Study of Japanese American Women's Perceptions of Their Struggle to Achieve Positive Identities as Americans of Asian Ancestry." Ph.D. Diss. Ann Arbor: University of Massachusetts, 1981.

Kitano, Harry H. L. *Japanese Americans: The Evolution of a Subculture.* Englewood Cliffs, NJ: Prentice-Hall, 1976.

Kitashima, Tsuyaku "Sox." *Birth of an Activist, The Sox Kitashima Story.* San Mateo, CA: Asian American Curriculum Project, 2003.

Kochiyama, Yuri. *Passing It On.* Berkeley: University of California Press, 2004.

Kuida, Jennifer, Martha Nakagawa, and Sharon Yamato, eds. *"Keep It Going, Pass It On" Poetry Inspired by the Manzanar Pilgrimages.* Los Angeles: Manzanar Committee, 2004.

Kurashige, Lon. *Japanese American Celebration and Conflict: A History of Ethnic Identity and Festival in Los Angeles, 1934–1990.* Berkeley: University of California Press, 2002.

Kurashige, Scott Tadao. "Transforming Los Angeles: Black and Japanese Americans Struggles for Racial Equality in the Twentieth Century." Ph.D. Diss. University of California, Los Angeles, 2002.

Kvammen, Elizabeth [Lechner]. "German Americans Interned During WWII." Letter to *Los Angeles Times,* December 18, 2002.

Lelyveld. Nita. "Old Market Closes Doors for Last Time," *Los Angeles Times,* August 1, 2004.

Lim, Deborah K. *The Lim Report: A Research Report of Japanese Americans in American Concentration Camps during World War II.* Kearney, NE: Morris Publishing. Original version, unedited by JACL.

Margalit, Avishai. *The Ethics of Memory.* Cambridge and London: Harvard University Press, 2002.

Marquez, Letisia and Wendy Soderburg. "Former Internees Make Sure No One Forgets." *UCLA Today,* February 24, 2004.

Mass, Amy. "Psychological Effects of the Camps on Japanese Americans." In Daniels, Taylor and Kitano, eds., *Japanese Americans from Relocation to Redress.* Seattle: University of Washington Press, rev. ed., 1991.

Materson, Daniel M. with Sayaka Funada-Classen. *The Japanese in Latin America.* Urbana: University of Illinois Press, 2004.

Matsumoto, Valerie. *Farming the Home Place: A Japanese American Community in California, 1919–1942.* Ithaca, N.Y: Cornell University Press, 1993.

Miller, Merle. *Plain Speaking, an Oral Biography of Harry S. Truman,* New York: Tess Press, an imprint of Black Dog and Leventhal Publishers, Inc. 1974.

Mitson, Betty E. "Looking Back in Anguish: An Oral History and Japanese American Evacuation." *Oral History Review* 2 (1974): 24–51.

Modell, John. *The Economics and Politics of Racial Accommodation: The Japanese of Los Angeles, 1900–1942.* Urbana: University of Illinois Press, 1977.

Moore, Melanie. "Value Change across Three Generations of Japanese Americans: The Effects of Culture, Social Structure and Identity." University of Washington, Ph.D. Diss., 1991.

Muller, Eric L. *Free to Die for Their Country: The Story of Japanese American Draft Resisters in World War II.* Chicago: The University of Chicago Press, 2001.

Murakawa, Phyllis. "Baachan." In *Nanka Nikkei Voices, Vol. II, Turning Points.* Los Angeles: Japanese American Historical Society of Southern California, 2002, 78–80.

Myer, Dillon S. *Uprooted Americans: The Japanese Americans and the War Relocation Center during World War II.* Tucson, AZ: University of Arizona Press, 1971.

Nagata, Donna. *Legacy of Injustice: Exploring the Cross-Generational Impact of the Japanese American Internment.* New York: Plenum Press, 1993.

Nakagawa, Martha. "Rebels with a Just Cause." *Rafu Shimpo,* December 11, 1997.

——. "Sakae Ishihara: A Marked Man." *Rafu Shimpo,* December 11, 1997.

Nakano, Mei T. *Japanese American Women: Three Generations, 1890–1990.* Berkeley: Mina Press Publishing and San Francisco: National Japanese American Historical Society, 1990.

Niiya, Brian, ed. *Nanka Nikkei Voices, Vol. I: Resettlement Years, 1945–1955.* Los Angeles: Japanese American Historical Society of Southern California, 1998.

——. *Encyclopedia of Japanese American History: An A to Z Reference from 1968 to the Present.* Los Angeles: Japanese American National Museum, 2001.

——. *Nanka Nikkei Voices, Vol. II: Turning Points.* Los Angeles: Japanese American Historical Society of Southern California, 2002.

——. *Nanka Nikkei Voices, Vol. III: Little Tokyo, Changing Times. Changing Faces.* Los Angeles: Japanese American Historical Society of Southern California, 2004.

Noriyuki, Duane. "Stories in the Dust." *Los Angeles Times,* July 31, 2002.

Okihiro, Gary Y. "Filling the Gaps: Japanese Americans and World War II." *Oral History Review* 15 (Fall 1987): 159–163.

Oliver, Myrna. "Harry Ueno, 97; Hero to Japanese Americans in Internment Camps." *Los Angeles Times,* December 21, 2004.

Our World. Manzanar, California: Manzanar High School, 1943–44.

Reflections in Three Self-Guided Tours of Manzanar. Los Angeles: Manzanar Committee, 1998.

Riley, Karen L. *Schools behind Barbed Wire: The Untold Story of Wartime Internment and the Children of Arrested Enemy Aliens.* Lanham, MD: Rowman and Littlefield, 2002.

Robinson, Greg. *By Order of the President: FDR and the Internment of Japanese Americans.* Cambridge: Harvard University Press, 2001.

Sahagun, Louis . "Owens Valley Residents, DWP Locked in Standoff." *Los Angeles Times,* January 9, 2006.

——. "Judge Threatens DWP Sanctions over Owens River Flow." *Los Angeles Times,* June 25, 2006.

——. In Owens Valley Water Again Flows. *Los Angeles Times,* December 7, 2006.

Schlesinger, Jr., ed. *The Almanac of American History.* Greenwich, CT: Bison Books Corp., 1983.

Shigekuni, Phil. "My Resettlement Experience." In *Nanka Nikkei Voices, Vol. I, Resettlement Years, 1945–1955.* Los Angeles Japanese American Historical Society of Southern California, 1998, 71–73.

Simon, Richard. "Robert Matsui, 63. Lawmaker Fought for WWII Reparations." *Los Angeles Times,* January 2, 2005.

Skelton, George. "A 'Spectacular' Leader's Grievous Flaw." *Los Angeles Times,* May 3, 2004.

Smith, Page. *Democracy on Trial: The Japanese American Evacuation and Relocation during World War II.* New York: Simon and Schuster, 1995.

Starr, Kevin. *Embattled Dreams: California in War and Peace, 1940–1950.* Oxford: Oxford University Press.

Stewart, Jocelyn W. "Manzanar Icon Now More Than a Memory." *Los Angeles Times,* September 18, 2005.

Takahashi, Jere. *Nisei/Sansei: Shifting Japanese American Identities and Politics.* Philadelphia: Temple University Press, 1997.

Takemoto, Mary Ann Michiko. "Family Environment, Social Support, Coping and Acculturation in Japanese Americans." Indiana University, Ph.D. Diss., 1987.

Takezawa, Yasuko I. *Breaking the Silence: Redress and Japanese American Ethnicity.* Ithaca: Cornell University Press, 1995.

Tamaki, Julie. "New Lease on Life for Little Tokyo Landmark." *Los Angeles Times,* January 11, 2004.

Tateishi, John. *And Justice for All: An Oral History of the Japanese American Detention Camps.* New York: Random House, 1984.

The Manzanar Pilgrimage: A Time for Sharing. Los Angeles: Manzanar Committee, 1981.

Thomas. Dorothy Swaine. *The Salvage: Japanese American Evacuation and Resettlement.* Berkeley: University of California Press, 1952.

Thomas, Dorothy Swaine and Richard S. Nishimoto. *The Spoilage: Japanese American Evacuation and Resettlement.* Berkeley: University of California Press, 1946.

Turley, Jonathan. "60 Years On, Again Battling an Abomination of Power." *Los Angeles Times,* November 17, 2003.

Unrau, Harlan D. *The Evacuation and Relocation of Persons of Japanese Ancestry during World War II: A Historical Study of the Manzanar Relocation.* Historic Resource Study/ Special History Study. Vols. I and II. Washington, D.C: National Park Service, United States Department of the Interior, 1996.

"U. S. At War." *Los Angeles Examiner,* December 8, 1941.

Waugh, Isami Arifuku. "Hidden Crime and Deviance in the Japanese American Community, 1920–1946." University of California Berkeley, Ph.D. Diss., 1978.

Weglyn, Michi Nishiura. *Years of Infamy: The Untold Story of America's Concentration Camps.* Updated ed. Seattle: University of Washington Press, 1996.

Wehrey, Jane. *Voices from This Long Brown Land: Oral Recollections of Owens Valley Lives and Manzanar Pasts.* New York: Palgrave MacMillan, 2006.

Woo, Elaine. "John Nason, 96, Got Nisei Students into College during War." *Los Angeles Times,* December 7, 2001.

Yamano, Tina Kazumi. "Brooding Silence: A Cross-Generational Study of Informal Learning, Socialization and Child-Rearing Practices in a Japanese American Family." University of California Los Angeles, Ph.D., 1994.

Yamamoto, Takenori. "Coming to Los Angeles." In *Nanka Nikkei Voices, Vol. III, Resettlement Years, 1945–1955.* Los Angeles: Japanese American Historical Society of Southern California, 2004, 40–41.

Yamashita, Kanshi Stanley. "Little Tokyo Eons Ago." In *Nanka Nikkei Voices, Vol. III.* Los Angeles: Japanese American Historical Society of Southern California, 2003, 31.

Yanagisako, Sylvia Junko. *Transforming the Past: Tradition and Kinship Among Japanese Americans.* Stanford, CA: Stanford University Press, 1985.

Yew, Chay. *Question 27, Question 28.* Theatrical production performed by Mark Taper Forum Asian American Workshop. East-West Players, Los Angeles. June 20, 2004.

Yoneda, Karl. *Ganbatte: The Sixty-Year Struggle of a Kibei Worker.* Los Angeles: UCLA Asian American Studies Center, 1983.

Yoo, David K. *Growing Up Nisei: Race, Generation, and Culture among Japanese Americans of California, 1924–49.* Urbana: University of Illinois Press, 2000.

Index